THE LIFE RECOVERY® DEVOTIONAL

STEPHEN ARTERBURN | DAVID STOOP

THE
Life Recovery®
DEVOTIONAL

Thirty Meditations from Scripture
for Each Step in Recovery

TYNDALE HOUSE PUBLISHERS, INC.
CAROL STREAM, ILLINOIS

Library of Congress Cataloging-in-Publication Data

Arterburn, Stephen, date.
    The life recovery devotional : thirty meditations from Scripture for each step in recovery / Stephen Arterburn and David Stoop. —New repackage.
        p. cm.
    Originally published: The twelve step life recovery devotional / David Stoop, Stephen Arterburn. c1991.
    ISBN 978-1-4143-3004-4 (sc)
    1. Twelve-step programs—Religious aspects—Christianity—Meditations. 2. Bible—Meditations. I. Stoop, David A. II. Stoop, David A. Twelve step life recovery devotional. III. Title.
    BV4596.T88A78 2009
    242′.4—dc22   2008054374

Printed in the United States of America

15   14   13   12   11   10   09
7   6   5   4   3   2   1

DEDICATION

This devotional is dedicated to all fellow strugglers who have had
the courage to face the truth about themselves, the humility to
abandon their flawed attempts at living, and the willingness to find
God's truth and live accordingly.

CONTENTS

THE TWELVE STEPS OF ALCOHOLICS ANONYMOUS

(1) We admitted we were powerless over alcohol—that our lives had become unmanageable.

(2) Came to believe that a Power greater than ourselves could restore us to sanity.

(3) Made a decision to turn our will and our lives over to the care of God *as we understood Him*.

(4) Made a searching and fearless moral inventory of ourselves.

(5) Admitted to God, to ourselves and to another human being the exact nature of our wrongs.

(6) Were entirely ready to have God remove all these defects of character.

(7) Humbly asked Him to remove our shortcomings.

(8) Made a list of all persons we had harmed, and became willing to make amends to them all.

(9) Made direct amends to such people wherever possible, except when to do so would injure them or others.

(10) Continued to take personal inventory and when we were wrong promptly admitted it.

(11) Sought through prayer and meditation to improve our conscious contact with God, *as we understood Him*, praying only for knowledge of His will for us and the power to carry that out.

(12) Having had a spiritual awakening as the result of these steps, we tried to carry this message to alcoholics, and to practice these principles in all our affairs.

The Twelve Steps are reprinted and adapted with permission of Alcoholics Anonymous World Services, Inc. Permission to reprint and adapt the Twelve Steps does not mean that AA has reviewed or approved the contents of this publication, nor that AA agrees with the views expressed herein. AA is a program of recovery from alcoholism—use of the Twelve Steps in connection with programs and activities which are patterned after AA, but which address other problems, does not imply otherwise.

THE TWELVE STEPS

1. We admitted that we were powerless over our dependencies and that our lives had become unmanageable.
2. We came to believe that a Power greater than ourselves could restore us to sanity.
3. We made a decision to turn our wills and our lives over to the care of God.
4. We made a searching and fearless moral inventory of ourselves.
5. We admitted to God, to ourselves, and to another human being the exact nature of our wrongs.
6. We were entirely ready to have God remove these defects of character.
7. We humbly asked God to remove our shortcomings.
8. We made a list of all persons we had harmed and became willing to make amends to them all.
9. We made direct amends to such people wherever possible, except when to do so would injure them or others.
10. We continued to take personal inventory, and when we were wrong, promptly admitted it.
11. We sought through prayer and meditation to improve our conscious contact with God, praying only for knowledge of his will for us and the power to carry it out.
12. Having had a spiritual awakening as the result of these steps, we tried to carry this message to others and to practice these principles in all our affairs.

The Twelve Steps in this devotional book have been adapted from the Twelve Steps of Alcoholics Anonymous.

ACKNOWLEDGMENTS

A lot of people have played a part in the creation of this devotional, but we want to especially thank Connie Neal, for letting us draw from her own recovery, and Mark Norton at Tyndale House Publishers, for bringing it all together.

INTRODUCTION

It's impossible to go through life without experiencing hurt, especially in the invisible world of our thoughts and emotions. We all respond differently to these hurts. Some of us try to avoid feeling the pain by turning to harmful behaviors or addictive substances—hoping to numb the hurts within. Others of us try to distance ourselves from the pain by throwing ourselves into more noble pursuits—hoping to stay busy enough to silence the painful memories from our past.

Over the years, millions have found help and hope by working through the Twelve Steps of Alcoholics Anonymous. More recently, many who have not been addicted to alcohol or another addictive chemical also have found healing through these steps. *The Life Recovery Devotional* has been designed for all of us whose lives have in some way been touched by addictions or other compulsive behaviors.

All of the Twelve Steps are rooted in spiritual principles that are displayed prominently in God's Word. And each meditation in this book is based upon biblical truths that will lead us to freedom from the prisons of our addictions and compulsions. This fits with our desire to bring recovery back to the Bible.

These biblical meditations have been written and edited by people who are in recovery. Some of them are focused more toward those of us struggling with addictions; others deal with issues common among those living alongside those with addictions and compulsions. Although we may go about dealing with our problems in very different ways, we're all trying to deal with the pain of growing up in a broken world. Reading these meditations will help us understand the struggles that are common to all of us in recovery. Sharing the truths we encounter will encourage our growth and lead us out of our isolation and loneliness.

This book contains thirty meditations for each of the Twelve Steps, plus five additional meditations to use when starting over after a relapse. There are no wrong ways to use this book (unless it is used to point a finger at someone else). Some of us may choose to read one meditation each day for a year, progressing a step each month. Others may find it more helpful to read through the meditations for a single step several times before progressing to the next. Our recovery is the goal; use the book with this in mind! And this devotional will be helpful whether or not we're active in Twelve Step groups.

Working through the Twelve Steps will unite us with millions of others who are working through their programs. Looking for help in God's Word will unite us with God and the power he offers for our healing. He longs to bring us good news, to heal our broken hearts, to comfort those of us who mourn, and to free us from the bondage of our past. "For I know the plans I have for you," says the LORD. "They are plans for good and not for disaster, to give you a future and a hope" (Jeremiah 29:11).

STEP ONE

We admitted that we were powerless over our dependencies
and that our lives had become unmanageable.

*Jesus said, "I tell you the truth, anyone who doesn't receive
the Kingdom of God like a child will never enter it"
(Mark 10:15).*

Day 1

Like Little Children
Bible Reading: Mark 10:13-16

> We admitted that we were powerless over our dependencies
> and that our lives had become unmanageable.

For many of us in recovery, memories of childhood are memories of the terrors associated with being powerless. If we were raised in families that were out of control, where we were neglected, abused, or exposed to domestic violence and family dysfunction, the thought of being powerless might be unreasonably frightening. We may have silently vowed never again to feel as vulnerable as we did when we were children.

Jesus tells us that the first step into the Kingdom of God is to become like a little child, and this involves being powerless. He said, "I tell you the truth, anyone who doesn't receive the Kingdom of God like a child will never enter it" (Mark 10:15).

In any society, children are the most dependent members. They have no inherent power for self-protection; no means to insure that their lives will be safe, comfortable, or fulfilling. Little children are singularly reliant on the love, care, and nurture of others for their most basic needs. They *must* cry out even though they may not know exactly what they need. They *must* trust their lives to someone who is more powerful than they, and hopefully, they will be heard and lovingly cared for.

We, too, must dare to admit that we are truly powerless if our lives are to become healthy. This doesn't mean we have to become victims again. Admitting our powerlessness is an honest appraisal of our situation in life and a positive step toward recovery.

Discovering our powerlessness is the first step toward wholeness.

Day 2

A Humble Beginning
Bible Reading: 2 Kings 5:1-15

> We admitted that we were powerless over our dependencies
> and that our lives had become unmanageable.

I t can be very humiliating to admit that we are powerless, especially if we are used to being in control. We may be powerful in some areas of our lives, but out of control in terms of our addictive/compulsive behaviors. If we refuse to admit our powerlessness, we may lose everything. That one unmanageable part of our lives may infect and soon destroy everything else.

The experiences of a man named Naaman illustrate how this is true (2 Kings 5:1-15). He was a powerful military and political figure, a man of wealth, position, and power. He also had leprosy, which promised to bring about the loss of everything he held dear. Lepers were made outcasts from their families and society. Ultimately, they faced a slow, painful, and disgraceful death.

Naaman heard that there was a prophet in Israel who could heal him. He found the prophet and was told that in order to be healed he needed to dip himself seven times in the Jordan River. He went away outraged, having expected his power to buy him an instant and easy cure. In the end, however, he acknowledged his powerlessness, followed the instructions, and recovered completely.

Our "disease" is as life threatening as the leprosy in Naaman's day. It slowly separates us from our families and leads toward the destruction of everything important to us. There is no instant or easy cure. The only answer is to admit our powerlessness, humble ourselves, and submit to the process that will eventually bring us recovery.

We must let go in order to hold on to the things dear to us.

A Haunting Weakness
Bible Reading: Romans 7:15-20

> We admitted that we were powerless over our dependencies
> and that our lives had become unmanageable.

A key to recovery is breaking through our denial and admitting our powerlessness. We may want to pretend that all of our struggles are in the past, especially after we begin to "understand the problem." If we are going to maintain our sobriety, however, we need to continually work the first step, remembering that powerlessness is a part of the human condition.

The apostle Paul expressed some thoughts that probably sound like something we might have written ourselves. He says, "I don't really understand myself, for I want to do what is right, but I don't do it. Instead, I do what I hate. But if I know that what I am doing is wrong, this shows that I agree that the law is good. So I am not the one doing wrong; it is sin living in me that does it. And I know that nothing good lives in me, that is, in my sinful nature. I want to do what is right, but I can't. I want to do what is good, but I don't. I don't want to do what is wrong, but I do it anyway. But if I do what I don't want to do, I am not really the one doing wrong; it is sin living in me that does it" (Romans 7:15-20).

The apostle Paul spoke in the present tense about his own condition. And he spoke for all of us. We will never escape the struggle of being human and susceptible to the pull of our lower nature. Admitting this is the first step toward wholeness.

Powerlessness is part of what it means to be human.

Day 4

Dangerous Self-Deception

Bible Reading: Judges 16:1-31

> We admitted that we were powerless over our dependencies
> and that our lives had become unmanageable.

W hen we refuse to admit our powerlessness we are only deceiving ourselves. The lies we tell ourselves and others are familiar: "I could stop any time I want to." "I'm in control; this *one* won't hurt anything." And all the while, we are inching closer to disaster.

Samson was one of Israel's judges. As a child, he had been dedicated to God, and God had gifted him with supernatural strength. But Samson had a lifelong weakness; it had to do with the way he related to women. Samson was especially blinded to the dangers he faced in his relationship with Delilah. His enemies were paying her to discover the secret of his strength. Three times she begged him to let her in on his secret. Each time she set him up and tried to hand him over to the enemy. Three times Samson lied to her and was able to escape. But each time he got closer to telling her the truth. In the end, Samson revealed his secret, was taken captive, and died a slave in enemy hands (Judges 14–16).

Samson's real problem can be found in the lies he told himself. By not admitting his powerlessness, he remained blind to the obvious danger his addiction was leading him into. This caused him to gradually inch his way toward an untimely death.

We need to be careful not to fall into the same trap. As we learn to acknowledge our powerlessness over our addictive/compulsive tendencies on a daily basis, we will become more aware of behaviors that will likely lead to our downfall.

※

> When we lie to ourselves, a dangerous blindness begins
> to grow within us.

Day 5

The Paradox of Powerlessness
Bible Reading: 2 Corinthians 4:7-10

We admitted that we were powerless over our dependencies
and that our lives had become unmanageable.

We may be afraid to admit that we are powerless and that
our lives are unmanageable. If we admit that we are
powerless, won't we be tempted to give up completely
in the struggle against our addiction? It doesn't seem to make sense
that we can admit powerlessness and still find the power to go
on. This paradox will be dealt with as we go on to Steps Two and
Three.

Life is full of paradoxes. The apostle Paul tells us, "We now
have this light shining in our hearts, but we ourselves are like
fragile clay jars containing this great treasure. This makes it clear
that our great power is from God, not from ourselves. We are
pressed on every side by troubles, but we are not crushed. We are
perplexed, but not driven to despair" (2 Corinthians 4:7-8).

The picture here presents a contrast between a precious
treasure and the simple clay jar in which the treasure is stored. The
living power poured into our lives from above is the treasure. Our
human lives, with all the everyday pressures and problems, are represented by the clay jar, an earthen container. As human beings,
we have inherent weaknesses.

Once we recognize the paradox of powerlessness it can be
quite a relief. We don't have to always be strong or pretend to be
perfect. We can live a real life, with daily struggles, in a human
body beset with weakness, and still find the power from above to
keep going without being crushed and broken.

Our powerlessness displays the magnificent power of God.

Day 6

Difficult Losses
Bible Reading: John 15:1-8

We admitted that we were powerless over our dependencies
and that our lives had become unmanageable.

S ome of us have seen everything we have produced in life go
up in smoke because of our addictions. If it hasn't happened
to us, surely we've seen others who have lost all that they
have worked for: home, career, family, health, finances, and friendships. During the times when life becomes unmanageable, we are
faced with the fact that we are not self-sufficient. Sometimes our
losses (or even potential losses) can act to spur us on toward taking
the first step on the road to recovery.

All of us have times of weakness; none of us are self-
sufficient. Jesus recognized this when he said, "Yes, I am the vine;
you are the branches. Those who remain in me, and I in them,
will produce much fruit. For apart from me you can do nothing.
Anyone who does not remain in me is thrown away like a useless
branch and withers. Such branches are gathered into a pile to be
burned" (John 15:5-6).

Some of us have already lost many of the good things our
lives produced. For us it is a matter of facing the losses, admitting
that we can't make it on our own, and starting to grow again. For
others of us, things may still look rewarding, but if we don't deal
honestly with the effects of our addictions we risk seeing the fruits
of our lives burned up. It's hard to give up our pride and admit that
on our own we "can do nothing." Perhaps, by considering the possible losses and the value of our previous investments, we will be
able to "hit bottom" before we lose everything.

❧

Apart from God, our efforts cannot bear fruit.

Day 7

The End of Ourselves

Bible Reading: Psalm 116:1-19

> We admitted that we were powerless over our dependencies
> and that our lives had become unmanageable.

For some of us, we have to stare death in the face before we can admit our need for help. We may experience a crisis where we literally come close to death. Or we may be overwhelmed by depression, suicidal tendencies, and self-destructive behaviors. Sometimes it is our hopelessness and despair that act as a springboard, driving us into recovery. When we realize that we are at the end of ourselves, we may find the humility to reach out and accept the help we need.

King David, whom God loved dearly, felt this way, too. He once said, "The pains of death surrounded me, and the pangs of Sheol laid hold of me; I found trouble and sorrow. Then I called upon the name of the LORD: 'O LORD, I implore You, deliver my soul!' . . . What shall I render to the LORD for all His benefits toward me? I will take up the cup of salvation, and call upon the name of the LORD" (Psalm 116:3-4, 12-13, NKJV). David had hit bottom. He had finally come to the point of realizing that he had nothing to offer except an empty cup, a life in need of salvation. What did he have left to offer? All he had was "a sacrifice of thanksgiving" (vs. 17).

When we have reached our darkest hour and feel that all hope is lost, we may be closer to the help we need than ever before. When death stares us in the face and we realize that our cup is empty, we can lift up our empty cup by admitting our powerlessness, and thus, open up to salvation. In time, we, too, will be able to be thankful once again.

❧

Staring death in the face can be a starting point for recovery.

Day 8

No-Win Situations
Bible Reading: Genesis 16:1-15

We admitted that we were powerless over our dependencies
and that our lives had become unmanageable.

S ometimes we are powerless because of our station in life. We
may be in a situation where other people have power over
our lives. We may feel that we're trapped by the demands
of others, and that there's no way to please them all. It's a double
bind: to please one is to disappoint another. Sometimes when we
feel stuck and frustrated with our relationships, we look for a measure of control by escaping through our addictive behaviors.

Hagar is a picture of powerlessness. She had no rights. As
a girl, she was a slave to Sarai and Abram. When they were upset
because Sarai could not bear children, she was given to Abram as
a surrogate. When she did become pregnant, as they had wanted,
Sarai was so jealous that she beat the girl and she ran away. All
alone, out in the wilderness, she was met by an angel who told her,
"Return to your mistress, and submit to her authority. . . . I will
give you more descendants than you can count. . . . You are now
pregnant and will give birth to a son. You are to name him Ishmael
(which means 'God hears'), for the LORD has heard your cry of distress" (Genesis 16:9-11).

When we are caught in no-win situations, it's tempting
to run away through our addictive/compulsive escape hatches.
At times like these, God is there and he is listening to our woes.
We need to learn to express our pain to God, instead of just trying to escape. He hears our woes and is willing to give us hope for
the future.

❊

It is wise to turn and face our problems, accepting God's
promise of help.

Day 9

Promises for Children
Bible Reading: Genesis 21:1-21

> We admitted that we were powerless over our dependencies and that our lives had become unmanageable.

There is a special kind of powerlessness experienced when we're unable to take care of the needs of our children or others who are dependent on us. For those of us raised in dysfunctional families, there are grief and fear associated with watching our children suffer, as the effects of our own past fall upon them.

With God's help, Hagar had faced her life with Abraham and Sarah. When Sarah was finally able to give birth to her own son, she demanded that Hagar and Ishmael be thrown out of the family. In response, Abraham "got up early the next morning, prepared food and a container of water, and strapped them on Hagar's shoulders. Then he sent her away with their son, and she wandered aimlessly in the wilderness of Beersheba. When the water was gone, she put the boy in the shade of a bush. Then she went and sat down by herself about a hundred yards away. 'I don't want to watch the boy die,' she said, as she burst into tears. But God heard the boy crying, and the angel of God called to Hagar from heaven, 'Hagar, what's wrong? Do not be afraid! God has heard the boy crying as he lies there. Go to him and comfort him, for I will make a great nation from his descendants.' Then God opened Hagar's eyes, and she saw a well full of water. She quickly filled her water container and gave the boy a drink" (Genesis 21:14-19).

God doesn't forget his promises toward us or our children. When we are powerless to help them, God is listening to their cries and ours. We can expect God's help when we are powerless to help our children. He loves them even more than we do.

Our problems won't seem so impossible if we let
God handle them.

Hope amidst Suffering

Bible Reading: Job 6:2-13

> We admitted that we were powerless over our dependencies and that our lives had become unmanageable.

There are times when we are so confused and overwhelmed by the pain in our lives that we wish we could die. No matter what we do, we are powerless to change things for the better. The weight of the sadness seems too heavy to bear. We can't see why our heart just doesn't break and allow death to free us.

Job felt that way. He'd lost everything, even though he had always done what was right. His ten children were dead. He had lost his business, his riches, and his health. And all this happened in a matter of days! He was left with a sharp-tongued wife and three friends who blamed him for his own misfortune. Job cried out, "If my misery could be weighed and my troubles be put on the scales. . . . Oh, that I might have my request, that God would grant my desire. I wish he would crush me. I wish he would reach out his hand and kill me.. . . . I don't have the strength to endure. I have nothing to live for. Do I have the strength of a stone? Is my body made of bronze? No, I am utterly helpless, without any chance of success" (Job 6:2, 8-9, 11-13).

Job didn't know that the end of his life would be even better than it had been at the beginning. God restored everything he had lost, and then some. "Then he died, an old man who had lived a long, full life" (Job 42:17). Even when we're pressed to the point of death, there is still hope that our lives will change. Our recovery could be so complete that the final line written about us might read: "Then they died, having lived long, full lives." We must remember: life can be good again!

❧

Trusting God in difficult times will stretch our faith.

Day 11

A Time to Choose
Bible Reading: Acts 9:1-9

We admitted that we were powerless over our dependencies and that our lives had become unmanageable.

There are important moments in life that can bring about changes in our very destiny. These are often times when we are confronted with how powerless we really are over our own lives. These moments can either destroy us or forever set the course of our lives in a much better direction.

Saul had such a moment. After Jesus' ascension, Saul took it upon himself to rid the world of Christians. As he took off on his quest, "a light from heaven suddenly shone down around him. He fell to the ground and heard a voice saying to him, 'Saul! Saul! Why are you persecuting me? . . . I am Jesus, the one you are persecuting! Now get up and go into the city, and you will be told what you must do.' . . . When he opened his eyes he was blind. So his companions led him by the hand to Damascus. He remained there blind for three days and did not eat or drink" (Acts 9:3-6, 8-9).

Paul—as he was called later—was suddenly confronted with the fact that his life wasn't as perfect as he thought. Self-righteousness had been his trademark. By letting go of his illusions of power, however, he soon became one of the most powerful men ever: the apostle Paul. When we're confronted with the fact that our lives aren't in our control, we have a choice. We can continue in denial and self-righteousness, or we can face the fact that we have been blind to some important issues. If we become willing to be led into recovery and a whole new way of life, we will find true power.

❦

Moments of crisis present us with opportunities for great change.

Day 12

Desperate for Love
Bible Reading: Genesis 29:16-35

We admitted that we were powerless over our dependencies
and that our lives had become unmanageable.

We'll do almost anything to gain the love we need (which may have been denied us as children or in our marriage). Maybe the pain and sadness over our powerlessness to attract the love we desperately need drive us to find a way to deaden the pain.

Leah was a plain girl with a beautiful younger sister and a scheming father. Her father tricked Jacob into marrying Leah. He then allowed Jacob also to have her sister, Rachel. "So Jacob slept with Rachel, too, and he loved her much more than Leah. . . . When the LORD saw that Leah was unloved, he enabled her to have children, but Rachel could not conceive. So Leah became pregnant and gave birth to a son. She named him Reuben, for she said, 'The LORD has noticed my misery, and now my husband will love me.' She soon became pregnant again and gave birth to another son. She named him Simeon, for she said, 'The LORD heard that I was unloved and has given me another son.' Then she became pregnant a third time and gave birth to another son. She named him Levi, for she said, 'Surely this time my husband will feel affection for me, since I have given him three sons!'" (Genesis 29:30-34).

We may be powerless to make someone love us, spending our lives trying to produce something to make us worthy of their love. This need might gnaw away at us and lead to relapse when the pain becomes overwhelming. When people won't love us, we can learn to draw upon the love of God. He loves us as we are.

❧

Drawing on God's unconditional love and grace can fill
our need to be wanted.

Day 13

Emotional Time Bombs
Bible Reading: 2 Samuel 13:1-24

> We admitted that we were powerless over our dependencies
> and that our lives had become unmanageable.

T here are times when we become deeply upset by the injustices of life, the abuses kept as family secrets, the feelings buried alive, and our vows to get even. In such times, we often become powerless over the strength of our inner turmoil. All we can feel is the resolve to act out our hatred. We can't control feelings.

Absalom became powerless over his hatred and rage. It ultimately controlled his life to the point that he fought to overthrow his father's rule. He was outraged when his half brother raped his sister, Tamar. When King David did nothing to avenge his daughter, Absalom vowed revenge in his heart. He waited until the time was right and murdered the guilty brother. This sequence of abuse, family secrecy, denial, unprocessed feelings, and revenge destroyed Absalom's relationship with his father. He never forgave David and died in a military rebellion against him (2 Samuel 13:1–18:33).

We may use our addictive/compulsive behaviors to distract us from the deep, unresolved family issues that cut us to the heart. There may be so many strong emotions, which we don't know how to process appropriately, that we simply try to stuff them down inside. Eventually these feelings are expressed in some way. We need to confront the family secrets, express our feelings, convict the guilty, and work through forgiveness. If we try to ignore them, we will be controlled by these explosive hidden emotions.

❧

> Hatred leads to disaster; accepting our powerlessness
> leads to recovery and wholeness.

Day 14

Destructive Pride
Bible Reading: Acts 8:9-23

We admitted that we were powerless over our dependencies
and that our lives had become unmanageable.

For many of us, personal power is used as the foundation for
our self-esteem. We become used to getting things our way,
through whatever influences we have at our disposal (money,
power, sex, love, etc.). It can be very unsettling to arrive at a place
in life where we can't buy the power we need. For those of us who
use power to bolster our self-esteem, admitting powerlessness will
require a foundational change.

"A man named Simon had been a sorcerer. . . . Everyone,
from the least to the greatest, often spoke of him as 'the Great
One—the Power of God.' . . . Then Simon himself believed [that
Jesus was the Messiah]. . . . When Simon saw that the Spirit was
given when the apostles laid their hands on people, he offered
them money to buy this power. . . . But Peter replied, 'May your
money be destroyed with you for thinking God's gift can be bought!
You can have no part in this, for your heart is not right with God.
Repent of your wickedness and pray to the Lord. Perhaps he will
forgive your evil thoughts, for I can see that you are full of bitter
jealousy and are held captive by sin'" (Acts 8:9-10, 13, 18-23).

Simon realized he was powerless in this situation. He admitted his pride and powerlessness and was able to change. We need
to be aware of how pride can hinder us. We can't buy our way out
of addiction. No matter how "powerful" we are in worldly terms,
our recovery will come by working a program, day by day.

🌱

Our recovery can only begin as we "give up" our
efforts and our pride.

Serenity despite Powerlessness

Bible Reading: Luke 1:26-56

We admitted that we were powerless over our dependencies
and that our lives had become unmanageable.

T here are times in life when we are powerless over the circumstances around us. We're not in the driver's seat. We
have to do things someone else's way. And often, the whole
experience is uncomfortable and frightening. During these times
we can find hope and serenity in the promises of God.

Mary was in her early teens when destiny took her by the
hand. She was greeted by an angel who announced that she had
been chosen by God to be the mother of the Messiah. She found
herself pregnant, much to the confusion of her fiancé, family,
friends, and neighbors. After the angel returned to visit her fiancé,
he believed Mary's story and married her. When the time came to
give birth, she and Joseph were required to travel the long, difficult
journey to Bethlehem. There, in a smelly stable carved out of the
side of a rocky hill, she delivered the baby. No one but her husband
was there to attend Jesus' birth (Luke 1:26–2:20).

What power did she have over her circumstances? She was
powerless under the will of God, the decree of the state, the limitations of their financial poverty, and the demands of her body. And
yet, by holding on to the promises God had given her, she found
serenity in her powerlessness and gave birth to the Savior. When
we are powerless, we can find serenity by holding on to the promises of God. When we do this, we will find new life and salvation
being born again into our lives.

No matter what our circumstances, God meets us
there with his grace.

Day 16

Self-Control versus Willpower
Bible Reading: Galatians 5:16-23

We admitted that we were powerless over our dependencies
and that our lives had become unmanageable.

There's a struggle going on inside of us—a fight for control.
Our willpower fails us repeatedly. Where can we turn when
we realize that we can't control ourselves?

The apostle Paul says, "Let the Holy Spirit guide your lives.
Then you won't be doing what your sinful craves. The sinful nature wants to do evil, which is just the opposite of what the
Spirit wants. And the Spirit gives us desires that are the opposite
of what the sinful nature desires. These two forces are constantly
fighting each other, so you are not free to carry out your good
intentions. . . . But the Holy Spirit produces this kind of fruit in
our lives: love, joy, peace, patience, kindness, goodness, faithfulness, gentleness, and self-control" (Galatians 5:16-17, 22-23).

Self-control is not willpower. It's not something we get
by gritting our teeth and forcing ourselves to "just say no." Self-
control is called a fruit. Fruit doesn't instantly pop out on the tree.
As the tree grows and seasons pass, the fruit naturally develops. As
we continue to follow God's guidance, taking one step at a time,
our self-control will naturally grow. Our job is to stay connected to
God. It's the Holy Spirit's job to produce the fruit of self-control.

❧

As God takes control of our lives, self-control will be
the natural result.

Day 17

Victim or Victor?
Bible Reading: 1 Samuel 17:20-49

We admitted that we were powerless over our dependencies
and that our lives had become unmanageable.

There will be times in life when right and wrong stand in
stark contrast. Even when we know what's right and how
things should be changed, the power may seem to be on
the wrong side. We may feel powerless even though we know we
are standing for what is right. But even when this is true, we still
shouldn't give up. Sometimes situations where we feel powerless
can prompt action that changes everything for the better.

David observed as "Goliath, the Philistine champion from
Gath, came out from the Philistine ranks. Then David heard him
shout his usual taunt to the army of Israel. As soon as the Israelite
army saw him, they began to run away in fright. 'Have you seen
the giant?' the men asked. 'He comes out each day to defy Israel.'"
David convinced the king to let him fight the giant his own way.
He shouted to Goliath, "'You come to me with sword, spear, and
javelin, but I come to you in the name of the LORD of Heaven's
Armies—the God of the armies of Israel, whom you have defied.
Today the LORD will conquer you'" (1 Samuel 17:23-25, 45-46).

The army saw themselves as helpless victims. Their powerlessness paralyzed them so they just stood there and took the abuse.
David took courageous action to recover their dignity. There are
times when we need courage and God's help to fight against the
tendency to remain a victim. We need to stand up for our human
dignity and respond in new ways if we are to claim our recovery.

With God by our side there is no need to wait;
we can move forward into our recovery.

Day 18

Painful Abandonment
Bible Reading: Isaiah 54:1-8

We admitted that we were powerless over our dependencies
and that our lives had become unmanageable.

Many of us know the deep sorrow and shame that come
from being abandoned. Those we should have been able
to depend on weren't there for us. We may have lost them
through an untimely death; or perhaps they were there in body
but out of our reach emotionally because of their own addictions.
We know the deep, unspeakable fear that can reach up and grab
hold of us at any moment. We may have used our own compulsive
behaviors to find comfort and distance from our feelings of abandonment.

Here's the Lord's message to those who have experienced
the loss of an important relationship: "Sing, O childless woman!
. . . For the desolate woman now has more children than the
woman who lives with her husband! . . . Fear not; you will no
longer live in shame. Don't be afraid; there is no more disgrace for
you. You will no longer remember the shame of your youth and
the sorrows of widowhood. For your Creator will be your husband;
the LORD of Heaven's Armies is his name! He is your Redeemer,
the Holy One of Israel, the God of all the earth. For the LORD has
called you back from your grief" (Isaiah 54:1, 4-6).

God wants to give us such confidence in our relationship
with him that we can be free of the fear of abandonment and overcome its scars. He can make up to us all that we have missed in our
past relationships. He can fill the shoes of the one who isn't there
for us. There is a season for grieving the losses, but the Lord can
call us back from grief and give us renewed joy.

❧

God delivers us from shame and abandonment,
welcoming us to the joy of recovery.

Day 19

God's Power
Bible Reading: Isaiah 42:21-25

> We admitted that we were powerless over our dependencies and that our lives had become unmanageable.

Many of us believe that God's law is good and that it provides helpful moral standards. We may try hard to be perfect, but find ourselves frustrated. Some of us may be troubled by this, and we probably avoid thinking about it. We try not to feel the shame and guilt that come with violating these values that we've taken as our own. We may pretend that everything is fine with us and focus on another person's addiction to avoid our own inner conflict.

Isaiah tells us, "Because he is righteous, the LORD has exalted his glorious law. But his own people have been robbed and plundered, enslaved, imprisoned, and trapped. They are fair game for anyone. . . . The people would not walk in his path, nor would they obey his law" (Isaiah 42:21-22, 24). The words translated *obey* literally mean "take it to heart." God wanted his people to take his law to the depth of their being. This is the part of us where we feel, think, and choose.

The law of God is designed to magnify God's righteousness, not ours! "We are all infected and impure with sin. When we display our righteous deeds, they are nothing but filthy rags" (Isaiah 64:6). When we are powerless over sin to the point where we become enslaved and unprotected, God wants us to "take it to heart." When we allow ourselves to feel and think and choose in response to our own powerlessness, we are on our way to finding God's power, the only power that leads to freedom.

Our powerlessness leads us directly to God's power.

Day 20

Our Limitations
Bible Reading: Galatians 3:19-26

We admitted that we were powerless over our dependencies and that our lives had become unmanageable.

Many of us begin our recovery by seeing that we've been powerless to measure up to God's laws. Some of us, however, expect that once we're well on the road to recovery we'll start keeping the laws of God. And we hope that this will guarantee our standing with God on the basis of our good works. We start with a recognition of our powerlessness, but hope for the day when we will no longer be powerless. Surely our standing before God must be somewhat dependent upon our keeping of the law! Otherwise, why would he have given us his laws in the first place?

The apostle Paul answers by saying, "Why, then, was the law given? It was given alongside the promise [of salvation through faith] to show people their sins. . . . If the law could give us new life, we could be made right with God by obeying it. But the Scriptures declare that we are all prisoners of sin, so we receive God's promise of freedom only by believing in Jesus Christ. . . . The law was our guardian until Christ came; it protected us until we could be made right with God through faith" (Galatians 3:19, 21-22, 24).

The law of God is an eternal reminder of our true powerlessness—our ongoing need for a Savior and for the power of God. Our failures should point us back to the only one able to help us recover.

✖

God sets us free from our failures and places us on the path toward recovery.

Day 21

Powerless and Abused
Bible Reading: Judges 19:12-30

> We admitted that we were powerless over our dependencies
> and that our lives had become unmanageable.

There are societal forces beyond our control. We live in times when sexual abuse is commonplace and security in relationships is hard to find. We may know the agony of being sexually abused or bear the shame of allowing someone else to be victimized when we were in a position to protect them. A deep sense of powerlessness is experienced in this kind of situation.

Before Israel had a king, there was no law and order; "all the people did whatever seemed right in their own eyes" (Judges 21:25). A horrifying story is told of a young woman who was brutally gang-raped. Her husband had allowed her to be taken by a group of men who had been trying to attack and rape him. He "took hold of his concubine and pushed her out the door. The men of the town abused her all night. . . . When her husband opened the door to leave, there lay his concubine with her hands on the threshold" (Judges 19:25-27). The girl died there on the doorstep. Her death became a rallying cry for reform, but she had been lost. Her husband was left with terrible shame and guilt. The man and his young wife were both victims, suffering the pain of powerlessness in a crime-filled society.

If we have been victims of sexual abuse, we must begin by acknowledging that we were powerless. Although we suffered the abuse, we were not the cause of it. This realization is an important key to our recovery.

> Recovery from being a victim begins by recognizing
> our powerlessness.

Day 22

Secure Love

Bible Reading: Song of Solomon 5:1-8

We admitted that we were powerless over our dependencies
and that our lives had become unmanageable.

The search for love and permanent security in relationships is
deep within all of us. Even though we may be in a relationship where we are loved, we may deeply fear the loss of that
love. This is especially true if we've been abandoned in the past or
had our love betrayed.

The Song of Solomon is a love poem dedicated to the girl
Solomon loved. He describes a nightmare she had: "I opened to
my lover, but he was gone! My heart sank. I searched for him but
could not find him anywhere. . . . Make this promise, O women
of Jerusalem—If you find my lover, tell him I am weak with love"
(Song of Solomon 5:6, 8). The fear of separation darkened the
girl's joy at being deeply loved. At the end of the poem she says,
"Place me like a seal over your heart, like a seal on your arm. For
love is as strong as death, its jealousy as enduring as the grave"
(Song of Solomon 8:6).

We are all haunted by a deep need for a "permanent
betrothal," a secure love that won't escape us. When we lose a
close and intimate relationship, we become lovesick. We feel
powerless over the forces driving us in search of permanent and
true love. No matter how much a person loves us, our needs seem
deeper. Perfect love that never leaves can only be found in the
one who is *Love*. When we are powerless over the forces of love
or over our own obsessions, we need to look to God to satisfy our
deepest longings so that fear and dissatisfaction don't become
a trap.

God can—and will—satisfy our deepest longings.

Day 23

Breaking the Cycle

Bible Reading: Ecclesiastes 1:1-18

> We admitted that we were powerless over our dependencies
> and that our lives had become unmanageable.

Human existence consists of a series of patterns. Our world goes around the sun in an unending orbit; it spins on its axis with tireless regularity. Dysfunctional family patterns seem to resurface generation after generation in a wearying march of repetitious pain. We may grow tired and wonder if there's really any escape from the merry-go-round of addictive behavior and suffering.

King Solomon examined life and was discouraged by some of his observations. "Generations come and generations go, but the earth never changes. The sun rises and the sun sets, then hurries around to rise again. The wind blows south, and then turns north. Around and around it goes, blowing in circles. Rivers run into the sea, but the sea is never full. Then the water returns again to the rivers. . . . Everything is wearisome beyond description. . . . No matter how much we hear, we are not content" (Ecclesiastes 1:4-8).

Life can seem like one meaningless, wearying cycle after another. Solomon observed that our lives can be spent without ever going anywhere. He also wrote these instructions: "Follow the steps of good men instead, and stay on the paths of the righteous" (Proverbs 2:20). Throughout the Bible we see that life can be linear, leading somewhere. Even though we are powerless to stop all the destructive cycles around us, we can take our own steps in the direction of recovery and a new way of life.

> Our efforts just add to the destructive cycles in life;
> only God can break them.

Day 24

Starting with Ourselves
Bible Reading: Ecclesiastes 3:15–4:3

> We admitted that we were powerless over our dependencies
> and that our lives had become unmanageable.

S ome of us avoid or cope with our own pain by trying to fix
the world. We try to right every wrong, heal every wound,
point out every injustice. We spend our time demanding
that the world system reform. We may also dedicate ourselves to
rescuing and reforming those we love. Our zealousness to set the
world aright can be a means of denying that we are powerless
to do so.

Solomon said, "I also noticed that under the sun there is
evil in the courtroom. Yes, even the courts of law are corrupt! I said
to myself, 'In due season God will judge everyone, both good and
bad, for all their deeds.' . . . I observed all the oppression that takes
place under the sun. I saw the tears of the oppressed, with no one
to comfort them. The oppressors have great power" (Ecclesiastes
3:16-17; 4:1). He saw that the world was not as it should be. He
also recognized that it was God's job to judge and overcome the
injustices in our world.

When we set out to save the world we err by taking on a
role that belongs to God. What we gain by taking on such a massive task is the guarantee that we'll always be busy. Then we'll
never have the time or energy to face our own issues. The Bible
makes it clear that the world will never be right until Jesus Christ
returns to make it so. We need to accept the fact that we are powerless to do his job. However, when we focus on our own recovery,
fixing ourselves instead of everyone else, we will then be able to be
more effective in helping others, too.

If we try to fix the world before fixing ourselves,
we'll do both badly.

Magical Thinking

Bible Reading: Ecclesiastes 5:10-12

> We admitted that we were powerless over our dependencies
> and that our lives had become unmanageable.

T his is one of the rules that governs a dysfunctional family:
Always blame someone or something whenever things get
out of control. We might say, "If only I weren't poor, then
I could handle life." We might dream of how all our problems
would be resolved if only we were rich. But by blaming our lack
of wealth, we fail to take responsibility for coping with life.

Solomon was one of the richest men who ever lived. He
had this to say on the subject: "Those who love money will never
have enough. How meaningless to think that wealth brings true
happiness! The more you have, the more people come to help you
spend it. So what good is wealth—except perhaps to watch it slip
through your fingers! People who work hard sleep well, whether
they eat little or much. But the rich seldom get a good night's
sleep" (Ecclesiastes 5:10-12).

Solomon, along with many affluent people of our day, is
living proof that riches don't solve our problems or guarantee
happiness. Wealthy people are just as powerless over their lives
and addictions as poor people. Accepting this reality can help us
to face the fact that it is not anything external that keeps us from
recovery. We don't need to wait until we have more money to
begin coping with our lives and our compulsive behaviors. The
sooner we stop all the blaming and begin to acknowledge the true
powerlessness of the human condition, the sooner we'll recover.

❧

No matter how much or how little we have, it will
never be "enough."

Chasing the Wind

Bible Reading: Ecclesiastes 2:1-11

We admitted that we were powerless over our dependencies
and that our lives had become unmanageable.

We may have gotten involved in our addictive behavior on an experimental basis at first. We wanted to taste life's pleasures and find the fun and excitement. For a while the "partying" makes us feel good; but when we pull back to look at our lives we realize that we're not really getting any closer to fulfillment.

Solomon set out to taste all of life's pleasures, and he had the means to do so without limit. He writes, "I said to myself, 'Come on, let's try pleasure. Let's look for the "good things" in life.' But I found that this, too, was meaningless. So I said, 'Laughter is silly. What good does it do to seek pleasure?'" Solomon systematically explored drinking, looking for wisdom, toying with folly, trying to find fulfillment through public works projects and empire building, collecting slaves, silver and gold, enhancing his sense of power, involvement in the cultural arts and vast sexual exploits. He then explains, "Anything I wanted, I would take. I denied myself no pleasure. I even found great pleasure in hard work, a reward for all my labors. But as I looked at everything I had worked so hard to accomplish, it was all so meaningless—like chasing the wind. There was nothing really worthwhile anywhere" (Ecclesiastes 2:1-2, 10-11).

Like Solomon, we, too, may be chasing the wind and getting nowhere. The futility of being driven to excess in our "chasing around," whether in work or play, can cause us to miss the true purpose of our existence and the fulfillment we seek.

❦

Our addictions are like the wind: we may feel them as they pass,
but we can never hold on to them.

Day 27

A Balanced Life

Bible Reading: Ecclesiastes 7:14-17

We admitted that we were powerless over our dependencies
and that our lives had become unmanageable.

For those of us raised in chaotic situations our response may
be to try to maintain control of something . . . anything! We
may become rigid and controlling of our children, or insist
on having control in our homes or work relationships. Perhaps we
focus on our eating habits or develop rituals for living that give us
the feeling of being in control of our own lives.

King Solomon tells us, "Enjoy prosperity while you can, but
when hard times strike, realize that both come from God. Remember that nothing is certain in this life. I have seen everything in
this meaningless life, including the death of good young people
and the long life of wicked people. . . . For there is a time and
a way for everything, even when a person is in trouble. Indeed,
how can people avoid what they don't know is going to happen?"
(Ecclesiastes 7:14-15; 8:6-7).

It's understandable that we would want to develop a security
system to protect our lives in response to our past powerlessness
and the pain it brought. Maintaining control can serve to make us
feel safer in an uncertain world. However, it can also pose a trap
for us, if we must always have control in order to cope. We need to
balance our understanding of life to realize that life is uncertain.
We will not always be in situations where we have the power and
control we need to make us feel safe. This balance can keep us on
track, even when an unexpected loss of power occurs.

❧

If we must always be in control, we're out of control.

28

Day 28

Powerless over Death
Bible Reading: Ecclesiastes 7:1-4

We admitted that we were powerless over our dependencies
and that our lives had become unmanageable.

From the moment of birth, we all are living under the sentence of death. For some of us there is the added burden of knowing we are going to die as the result of previous risky behavior related to our addictions. Others of us realize that our addictions could kill us if they are not brought under control. We are all powerless over death. The understanding of this can actually be beneficial for us.

King Solomon wisely noted, "The day you die is better than the day you are born. Better to spend your time at funerals than at parties. After all, everyone dies—so the living should take this to heart. Sorrow is better than laughter, for sadness has a refining influence on us. A wise person thinks a lot about death, while a fool thinks only about having a good time. . . . None of us can hold back our spirit from departing. None of us has the power to prevent the day of our death. There is no escaping that obligation, that dark battle" (Ecclesiastes 7:1-4; 8:8).

Realizing that we are powerless over the inevitable approach of death should have a sobering effect on us all. Death has a way of revealing our powerlessness and uncovering hidden sorrow as nothing else can. Thinking about the end of life, however, should also help us realize how precious each day of life actually is. The sorrow of approaching death can help us by revealing what is really important in life and by strengthening our commitment to recovery.

We all live under the sentence of death; we should make
the most of each and every day.

Day 29

When Heroes Lose
Bible Reading: Ecclesiastes 9:11-12

We admitted that we were powerless over our dependencies and that our lives had become unmanageable.

Some of us who grew up in dysfunctional families vowed to escape their downward pull. We may have become the "family hero," the one who "was going to make it." We set out believing in some formula for success, maybe even based on scriptural principles. We have told ourselves, "If I only do thus and such, I will have to be successful." It feels very safe as long as our beliefs match with our experience.

Solomon relates, "I have observed something else under the sun. The fastest runner doesn't always win the race, and the strongest warrior doesn't always win the battle. The wise sometimes go hungry, and the skillful are not necessarily wealthy. . . . It is all decided by chance, by being in the right place at the right time. People can never predict when hard times might come. Like fish in a net or birds in a trap, people are caught by sudden tragedy" (Ecclesiastes 9:11-12).

Life doesn't always follow our rules or any other set of rules that might help us predict how things will happen. Even the truth of the Bible leaves room for a struggle between the forces of good and evil. There are times when we do our best, try our hardest to be good, and apply ourselves completely. But life still doesn't work out the way we think it should. Our lives are interwoven with the lives of others in a world that isn't always fair. Regardless of how hard we try, we cannot predict with certainty or guarantee the exact journey we will take through life.

This world grants only one guarantee—our powerlessness.

Day 30

Powerless to Understand

Bible Reading: Lamentations 5:7-22

> We admitted that we were powerless over our dependencies
> and that our lives had become unmanageable.

W hen the bottom falls out of our world, we grapple with confusion. We try to understand what is happening and why it's happening to us. Is it our fault? What did we do wrong? We look for someone to blame. We search for meaning in the madness. We stagger in our attempt to make some sense of it all.

After the destruction of Jerusalem the prophet Jeremiah poured out his heart to God. He described the horrifying conditions that fell upon the people he loved. He cried out, "Our ancestors sinned, but they have died—and we are suffering the punishment they deserved! . . . The garlands have fallen from our heads. . . . But LORD, you remain the same forever! Your throne continues from generation to generation. Why do you continue to forget us? Why have you abandoned us for so long? Restore us, O LORD, and bring us back to you again! Give us back the joys we once had! Or have you utterly rejected us? Are you angry with us still?" (Lamentations 5:7, 16, 19-22).

Even this great prophet of God was often powerless to understand the meaning of the troubling events in his life. Whose fault was it? Why did this have to happen to us and our loved ones? When we are powerless to understand, it is wise to follow Jeremiah's example and turn to God. God is always there. He understands when we can't. He has promised that "he will listen to the prayers of the destitute" (Psalm 102:17).

❧

> Though we can't always understand the events of life,
> we can know that God does.

STEP TWO

We came to believe that a Power greater than ourselves could restore us to sanity.

"Faith is the confidence that what we hope for will actually happen"
(Hebrews 11:1).

Grandiose Thinking
Bible Reading: Daniel 4:19-33

> We came to believe that a Power greater than ourselves
> could restore us to sanity.

When we're caught up in our addiction, it's common for us to deceive ourselves with grandiose thinking. We may believe that we're above it all, a god unto ourselves, accountable to no one.

In his day, Nebuchadnezzar, king of ancient Babylon, was the most powerful ruler on earth. He believed himself to be a god and demanded worship as such. God said to him, "The Most High has declared . . . [that] you will be driven from human society, and you will live in the fields with the wild animals . . . until you learn that the Most High rules over the kingdoms of the world and gives them to anyone he chooses" (Daniel 4:24-25).

All this happened just as predicted. At the end of the king's time in exile, he said, "I . . . looked up to heaven. My sanity returned, and I praised and worshiped the Most High and honored the one who lives forever. . . . When my sanity returned to me, so did my honor and glory and kingdom . . . with even greater honor than before. Now I, Nebuchadnezzar, praise and glorify and honor the King of heaven. All his acts are just and true, and he is able to humble the proud" (Daniel 4:34, 36-37).

We must remember that we are not God. We're accountable to a higher Power who can remedy our "madness" and restore our lives to be even better than before our season of insanity.

❧

> God is not going to shape our lives until we
> acknowledge him as God.

Day 2

Healing Faith
Bible Reading: Luke 8:43-48

We came to believe that a Power greater than ourselves
could restore us to sanity.

F aith is a key to successfully working the second step. For some
of us faith comes easily. For others, especially if we have experienced betrayal, it may be more difficult. Sometimes we must
exhaust all of our own resources in trying to overcome our addictive "disease" before we will risk believing in a higher Power.

When Jesus was on earth he was renowned for his healing
power. Crowds of sick people constantly pressed in on him. One
day there was "a woman in the crowd [who] had suffered for twelve
years with constant bleeding, and she could find no cure. Coming
up behind Jesus, she touched the fringe of his robe. Immediately,
the bleeding stopped." Jesus realized that someone had deliberately
touched him because he felt the healing power go out from him.
When the woman confessed that she was the one who had been
healed, Jesus said, "Your faith has made you well. Go in peace"
(Luke 8:43-48).

In order to recover we need to follow the example of this
woman. We cannot afford to stand back, hoping for a "cure," and
avoid deliberate action because of our lack of faith. We may have
lived with our condition for many years, spending our resources on
promising "cures" without success. When we can come to believe
in a Power greater than ourselves and have the faith to take hold
of our own recovery, we will find the healing power we've been
looking for.

❧

What a difference between knowing about Jesus and
reaching out to touch him!

34

Restoration
Bible Reading: Luke 15:11-24

> We came to believe that a Power greater than ourselves
> could restore us to sanity.

I n the natural progression of addiction our lives necessarily
degenerate. In one way or another, many of us wake up one
day to realize that we are living like animals. How this is true
depends on the nature of our addiction. Some of us may be living like animals in terms of our physical surroundings. Others of
us may be slaves to our animal passions—powerful emotions that
dehumanize us.

A young man took an early inheritance and wandered away
from home. When the money was spent, the women just a memory,
and the "high" long gone, he resorted to slopping pigs to earn a
meager living. When he became so hungry that he was eyeing
the pig's slop with envy, he realized he had a problem. "When he
finally came to his senses, he said to himself, 'At home even the
hired servants have food enough and to spare, and here I am dying
of hunger! I will go home to my father. . . .' So he returned home
to his father. And while he was still a long way off, his father saw
him coming. Filled with love and compassion, he ran to his son,
embraced him, and kissed him" (Luke 15:17-18, 20).

The fact that we are able to recognize our lives as degenerate or insane proves that there is hope for a better way of life. We
are reminded of a time when life was good and we long to have it
restored. When we turn in the direction of one who is more powerful, who represents the memory of something better, we will find
the Power that can restore us to sanity.

❧

> God doesn't force us to come to him; he simply
> waits for us to come to our senses.

Day 4

Hope in Faith
Bible Reading: Hebrews 11:1-10

> We came to believe that a Power greater than ourselves
> could restore us to sanity.

S tep Two is often referred to as "the hope step." In coming to believe that a Power greater than ourselves can restore us to sanity, we must remember what it was like to live sanely, and have the faith to hope that sanity can return.

"What is faith?" the Bible asks. "Faith is the confidence that what we hope for will actually happen; it gives us assurance about things we cannot see" (Hebrews 11:1). How can we be confident that something we want is going to happen, especially if all of our hopes have been dashed? How can we risk believing that the life we hope for is waiting for us around the bend?

The Bible tells us that the key is in the nature of the higher Power we look to. We are told, "Anyone who wants to come to him must believe that God exists and that he rewards those who sincerely seek him" (Hebrews 11:6). If we see God as one waiting to reward us, we will be more eager to look for him. If our faith has not matured to that point yet, we can ask for help. There was one man who came to Jesus and asked him to help his young son who was afflicted by a demon. He said to Jesus, "'Have mercy on us and help us, if you can.' 'What do you mean, "If I can"?' Jesus asked. 'Anything is possible if a person believes.' The father instantly cried out, 'I do believe, but help me overcome my unbelief!'" (Mark 9:22-24). We can start by asking God to help us to have more faith. Then we can ask him for the courage to hope for a better future.

Faith starts when we believe God is who he is.

36

Day 5

Internal Bondage
Bible Reading: Mark 5:1-13

> We came to believe that a Power greater than ourselves
> could restore us to sanity.

When we are under the influence of our addiction, it may feel like its hold has supernatural force. We may give up on living, throwing ourselves into self-destructive behaviors with wild abandonment. People also may give up on us. They may divorce themselves from us, as though we were already dead. Whether our "insanity" is self-induced or even if it has a more sinister origin, there is power to restore us to sanity.

Jesus helped a man who was known to be acting insanely. "This man lived among the burial caves and could no longer be restrained, even with a chain. Whenever he was put into chains and shackles—as he often was—he snapped the chains from his wrists and smashed the shackles. No one was strong enough to subdue him. Day and night he wandered among the burial caves and in the hills, howling and cutting himself with sharp stones" (Mark 5:3-5). Jesus went into the graveyard and assessed the situation. He dealt with the forces of darkness that were afflicting him and restored the man to sanity. He then sent him home to his friends and family.

We may be so far gone that we have broken all restraints. We struggle to be free from the control of society and loved ones. Then we discover that our bondage doesn't come from outside sources. All hope seems lost; but if there is still life there is still hope. God can come into our "burial caves," too, and restore us to sanity.

> Only a Power greater than ourselves can free us
> from our bondage.

Day 6

Filling the Emptiness
Bible Reading: Luke 8:35-39

> We came to believe that a Power greater than ourselves
> could restore us to sanity.

Some of us enter recovery because of the intervention of those who love us. We are confronted and persuaded to break from our addiction. Perhaps, we have received spiritual help and been delivered from demonic influences as well. Intervention can be a very helpful starting place but we cannot afford to stop there.

With the demon-possessed man who lived among the tombs, Jesus came into his territory and confronted him. There is no record that the man was seeking help before this "intervention." After the encounter, the crowd "saw the man . . . sitting at Jesus' feet, fully clothed and perfectly sane" (Luke 8:35).

Most of us would stop right there, but if we did, we would probably end up in worse shape than before. Jesus explains, "When an evil spirit leaves a person, it goes into the desert, searching for rest. But when it finds none, it says, 'I will return to the person I came from.' So it returns and finds that its former home is all swept and in order Then the spirit finds seven other spirits more evil than itself, and they all enter the person and live there. And so that person is worse off than before" (Luke 11:24-26).

If we are to remain free, we must go beyond just accepting deliverance. It's not enough to just let Christ clean us up. We must use our season of sobriety to go back and deal with filling up the empty, broken places in our hearts and lives.

> Recovery is a beginning of restoration; but to be in
> recovery, we need to continue what we begin.

Finding Support
Bible Reading: Galatians 6:1-5

> We came to believe that a Power greater than ourselves
> could restore us to sanity.

For some of us the higher Power we turn to first is the power of something we can see and feel. When we find a group of supportive people, who understand our struggle and care about our recovery, we can turn to them to help us on the road toward restoration.

The apostle Paul wrote about the value of people helping people. He instructed, if someone "is overcome by some sin, you who are godly should gently and humbly help that person back onto the right path. And be careful not to fall into the same temptation yourself" (Galatians 6:1). Some versions say, "restore such a one in a spirit of gentleness" (NKJV). In the original biblical language, the word *restore* means to allow a broken bone to set and heal properly. Paul was calling to mind a picture of people lifting up and carrying a person who had been injured. It implies that they will continue to uphold the suffering person until the injury has had time to heal.

We can't recover all alone any more than someone with a broken leg can heal properly while walking around without any support. We need support from people who are willing to gently bear us up and walk beside us until we've had time to heal.

The verse warns those giving the support that they should remember their own capacity for falling. It is important for us to turn to people who have some understanding of their own brokenness, who will be able to act in a "spirit of gentleness."

❦

> No one is ever independent enough to not need
> help from others.

Day 8

Coming to Believe

Bible Reading: Romans 1:18-20

> We came to believe that a Power greater than ourselves
> could restore us to sanity.

To say that we "came to believe" in anything describes a process. Belief is the result of consideration, doubt, reasoning, and concluding. Forming beliefs shows the mark of God's image in our lives. It involves emotion and logic. It leads to action. What's the process that leads to solid belief, which leads us to change our lives?

We start with our own experience. We see what doesn't work. Looking at the condition of our lives, we realize that there isn't enough power in ourselves to restore us to sanity. We try with all our might, but to no avail. When we're quiet enough to listen, we hear that little voice inside us saying, "There is a God and he's extremely powerful." The apostle Paul said it this way: "They know the truth about God because he has made it obvious to them" (Romans 1:19).

After looking at our internal weakness, we then need to look outside ourselves. We need to see that there are others who have struggled with addictions and recovered. We can see that they, too, were unable to heal themselves, yet they are able to live free of the addictive behavior. We conclude that there must be a greater Power that helped them. Since we can see the similarities between their struggle and our own, we come to believe that there must be a Power greater than ourselves that can restore us to sanity also. This is where many people are when they get to Step Two; and it's a good place to be on the way to recovery.

> God has put knowledge about himself inside each of us,
> but sometimes we can see him best in others.

God's Character
Bible Reading: Romans 1:21-23

> We came to believe that a Power greater than ourselves
> could restore us to sanity.

Most of us who have lived with addictions struggle with inner guilt. We may conclude that God is against us, and/or that we are against him. Our fear of rejection, coupled with the fear of having to give up an addiction that helps us cope, can cause us to distance ourselves from God. When this happens, our minds become confused. We concoct a long list of all the things we need to do in order to come to God. This list usually describes our version of what it means to be "good enough." And in our minds, it often disqualifies us from the hope of having a loving relationship with God.

The apostle Paul once wrote, "Yes, they knew God, but they wouldn't worship him as God or even give him thanks. And they began to think up foolish ideas of what God was like. As a result, their minds became dark and confused. Claiming to be wise, they instead became utter fools" (Romans 1:21-22).

If we have negative feelings toward God, we need to look carefully at the reasoning behind our conclusions. We may have concluded that we don't want, or can't accept, God. If we examine these conclusions and compare them with what the Bible really says about God, we may be happy to find that God is far more loving and accepting than we might have believed possible.

❧

> Addictions begin when we reject what we know about God;
> recovery begins when we rediscover it.

Day 10

Persistent Seeking
Bible Reading: Job 14:1-6

> We came to believe that a Power greater than ourselves
> could restore us to sanity.

One thing that may make it hard to believe in God is that life often seems unfair to us. We didn't ask to be born into a dysfunctional family! We didn't have any say over the abuses and injustices we suffered! We didn't choose our predisposition toward addiction! And yet we're held accountable over something we can't control on our own! This makes it hard to initially turn to God, as the Power to restore our sanity. He seems unreasonable in his demands!

Job understood these feelings. In the midst of his suffering he said, "How frail is humanity! How short is life, how full of trouble! We blossom like a flower and then wither. Like a passing shadow, we quickly disappear. Must you keep an eye on such a frail creature and demand an accounting from me? Who can bring purity out of an impure person?" (Job 14:1-4).

That's a good question—one which most people, especially addicts, have asked themselves in one form or another. Job persisted in his questioning because deep inside he believed God to be good and fair, even though life wasn't. He was honest with his emotions and questions, but he never stopped seeking God.

There's a good answer to the question posed by Job, one which will satisfy both our hearts and our minds. It will only be found, however, by those who are willing to work through the pain and unfairness of life, and still seek God. Those who seek him will find him, and the answers they seek as well.

❧

> No matter how unfair life may seem, God can offer
> hope in its darkest hours.

God's Solution

Bible Reading: Romans 3:21-26

> We came to believe that a Power greater than ourselves could restore us to sanity.

E ven though life may seem unfair to us, we also may feel justifiably guilty for all the pain we've caused others. We may struggle with a desire for fairness in life but also feel that if everything were as it should be, we'd deserve God's anger and punishment. When we fear punishment from God, we'll probably hesitate to approach him to ask for the power we need to recover.

There's a solution to the problem of needing God's power, but feeling that we don't deserve it. "Now God has shown us a way to be made right with him without keeping the requirements of the law. . . . God, with undeserved kindness, declares that we are righteous. He did this through Christ Jesus when he freed us from the penalty for our sins. For God presented Jesus as the sacrifice for sin. People are made right with God when they believe that Jesus sacrificed his life, shedding his blood. This sacrifice shows that God was being fair. . . . God did this to demonstrate his righteousness, for he himself is fair and just, and he declares sinners to be right in his sight when they believe in Jesus" (Romans 3:21, 24-26).

God figured out a way to remain just in an unfair world. He found a way to punish our sins without having to destroy our lives as the penalty. When we can accept that Jesus' death was payment for our sins, not his own, it solves the problem for us. It also gives us access to the greatest Power there is: God himself.

❦

God's solution is available to each of us, regardless of our failures.

Day 12

Never Hopeless
Bible Reading: John 11:37-45

> We came to believe that a Power greater than ourselves
> could restore us to sanity.

A s much as we want to believe that a Power greater than
ourselves can restore us to sanity, we may have to deal
with nagging doubts. We may see other people who have
recovered from their addictions and still wonder if we will be
able to recover as they did. We may fear that our lives are "too
far gone."

If anyone was too far gone to recover from anything, it was
Lazarus, a friend of Jesus. Lazarus had been dead and buried (without embalming) for four days when Jesus finally arrived on the
scene. "He arrived at the tomb, a cave with a stone rolled across its
entrance. 'Roll the stone aside,' Jesus told them. But Martha, the
dead man's sister, protested, 'Lord, he has been dead for four days.
The smell will be terrible.' Jesus responded, 'Didn't I tell you that
you would see God's glory if you believe?' So they rolled the stone
aside. Then Jesus looked up to heaven and said, 'Father, thank you
for hearing me. You always hear me, but I said it out loud for the
sake of all these people standing here, so that they will believe you
sent me.' Then Jesus shouted, 'Lazarus, come out!' And the dead
man came out, his hands and feet bound in graveclothes, his face
wrapped in a headcloth. Jesus told them, 'Unwrap him and let him
go!'" (John 11:38-44).

When we feel like our lives are too far gone we can remember Lazarus. Jesus wanted everyone to know that when God is in
the picture, no one is ever too far gone.

❧

Because of God's power, no one is beyond recovery.

Beyond Insanity
Bible Reading: 1 Samuel 21:10-15

> We came to believe that a Power greater than ourselves
> could restore us to sanity.

There are times in life when our "insanity" is useful to keep us alive or help us cope with a particularly difficult set of circumstances. We may have begun using our addictive/compulsive behavior as a survival mechanism. Maybe now we're stuck with the "craziness" just because it's familiar, even though its usefulness has long since passed. We may feel more comfortable with chaos than with "sanity" because it's all we've known.

Young David was fleeing from King Saul, who was trying to kill him to prevent him from taking over his throne. "David escaped from Saul and went to King Achish of Gath. But the officers of Achish were unhappy about his being there. 'Isn't this David, the king of the land?' they asked. 'Isn't he the one the people honor with dances, singing, "Saul has killed his thousands, and David his ten thousands"?' David heard these comments and was very afraid of what King Achish of Gath might do to him. So he pretended to be insane, scratching on doors and drooling down his beard. Finally, King Achish said to his men, 'Must you bring me a madman? We already have enough of them around here! Why should I let someone like this be my guest?' So David left Gath and escaped" (1 Samuel 21:10–22:1).

If David had continued to act insane after he was out of danger, he never would have become king or gone on to great victories. We, too, need to let go of the "insanity" that helped us cope in the past, and move on toward our own victories.

❊

Our insanity can end as soon as our recovery begins.

Day 14

Power from God

Bible Reading: Acts 2:1-18

> We came to believe that a Power greater than ourselves
> could restore us to sanity.

Maybe we've traveled this route before. This isn't the first time for us to begin recovery. We found courage once before, only to fail when the going got rough. Now we're starting over, but it's even harder than at first because we feel like a failure.

There is plenty of power, even for those who have failed on a grand scale. Peter didn't want to follow Jesus in the first place. Peter told Jesus to go away because Peter was aware of his own sinfulness. But Jesus wouldn't let him go. So Peter followed him, cautiously at first, then with bold confidence. When Jesus was arrested, Peter disappointed himself by denying that he even knew Jesus. Peter was afraid that he would be arrested, too.

After Jesus rose from the dead, he tried to help Peter feel better by reaffirming his love; but Peter's confidence was still sorely shaken. Then something happened that renewed Peter with power from on high. "All the believers were meeting together in one place. Suddenly, there was a sound from heaven like the roaring of a mighty windstorm, and it filled the house where they were sitting. . . . And everyone present was filled with the Holy Spirit. . . . Then Peter stepped forward with the eleven other apostles and shouted to the crowd" (Acts 2:1-2, 4, 14). Peter found the power to stand tall that day, and three thousand people found new life as a result.

Although we may have failed in the past, Peter is proof that there is no limit to the forgiveness and power available from God!

❧

> God's power brings stability and hope to our lives
> of fear and uncertainty.

Honest Grieving

Bible Reading: 1 Samuel 1:2-18

> We came to believe that a Power greater than ourselves
> could restore us to sanity.

Circumstances in life can be overwhelming. Yet at times, the grief we feel is misunderstood by those who observe us going through it. They may despise us, look down on us for our "weakness," or think we're losing our grasp on reality. On the contrary, when the pain of living becomes overwhelming, we aren't crazy to grieve. It would be crazy for us not to!

God looks on our hearts and has compassion for us in our times of grief, even when those around us don't understand. Hannah was overwhelmed by grief in response to a troubling family situation. "Once after a sacrificial meal at Shiloh, Hannah got up and went to pray. Eli the priest was sitting at his customary place beside the entrance of the Tabernacle. Hannah was in deep anguish, crying bitterly as she prayed to the LORD. . . . Seeing her lips moving but hearing no sound, [Eli] thought she had been drinking. 'Must you come here drunk?' he demanded. 'Throw away your wine!' 'Oh no, sir!' she replied. 'I haven't been drinking wine or anything stronger. But I am very discouraged, and I was pouring out my heart to the LORD. Don't think I am a wicked woman! For I have been praying out of great anguish and sorrow.' 'In that case,' Eli said, 'go in peace! May the God of Israel grant the request you have asked of him'" (1 Samuel 1:9-10, 13-17).

Sometimes what people see as insane behavior is really grief being expressed. At these times we need loving support to acknowledge our pain.

☘

> As we turn to face our pain and grief, we will
> discover that God is there with us.

47

Day 16

An Overwhelming Struggle

Bible Reading: Romans 8:35-39

We came to believe that a Power greater than ourselves could restore us to sanity.

Sometimes we may feel like giving up the struggle. We try, only to fall once again. We take two steps forward, but then stumble backwards. We feel condemned and fear that even God may give up on us. At times there are so many difficulties, so many issues to work through, so many patterns in our lives that have to be changed, we begin to feel like we're going crazy.

God acknowledges the difficulties we may face, but he also promises us victory in the end. The apostle Paul once wrote, "Overwhelming victory is ours through Christ, who loved us. And I am convinced that nothing can ever separate us from God's love. Neither death nor life, neither angels nor demons . . . not even the powers of hell can separate us from God's love. . . . Nothing in all creation will ever be able to separate us from the love of God that is revealed in Christ Jesus our Lord" (Romans 8:37-39). Paul also said, "I am certain that God, who began the good work within you, will continue his work until it is finally finished on the day when Christ Jesus returns" (Philippians 1:6).

When we feel like we're going crazy and don't think that we can handle life, God is there. He is determined not to give up on us. We can rely on his persistent love. God has promised to keep working on us until we are whole. There will still be crazy times, but with his help we can handle life, one day at a time.

Nothing can remove us from God's presence.

Day 17

A Little Faith
Bible Reading: Luke 17:5-6

> We came to believe that a Power greater than ourselves
> could restore us to sanity.

How many times have we wished that we could overcome the addictions and compulsions that keep us in bondage? We know what it is to struggle with the effects of addiction, and the craziness this brings to our lives. We may feel despair and wonder if there really is any way out of the insanity of our current circumstances. Maybe our plight is impossible, at least without God's help, but faith can make even the impossible happen.

"The apostles said to the Lord, 'Show us how to increase our faith.' The Lord answered, 'If you had faith even as small as a mustard seed, you could say to this mulberry tree, "May you be uprooted and thrown into the sea," and it would obey you!'" (Luke 17:5-6). Matthew also recorded Jesus' words: "If you had faith even as small as a mustard seed, you could say to this mountain, 'Move from here to there,' and it would move. Nothing would be impossible" (Matthew 17:20).

Faith is a mysterious commodity. Jesus says that if we have faith, real faith, it only takes a small amount to make a big difference. We may be exercising faith without even realizing it. It takes faith to believe that a Power greater than ourselves could restore us to sanity. It takes faith to work through the steps of a recovery program. It's comforting to know that God only needs a tiny bit of faith in order to work in powerful ways to restore our sanity.

Just a little faith can take root and grow, first underground
and then visibly.

Day 18

Worthy Promises
Bible Reading: Hebrews 6:12-18

We came to believe that a Power greater than ourselves
could restore us to sanity.

W e may believe that a Power greater than ourselves can
restore our sanity, but still wonder how long it's going to
take. Over time, we may grow discouraged at the length
of the process. We may have our spirits dampened by the chaos we
can't seem to escape. Some people report instant release from their
addictions and the accompanying craziness. But for most of us, it
will take patience to inherit the promise of a sane new life.

The book of Hebrews tells us: "You will follow the example
of those who are going to inherit God's promises because of their
faith and endurance. For example, there was God's promise to
Abraham. . . . God took an oath in his own name, saying: 'I will
certainly bless you, and I will multiply your descendants beyond
number.' Then Abraham waited patiently, and he received what
God had promised" (Hebrews 6:12-15). (The entire story of Abraham's life can be found in Genesis 11–25.)

The key point to consider here is that Abraham had to wait
twenty-five years to see God's promise fulfilled. There were times
he took matters into his own hands, times he probably wondered
if he had really received the promise at all, and times he laughed
in disbelief to think that the promise would ever come true. In the
end, "Abraham was now a very old man, and the LORD had blessed
him in every way" (Genesis 24:1). Just because our restoration
takes time doesn't mean our faith is in vain. Let's keep holding on!

❧

Since God is Truth, we can rest securely in his promises.

Day 19

A Desperate Faith
Bible Reading: Matthew 15:22-28

> We came to believe that a Power greater than ourselves
> could restore us to sanity.

Sometimes the insanity of living with our own addictions or with someone who is acting in bizarre ways can cause us to become desperate for help.

Jesus dealt with a woman who was driven to him out of desperation. "A Gentile woman who lived there came to [Jesus], pleading, 'Have mercy on me, O Lord, Son of David! For my daughter is possessed by a demon that torments her severely.' But Jesus gave her no reply, not even a word. Then his disciples urged him to send her away. . . . Then Jesus said to the woman, 'I was sent only to help God's lost sheep—the people of Israel.' But she came and worshiped him, pleading again, 'Lord, help me!' Jesus responded, 'It isn't right to take food from the children and throw it to the dogs.' She replied, 'That's true, Lord, but even dogs are allowed to eat the scraps that fall beneath their masters' table.' 'Dear woman,' Jesus said to her, 'your faith is great. Your request is granted.' And her daughter was instantly healed" (Matthew 15:22-28).

It took a lot of courage for this woman to even speak to Jesus because of the racism of their time. She was despised and ridiculed for seeking an end to her family's torment, but she didn't give up. She believed God was the only one who could help her and would not be deterred. Our own desperation can lead to a sincere faith that can be a tremendous help in recovery.

> When we realize that God is the only one who can help,
> nothing can block our recovery.

Day 20

God's Wisdom

Bible Reading: James 3:13-18

> We came to believe that a Power greater than ourselves
> could restore us to sanity.

When we get caught up in catering to our addictions, it's almost like we're a different person. It's like there are two of us tied up together. The Bible recognizes this dual nature in all of us. One part yearns for good and the other part of us is drawn toward corrupt desires and animal passions. The Bible describes a kind of "worldly" wisdom that justifies destructive behavior and leads to disorder, instability, and confusion.

We need to beware of this type of wisdom, which is characterized by jealousy and selfishness. James wrote, "For jealousy and selfishness are not God's kind of wisdom. Such things are earthly, unspiritual, and demonic. For wherever there is jealousy and selfish ambition, there you will find disorder and evil of every kind" (James 3:15-16).

This kind of thinking causes us to focus on what others are and have. It makes us want the same things for ourselves to the point where we are always dissatisfied. It is easy to become so consumed with our own desires that we become inconsiderate of others, often hurting the ones we love. This type of wisdom is inspired by the devil, and will lead to our ultimate destruction; his "purpose is to steal and kill and destroy" (John 10:10).

If we see that our thoughts are still dominated by these characteristics, we need to ask God to replace our "wisdom" with his wisdom. We can trust him to change our minds and our lives.

✿

> True wisdom restores our sanity and leads us
> to peace and wholeness.

Day 21

A Loving Father

Bible Reading: Proverbs 4:1-10

We came to believe that a Power greater than ourselves
could restore us to sanity.

Some people grow up in families where wisdom is modeled
and taught by their parents. They have the privilege of
receiving wise advice at home. Many of us grew up in families that were crazy. Our parents didn't provide wise guidance for
us. This deprivation can leave us wondering how we can fill up the
void of what we missed. We may feel like the rest of the human
race has passed us by. Some of us feel anger, resentment, and a
sense of shame because we never learned how to make wise choices. We may ask ourselves, *Shouldn't someone have shown me the way?*

Ideally, all of us should have had wise and godly instruction.
The book of Proverbs records a father instructing his son in the
way God intended. "For I, too, was once my father's son, tenderly
loved as my mother's only child. My father taught me, . . . 'Get
wisdom; develop good judgment. Don't forget my words or turn
away from them. Don't turn your back on wisdom, for she will protect you. Love her, and she will guard you'" (Proverbs 4:3-6).

For those of us who were left unprotected and unguarded
because of a parent's insane ways, it's not too late. We have a
Father in heaven who is eager to give us the wisdom we need.
James once wrote, "If you need wisdom, ask our generous God, and
he will give it to you. He will not rebuke you for asking" (James
1:5). God loves us tenderly, as a parent should. He is always there
for us, waiting to give us the wisdom we need whenever we ask.

God wants to encourage us with his love and compassion.

53

Day 22

Daring to Believe
Bible Reading: Joshua 1:1-9

We came to believe that a Power greater than ourselves
could restore us to sanity.

T here must have been a time when we had high hopes for a
promising life—before those hopes were dashed. But then,
through the crazy and chaotic circumstances of growing up,
we learned to settle for a life that was far less than what we had
once hoped for. We may have come to the conclusion that a sane,
good life is reserved for people better or stronger than ourselves.

God led the nation of Israel out of bondage in Egypt,
through the wilderness, and to the edge of the Promised Land. But
as they stood on the border, looking into the fruitful and prosperous
land of Canaan, they lacked the faith and courage to go in. Joshua
was one of the few who had the faith to enter, but because of the
others, he was held back. Forty years later the chance came again.
Just before he entered the land, the Lord told him, "Be strong and
courageous! Do not be afraid or discouraged. For the LORD your
God is with you wherever you go" (Joshua 1:9).

There is a Promised Land for each one of us. Jeremiah tells
us, "'For I know the plans I have for you,' says the LORD. 'They are
plans for good and not for disaster, to give you a future and a hope'"
(Jeremiah 29:11). We need to be courageous. We need to believe
that there can be good things in life for us. We, too, can be encouraged that regardless of the failures in our families and our past, we
can start again. We can find our way out of the chaos of the wilderness, into the Promised Land of sane and healthy living.

✤

We may not succeed by the world's standards, but we can
by God's standards, and his opinion lasts forever.

Day 23

Common Temptations

Bible Reading: 1 Corinthians 10:12-13

> We came to believe that a Power greater than ourselves
> could restore us to sanity.

E ntertaining belief in an addiction's magical cure often hinders recovery. One of the most common such beliefs is that someday we will finally be beyond the reach of temptation. Unfortunately, temptation is a permanent part of our world and of human experience. The Bible says, "The temptations in your life are no different from what others experience" (1 Corinthians 10:13). Not only is temptation all around us, it's within us as well. "Temptation comes from our own desires" (James 1:14). Even if we could rid ourselves of all external temptations, we'd still have to live with the destructive desires within our secret selves.

Even Jesus Christ himself faced temptation; and yet, he never sinned. Before he was tempted, he spent an extended period of time alone in the wilderness, and during that time he went without food. We are usually tempted the most during the times when we're lonely and hungry.

Facing temptation is a part of accepting reality. We need to accept that we will always be susceptible to temptation in our areas of weakness and predisposition. It is unrealistic to believe that our sinful nature will ever get better. When we put away the magical belief that temptation will disappear, we will be more aware and better able to avoid falling under temptation's power. We need to prayerfully seek God's help in dealing with this reality of life.

Temptations touch everyone; facing this fact is an
important step in recovery.

Day 24

A Day at a Time
Bible Reading: Matthew 6:25-34

We came to believe that a Power greater than ourselves
could restore us to sanity.

L iving one day at a time is a discipline we all have to focus on
when we're in recovery. It's easy to slip back into letting ourselves focus on worries about tomorrow, the "what ifs" and
the "if onlys." Each day brings with it a host of things we cannot
change. We face the continual reality of momentary circumstances
beyond our control. There is also the reality of who we are, human
beings confined within the slice of life we call today. It is tempting
to deny the present, but escaping reality is part of the insanity of
our addictive way of life.

Jesus once said, "Can all your worries add a single moment
to your life? . . . So don't worry about tomorrow, for tomorrow
will bring its own worries. Today's trouble is enough for today"
(Matthew 6:27, 34). The prophet Jeremiah said, "The faithful
love of the LORD never ends! His mercies never cease. Great is his
faithfulness; his mercies begin afresh each morning" (Lamentations 3:22-23). Since God's grace comes in daily doses, that's the
best way to face life.

We need to ask ourselves at every turn, Am I accepting this
present moment or am I pretending, trying to escape into the past
or the future? For each day, there is something to find joy in, and
there is strength promised for the troubles of that day. The psalmist wrote, "This is the day the LORD has made. We will rejoice
and be glad in it" (Psalm 118:24). We, too, can choose to find joy,
strength, and sanity when we accept today's realities.

✤

Our days can be filled with worry and anxiety or joy
and anticipation; it's our choice.

A Worthy Friend

Bible Reading: Job 33:23-32

> We came to believe that a Power greater than ourselves
> could restore us to sanity.

We may find ourselves in a pit of depression. We may be hiding in the dark, unable to work effectively, sick in body and mind, unable to cope, unable to pray, confused, and misunderstood.

Job's young friend Elihu noted how God can help one who is in this condition: "If an angel from heaven appears—a special messenger to intercede for a person and declare that he is upright—he will be gracious and say, 'Rescue him from the grave, for I have found a ransom for his life.' Then his body will become as healthy as a child's, firm and youthful again. When he prays to God, he will be accepted. And God will receive him with joy and restore him to good standing. He will declare to his friends, 'I sinned and twisted the truth, but it was not worth it. God rescued me from the grave, and now my life is filled with light.' Yes, God does these things again and again for people. He rescues them from the grave so they may enjoy the light of life" (Job 33:23-30).

When we are so drugged and/or depressed that we can't function, we have a friend to intercede for us before God. He made himself our substitute so that we don't have to die when life becomes overwhelming. God is in the business of restoring health to our bodies, reviving our darkened spiritual lives, renewing prayer, restoring us to our jobs, and making it so that we can face the light of day. When we're in the pit of depression we can be assured that God can bring us out because he has successfully done it for many others.

❧

God is in the business of restoring lives, and he
starts right where we are.

Bringing Order to Chaos
Bible Reading: Isaiah 40:25-31

We came to believe that a Power greater than ourselves
could restore us to sanity.

Wwe may be worn out by the overwhelming feelings that
dominate our lives and the chaos that wearies us. We
probably feel the need for someone who has the power
to bring order into our lives.

God leaves us this reminder: "'To whom will you compare
me? Who is my equal?' asks the Holy One. Look up into the heavens. Who created all the stars? He brings them out like an army, one
after another, calling each by its name. Because of his great power
and incomparable strength, not a single one is missing. O Jacob,
how can you say the LORD does not see your troubles? O Israel,
how can you say God ignores your rights? Have you never heard?
Have you never understood? The LORD is the everlasting God, the
Creator of all the earth. He never grows weak or weary. No one can
measure the depths of his understanding. He gives power to the
weak and strength to the powerless" (Isaiah 40:25-29).

Take a moment to ponder the vastness of the universe, the
innumerable stars and planets that all continue to move in perfect
order. Scientists marvel at how predictable and consistent the universe remains. Doesn't it make sense that the One who made the
universe and keeps every star in place can also have the power to
bring order into the chaos of our lives? He knows the weariness that
comes with disorder. He understands our need for safe, predictable
patterns in life. He, who made us, can bring order to our lives, too.

Even the strongest people get tired, but God's
strength never diminishes.

Risky Decisions
Bible Reading: Jonah 1:3-12

> We came to believe that a Power greater than ourselves
> could restore us to sanity.

We may do crazy things when we're caught up in stormy circumstances resulting from our own "out of control" behavior. We take risks that can have terrible consequences, but find that we've lost the power to choose otherwise.

Jonah made a risky decision that seems crazy by any definition! Let's try to learn something from his experience. Jonah was running away from God. He boarded a ship going the opposite direction from where God told him to go. "But the LORD hurled a powerful wind over the sea, causing a violent storm that threatened to break the ship apart." The sailors identified Jonah as the cause of the storm. "[Jonah] had already told them he was running away from the LORD. 'Oh, why did you do it?' they groaned. . . . 'What should we do to you to stop this storm?' 'Throw me into the sea,' Jonah said, 'and it will become calm again.' . . . Then the sailors picked Jonah up and threw him into the raging sea, and the storm stopped at once!" (Jonah 1:4, 10-12, 15).

When we follow our own ways, God may allow us to get caught up in a "storm." He often does this to help us face the insanity of the risks we take. Jonah was rescued and taken back to where God had intended him to go. God can rescue us out of our personal storms as well. He can take us back to a place where the available choices aren't life threatening or dangerous.

❧

Even when we go our own way, God is there with
us, ready to restore us.

Seasons of Darkness
Bible Reading: Psalm 6:1-10

> We came to believe that a Power greater than ourselves
> could restore us to sanity.

At times we get so caught up in our pain that we forget that life comes in seasons. No one is happy all the time. We may be paranoid and gloomy today, but that can change. Being upset and disturbed doesn't have to be forever.

When David was a young boy he lived a relatively carefree life, tending his father's sheep. He believed in his own goodness and expected the best. Later he realized his own frailties and faced many enemies. These pressures darkened his life. He cried out to God, "O LORD, don't rebuke me in your anger or discipline me in your rage. Have compassion on me, LORD, for I am weak. Heal me, LORD, for my bones are in agony. I am sick at heart. How long, O LORD, until you restore me? Return, O LORD, and rescue me. Save me because of your unfailing love. For the dead do not remember you. Who can praise you from the grave? I am worn out from sobbing. All night I flood my bed with weeping, drenching it with my tears" (Psalm 6:1-6). David did come out of this dark season of life and was able to share his experience, strength, and hope with others. He says of God, "He grants the desires of those who fear him; he hears their cries for help and rescues them" (Psalm 145:19).

If we're in a season of mental anguish, we need to remember that we haven't always felt this way and we won't always feel this way. We can cry out for help and expect God to rescue us. Someday we will share our experience and hope with others.

*When we are at the end of ourselves, God creates
a new beginning.*

Life from Death
Bible Reading: Ezekiel 37:1-14

We came to believe that a Power greater than ourselves
could restore us to sanity.

I t may be that our families have been governed by the craziness
of addiction for a long time. It may be that we have lost hope
of ever recovering; our hope may be just a skeleton, long dead.

God has demonstrated his power to restore in even the
most hopeless of situations. Consider this vision given to the
prophet Ezekiel. "I was carried away by the Spirit of the LORD to a
valley filled with bones. He led me all around among [them]. . . .
Then he said to me, 'Speak a prophetic message to these bones
and say, "Dry bones, listen to the word of the LORD! This is what
the Sovereign LORD says: Look! I am going to put breath into you
and make you live again! I will put flesh and muscles on you and
cover you with skin. I will put breath into you, and you will come
to life. Then you will know that I am the LORD.'" Ezekiel saw
these bones come to life. The Lord explained, "These bones represent the people of Israel. They are saying, 'We have become old,
dry bones—all hope is gone. Our nation is finished.' Therefore,
prophesy to them and say, 'This is what the Sovereign LORD says:
O my people, I will open your graves of exile and cause you to rise
again. Then I will bring you back to the land of Israel'" (Ezekiel
37:1-2, 4-6, 11-12).

Israel is the only nation in history that has been nearly
destroyed, the people exiled throughout the world, and then,
centuries later, reborn as a nation. If God was able to restore the
nation of Israel, surely he can restore our lives as well!

If God can give life to scattered bones, he can
restore our shattered lives.

Day 30

Confidence in God

Bible Reading: Amos 4:9-13

> We came to believe that a Power greater than ourselves
> could restore us to sanity.

Many of us began recovery experiencing one disaster after another. We probably wondered whether Someone was trying to tell us something. But as we came to believe that God's power could reach into our world in positive ways, we also received hope. We were able to exchange our fear of punishment for confidence in the power of God to restore us to sanity.

The Lord had allowed many disasters to befall the people of Israel, in hopes that they would return to him. God warned them of the evils that would result from continuing to resist his help, but they wouldn't listen. Finally, he said, "'Therefore, I will bring upon you all the disasters I have announced. Prepare to meet your God in judgment, you people of Israel!' For the LORD is the one who shaped the mountains, stirs up the winds, and reveals his thoughts to mankind . . . .The LORD God of Heaven's Armies is his name!" (Amos 4:12-13).

Ignoring the fact that God has power over our lives can be disastrous. He may try to get our attention by allowing us to experience the consequences of our wrong behaviors. We need to realize that God's ultimate goal is to lead us back to himself. Even the pain God allows us to suffer is designed to bring about our healing. His power is for our good; it isn't there to destroy us. Considering the mighty power of God, even in the natural realm, can encourage us. The one strong enough to form the mountains and the winds is willing to use his power to restore us to sanity.

> Even our greatest failures can be a means for God
> to make us his own.

STEP THREE

We made a decision to turn our wills and our lives
over to the care of God.

*Then Jesus said, "Come to me, all of you who are weary and carry
heavy burdens, and I will give you rest"
(Matthew 11:28).*

Submission and Rest

Bible Reading: Matthew 11:27-30

> We made a decision to turn our wills and our lives
> over to the care of God.

W hen our burdens become heavy and we see that our way of life is leading us toward death, we may finally become willing to let someone else do the driving. We've probably worked hard at trying to get our lives on the right track, but still feel like we always end up on a dead-end street.

Proverbs tells us, "There is a path before each person that seems right, but it ends in death" (Proverbs 14:12). When we began our addictive behaviors we were probably seeking a way to find pleasure or to overcome the pain of living. The way seemed right at first, but it became clear that we were on the wrong track. But then we were unable to turn around on our own. Jesus said, "Come to me, all of you who are weary and carry heavy burdens, and I will give you rest. Take my yoke upon you. Let me teach you, because I am humble and gentle at heart, and you will find rest for your souls" (Matthew 11:28-29).

To take on a yoke implies being united to another in order to work together. Those who are yoked together must go in the same direction, but by doing so, their work is made considerably easier. Jesus is saying that when we finally decide to submit our lives and our will to his direction, our burdens will become manageable. When we let him do the driving, we will be able to "find rest" for our souls. He knows the way and has the strength to turn us around and get us on the road toward life.

❧

> We all wear a yoke on our shoulders; the trick is in
> finding the right master.

Day 2

Releasing Worry

Bible Reading: Matthew 6:25-34

> We made a decision to turn our wills and our lives
> over to the care of God.

It is often our worries about the small details of life that lead to our undoing. Life's daily demands can be overwhelming. Perhaps, our "acting out" is a way of escaping. When we are sober, we are once again faced with the pressures of life. Learning to manage these in a new way is a key to maintaining our sobriety.

Jesus said, "I tell you not to worry about everyday life— whether you have enough food and drink, or enough clothes to wear. Isn't life more than food, and your body more than clothing? Look at the birds. They don't plant or harvest or store food in barns, for your heavenly Father feeds them. And aren't you far more valuable to him than they are? Can all your worries add a single moment to your life?

"And why worry about your clothing? Look at the lilies of the field and how they grow. They don't work or make their clothing. . . . And if God cares so wonderfully for wildflowers that are here today and thrown into the fire tomorrow, he will certainly care for you. . . .

"So don't worry at about these things. . . . Your heavenly Father already knows all your needs. Seek the Kingdom of God above all else, and live righteously, and he will give you everything you need. So don't worry about tomorrow, for tomorrow will bring its own worries. Today's trouble is enough for today" (Matthew 6:25-34).

Since God cares deeply for us, we can choose to live one day at a time and turn the details of our lives over to him.

God calls us to live one day at a time.

Day 3

Discovering God
Bible Reading: Acts 17:23-28

> We made a decision to turn our wills and our lives
> over to the care of God.

Before we can turn our lives over to God, we need to have an accurate understanding of who he is. It's crucial that our lives be turned over to the God who loves us, and not the "god" of this world who seeks only to deceive and destroy. The apostle Paul described the deceiver this way: "Satan, who is the god of this world, has blinded the minds of those who don't believe. They are unable to see the glorious light of the Good News. They don't understand this message about the glory of Christ, who is the exact likeness of God" (2 Corinthians 4:4). Has Satan deceived us? How can we be sure that we have a true understanding of God?

When Paul addressed the men of Athens he said, "I saw your many shrines. And one of your altars had this inscription on it: 'To an Unknown God.' This God, whom you worship without knowing, is the one I'm telling you about. . . . His purpose was for the nations to seek after God and perhaps feel their way toward him and find him—though he is not far from any one of us. For in him we live and move and exist" (Acts 17:23, 27-28).

Even though God may be unknown to us, he is near and willing to reveal himself. God has promised, "If you look for me wholeheartedly, you will find me" (Jeremiah 29:13). Turning over our will involves becoming willing to accept God as he is, instead of insisting on creating him in our own image. When we look for God with an open heart and mind, we will find him.

❧

As we seek God, he makes himself known to us.

Day 4

Belonging to God
Bible Reading: Daniel 3:14-27

> We made a decision to turn our wills and our lives
> over to the care of God.

Our decision to turn our will and our lives over to God will be tested. By making this decision we set our lives at odds with the crowd. This will include most of our old friends and maybe even members of our family. We should expect some heat and not be shocked when it comes. But God will be with us in the fire, to preserve us and to bring us through.

In the book of Daniel we meet three young Jewish men who were taken captive and relocated to a strange land. They entrusted their lives to God and refused to worship the idols of Babylon. Their resolve was so strong that when they were threatened with death by fire they replied, "If we are thrown into the blazing furnace, the God whom we serve is able to save us. . . . But even if he doesn't, we want to make it clear to you, Your Majesty, that we will never serve your gods." They were promptly bound with ropes and thrown into the furnace. The king was amazed at what he saw then. "'Look!' Nebuchadnezzar shouted, 'I see four men, unbound, walking around in the fire unharmed! And the fourth looks like a god!'" (Daniel 3:17-18, 25).

God was right there, taking the heat with them. The only thing they lost by turning their will and their lives over to him was the ropes that had bound them. Those were burned up in the flames. When we're challenged because of our decision to turn our lives over to God, we can expect God to be there for us, too.

Nothing can bind us when God wants us to be free.

Day 5

An Open Hand
Bible Reading: Matthew 16:24-28

> We made a decision to turn our wills and our lives
> over to the care of God.

Many of us who struggle with addictions have spent much of our strength just trying to hold on to our lives. Maybe we fear loosening our grip to let someone else take care of us. We may be doing a lousy job of caring for our own lives, but we still hesitate about letting go. Perhaps, we're afraid that if we do let go, no one will be there to take hold of us.

In the Old Testament we often hear about people being "consecrated" to God. This meant that they were making a decision to turn the remainder of their lives over to God for whatever purpose he desired. The root of this word literally means "an open hand" as opposed to a closed one. They had a ceremony to let go of what they were holding on to for their own lives, and to proclaim that God was welcome to take hold of them. Jesus told us, "If you try to hang on to your life, you will lose it. But if you give up your life for my sake, you will save it" (Matthew 16:25). By now we probably recognize that we were losing our lives anyway, no matter how hard we tried to hang on.

Once we decide to let go of the control of our will and our lives, something wonderful is promised. Jesus says of those who turn their lives over to him: "I give them eternal life, and they will never perish. No one can snatch them away from me" (John 10:28). When we finally find the courage to let go, God is waiting to grasp our lives firmly and hold them securely for all eternity.

❧

> Holding on, we lose what we have; letting go, we
> receive even more.

Day 6

Trusting God

Bible Reading: Numbers 23:18-24

> We made a decision to turn our wills and our lives
> over to the care of God.

I t is not uncommon to link our perceptions about God to our childhood experiences with people who played powerful roles in our lives. If we have been victimized in the past by people who were capricious, abusive, distant, uncaring, or incompetent, we may now anticipate these qualities in God.

Just because God is a Power greater than we are, and the people who victimized us represented a power greater than we were, it does not mean that God will harm us if we entrust our lives to him. Even Jesus tells us that he didn't entrust himself to men because he knew what was in their hearts. Nevertheless, he voluntarily turned his life over to the will of God the Father. "It is better to take refuge in the LORD than to trust in people" (Psalm 118:8).

We may have learned that when we place our confidence in people, our lives can be devastated by disappointment. We can't let this keep us from ever trusting again. In working Step Three we can make a healthy decision to turn our will and our lives over to the only one who is worthy of being trusted. The Bible tells us, "God is not a man, so he does not lie. He is not human, so he does not change his mind" (Numbers 23:19). And God has said, "I will never fail you. I will never abandon you" (Hebrews 13:5).

We realize that we can't make it all alone. This time we can stop being the victim. We can turn our lives over to someone who is really able to care for our needs.

❦

> We trust in many things, but it is best to trust in the only
> one worthy of our trust—God himself.

Day 7

Giving up Control
Bible Reading: Psalm 61:1-8

> We made a decision to turn our wills and our lives
> over to the care of God.

T he thought of turning our will and our lives over can be attractive. When we give in to our addictions aren't we giving control of ourselves over to another power? Aren't we, in some way, giving up personal responsibility for our lives? When we are overwhelmed or wanting to escape, our addictions can make us feel strong or safe, attractive, powerful, or happy. So, in a sense, we are very comfortable with the thought of giving up control of our will and our lives.

We can simply change our focus and turn our lives over to God instead of the sources we have turned to in the past. The apostle Paul touched on this contrast when he said, "Don't be drunk with wine, because that will ruin your life. Instead, be filled with the Holy Spirit" (Ephesians 5:18).

When we are overwhelmed and in need of some kind of escape, we have a new place to turn. King David declared, "The LORD is a shelter for the oppressed, a refuge in times of trouble. Those who know your name trust in you, for you, O LORD, do not abandon those who search for you" (Psalm 9:9-10).

David also wrote, "From the ends of the earth, I cry to you for help when my heart is overwhelmed. Lead me to the towering rock of safety, for you are my safe refuge, a fortress where my enemies cannot reach me" (Psalm 61:2-3).

God never changes; he is always present with us.

Day 8

Free to Choose
Bible Reading: Deuteronomy 30:15-20

> We made a decision to turn our wills and our lives
> over to the care of God.

Everyone has a life or death decision to make. We've been created with the supreme privilege of free will, the ability to choose. Even when we are in the bondage of our addiction we still have choices confronting us. When we are in recovery, we face the nagging lure of choosing to fall back into our addiction. The freedom to choose brings with it the burden of the results of our choices. And these choices affect our lives and the lives of our children. Free will is our blessing and our responsibility!

God spoke through Moses, saying, "Now listen! Today I am giving you a choice between life and death, between prosperity and disaster. For I command you this day to love the LORD your God and to keep his commands, decrees, and regulations by walking in his ways. If you do this, you will live . . . and the LORD your God will bless you. . . . But if your heart turns away and you refuse to listen, . . . then I warn you now that you will certainly be destroyed. . . . I call on heaven and earth to witness the choice you make. Oh, that you would choose life, so that you and your descendants might live! You can make this choice by loving the LORD your God, obeying him, and committing yourself firmly to him. This is the key to your life" (Deuteronomy 30:15-20).

Although we may feel out of control with respect to our addiction, we can choose to set our hearts in the direction of life. We can choose to love God and begin to walk in his ways.

> God doesn't force his will on us, but he is there if we
> decide to put ourselves in his hands.

71

Day 9

Single-Minded Devotion
Bible Reading: James 4:7-10

We made a decision to turn our wills and our lives
over to the care of God.

We may already have chosen to follow God's way, letting his ways define the overall direction for our lives. But even so, many of us still keep a part of our hearts hidden away from God. We have devoted this part of ourselves to gratifying our addictions, to doing things that are contrary to the will of God. This sets us up for living a double life, which can fill us with guilt, shame, and instability.

Even for those of us who have made the decision to give our hearts to God, we face new moments of decision every day. James was addressing Christians when he wrote, "So humble yourselves before God. Resist the devil, and he will flee from you. Come close to God, and God will come close to you. Wash your hands, you sinners; purify your hearts" (James 4:7-8).

When we choose to live the double life, it is easy to become doubtful that God hears us at all. James wrote, "For a person with divided loyalty is as unsettled as a wave of the sea that is blown and tossed by the wind. Such people should not expect to receive anything from the Lord. Their loyalty is divided between God and the world" (James 1:6-8).

When we resist the devil at every turn and choose to draw close to God, he will draw close to us. When we open up our hidden hearts and begin to make choices in favor of recovery, we will soon grow confident that God desires to help us.

❧

God has already defeated the devil; all we need
to do is choose the winning side.

Day 10

Redeeming the Past
Bible Reading: Isaiah 54:4-8

> We made a decision to turn our wills and our lives
> over to the care of God.

W e all come to God with a past. In turning our lives over to him, we need to give him our past with all its losses and shame. We need to hand over every moment of disgrace, every tear we've ever cried, every word we wish we could take back, all the broken promises, the loneliness, all the dreams that died, the dashed hopes, the broken relationships, our successes and failures, all of our yesterdays and the scars they've left in our lives.

Under Old Testament law, if someone lost freedom, property, or spouse because of a disaster or a debt, the next of kin was looked to as a "redeemer." If property had been lost because of an inability to pay, the redeemer would pay for it and return it to the original owner. If a woman lost her husband, the redeemer would marry her, providing her with protection and love. God tells us, "Fear not; you will no longer live in shame. Don't be afraid; there is no more disgrace for you. You will no longer remember the shame of your youth and the sorrows of widowhood. For your Creator will be your husband; the LORD of Heaven's Armies is his name! He is your Redeemer. . . . For the LORD has called you back from your grief" (Isaiah 54:4-6).

God is our redeemer, the restorer of our losses. We need to make him Lord of all, even of the days and dreams in our past. When we give God our past, he can make up for all that we've lost. He can rid us of the shame. He can fill the empty places in our hearts.

❧

> We sell ourselves into slavery; God removes our
> shame and buys us back.

Day 11

The Deal of a Lifetime
Bible Reading: Philippians 3:4-11

We made a decision to turn our wills and our lives
over to the care of God.

When we think of turning our lives over to God, it's not
unusual to try to polish up our credentials as best we
can before presenting them to him. We look at all the
worthwhile things we've done, how we've tried to be good, whatever we feel we have to offer. We don't really need to sort out the
good from the bad. God doesn't care what's in the mix, as long as
we give him the whole package.

Before Paul became a Christian he kept careful count of
his "good deeds" and took pride in his ancestry. When he finally
decided to turn his life over to the care of God, this is what he said:
"I once thought these things were valuable, but now I consider
them worthless because of what Christ has done. Yes, everything
else is worthless when compared with the infinite value of knowing
Christ Jesus my Lord. For his sake I have discarded everything else,
counting it all as garbage, so that I could gain Christ and become
one with him" (Philippians 3:7-9).

When we've made the decision to turn our will and our
lives over to God, we need to give him our whole life with all its
assets and liabilities. We can't earn his love by the "good stuff"
in our lives any more than we can discourage his love by all the
"bad stuff." It's a straight trade-in. We give him our whole life and
being. He gives us complete forgiveness, love, redemption, and
acceptance in the person of Jesus Christ. When we see what God is
offering us and the little we have to offer him, it's clear that we're
getting quite a deal!

God offers us far more than anyone could ever give in return.

Day 12

A Bright Future
Bible Reading: Luke 23:32-43

> We made a decision to turn our wills and our lives
> over to the care of God.

Perhaps we've become so disappointed that we've given up hope for the future altogether. We don't know what the future holds, but when we give our lives to God, he can be trusted with our future. Regardless of how bad our lives might be at the moment, we can still trust him to bring about glorious good in our lives.

Here's a story of a man who dared to trust God with his future. And he trusted God when it looked like he didn't even have a future to look forward to. "Two others, both criminals, were led out to be executed with him. When they came to a place called The Skull, they nailed him to the cross. And the criminals were also crucified—one on his right and one on his left. . . . One of the criminals hanging beside him scoffed, 'So, you're the Messiah, are you? Prove it by saving yourself—and us, too, while you're at it!' But the other criminal protested. 'Don't you fear God even when you have been sentenced to die? We deserve to die for our crimes, but this man hasn't done anything wrong.' Then he said, 'Jesus, remember me when you come into your Kingdom.' And Jesus replied, 'I assure you, today you will be with me in paradise'" (Luke 23:32-33, 39-43).

No matter what dire straits we may find ourselves in presently, we can give God our future and be assured that eternal life in paradise will far outweigh the sufferings of this present life. He can also transform our lives right now, making our future down here as bright as the heavenly one!

❦

> Even when everything seems dark and hopeless,
> God promises us a bright, new future.

Day 13

Never Lost

Bible Reading: Deuteronomy 8:1-18

> We made a decision to turn our wills and our lives
> over to the care of God.

The road that leads to recovery is often uncharted and dangerous. We may have been born into a family that was lost in a maze of dysfunction, and we have had to look for the way out. There are times of need, times of fear, times when we wonder if there is a God out there who cares at all.

The Israelites who were born in the wilderness must have experienced similar feelings. Their parents had sinned and were left to wander in the wilderness for forty years. The new generation had spent much of their lives going nowhere, and for no fault of their own. When the Israelites were about to enter the Promised Land, Moses showed how even there, God's care was present. He said, "Do not forget that he led you through the great and terrifying wilderness with its poisonous snakes and scorpions, where it was so hot and dry. He gave you water from the rock! He fed you with manna in the wilderness . . . to humble you and test you for your own good" (Deuteronomy 8:15-16).

Even when we seem lost, God is watching over us to protect our lives until we can get to a better place. He does take care of us in ways we may take for granted. Peter tells us, "Give all your worries and cares to God, for he cares about you" (1 Peter 5:7). Just being alive and in recovery shows that God cares for our lives!

> When lost in our personal deserts, we can be sure
> God is never far away.

Day 14

No One Is Worthless
Bible Reading: Matthew 25:14-30

> We made a decision to turn our wills and our lives
> over to the care of God.

When we've come out of a difficult season of life, we tend to think of our lives as a mess. But we need to realize that there is more in our lives than pain and problems; there is more to us than our addictions. If we've been treated as worthless, we may overlook our many assets—our talents, resources, and abilities. God wants these turned over to him, too.

Jesus told a story about a man who went away on a long trip. He left some "talents" to three of his servants to invest while he was away. (A talent was a unit of currency used in biblical times.) They were given differing amounts of money to invest in keeping with each of their abilities. Two of the servants used their money profitably. The third was afraid to try and buried his in the ground. When the master returned he was very pleased with the first two servants and rewarded them. He was very angry with the servant who just hid the money away, failing to make a return on it. The master had expected him to make the most of what he had been given (Matthew 25:14-30).

When we turn our lives over to God, that includes all the gifts he has entrusted to us. To say that we have no talents or abilities is an insult to the one who gave them to us. We're not worthless! We may have to dig around a bit to find those talents that have been buried while we were consumed by our craziness, but God expects us to find them and use them. This will improve our self-esteem and help in our recovery.

☙

God wants all of us because he loves all of us.

Day 15

Filled with Joy

Bible Reading: Acts 3:2-8

> We made a decision to turn our wills and our lives
> over to the care of God.

As we travel the road to recovery, we may feel like we've been reduced to begging for help. Our lives have been crippled by our own addictions and the addictions of others. We approach God's door, with heads down, because we feel desperate for the help he promises to give. But even though we come to God with our heads down, that's not how it has to stay.

Listen to this story about Peter and John's encounter with a man who felt this way: "As they approached the Temple, a man lame from birth was being carried in. Each day he was put beside the Temple gate, the one called the Beautiful Gate, so he could beg from the people going into the Temple. When he saw Peter and John about to enter, he asked them for some money. Peter and John looked at him intently, and Peter said, 'Look at us!' The lame man looked at them eagerly, expecting some money. But Peter said, 'I don't have any silver or gold for you. But I'll give you what I have. In the name of Jesus Christ the Nazarene, get up and walk!' Then Peter took the lame man by the right hand and helped him up. And as he did, the man's feet and ankles were instantly healed and strengthened. . . and [he] began to walk! Then, walking, leaping, and praising God, he went into the Temple with them" (Acts 3:2-8).

We may turn to God hoping for a meager handout to keep us going. But he has much more for us! He wants to give us such a full recovery that we are healed and transformed. He wants to take us from being the beggar at God's door, to being so full of joy that we can't keep from leaping and praising God.

❦

When we ask God for help, he gives us what we really need.

An Unfair World

Bible Reading: Genesis 39:1-23

> We made a decision to turn our wills and our lives
> over to the care of God.

T here are times when life treats us unfairly. We may protest the injustices, fall victim to self-pity, give in to a why-even-try kind of mentality, or sink into depression. We are invited to leave the injustices we experience in the hands of God.

If there's anyone in history who can complain of unfair treatment, it's Joseph. He was one of eleven brothers, the favorite of his father. In their jealousy, the ten older brothers sold Joseph as a slave into Egypt. Once a slave, Joseph devoted himself to doing a good job for his master and was quickly promoted. He was then propositioned by his master's wife, and when he refused her, was falsely accused of rape by this vindictive woman. Thrown into prison with no hope of release, he again did his best. He was soon running the administration of the whole prison. In the end, Joseph was freed and promoted to be prime minister of Egypt. In this position he was able to confront and forgive the brothers who had sold him into slavery so many years before (Genesis 37–45).

It takes courage and wisdom to maintain a healthy attitude when life isn't fair. This comes from trusting that God will take up our cause and vindicate us, as he has promised. We can't change the fact that we live in an imperfect world, where things aren't as they should be. Turning these matters over to God can help us change our response to the injustices of life and continue to focus on our recovery rather than remaining a victim.

Looking at circumstances brings despair; looking to God brings hope for recovery.

Unexpected Problems
Bible Reading: 2 Samuel 15:13-26

> We made a decision to turn our wills and our lives
> over to the care of God.

There are times in recovery when it seems like we've made it. We reach a place where we feel like we can relax and stop living one day at a time. Then life surprises us with an unexpected problem.

King David had reached a pinnacle of success. He had conquered giants, won many battles, captured the hearts of his people, and overcome enemies on every side. While he was in this comfortable position, life surprised him with a rebellion led by his own son. Here's what happened: "A messenger soon arrived in Jerusalem to tell David, 'All Israel has joined Absalom in a conspiracy against you!' 'Then we must flee at once, or it will be too late!' David urged his men. 'Hurry! If we get out of the city before Absalom arrives, both we and the city of Jerusalem will be spared from disaster. . . . If the LORD sees fit,' David said, 'he will bring me back to see the Ark and the Tabernacle again. But if he is through with me, then let him do what seems best to him'" (2 Samuel 15:13-14, 25-26).

King David wisely accepted what was happening and responded to reality, not to what he wished were true. It seems that David had gotten out of the habit of relying on God, day by day, but he quickly placed his life back in God's hands. God did protect him and returned him to the throne in Jerusalem. When life hits us with unexpected threats, we, too, can let that be a reminder to turn our lives back over to God.

When we think we've arrived, it's time to begin again.

Day 18

Doing God's Will
Bible Reading: 1 Samuel 24:1-11

> We made a decision to turn our wills and our lives
> over to the care of God.

Sometimes it's hard to tell the difference between the right thing to do and just an opportune moment. When we are working to make changes in our lives and relationships, we may be uncertain of what to do at times. When this happens, we need to rely on God's wisdom to help us make our decisions.

The jealousy and abuse of King Saul made young David's life miserable. Saul knew that God had chosen David to be king instead of him. Although David was a loyal subject, Saul tried to kill him. Once, when David was hiding in a cave, King Saul came in without knowing David was there. "'Now's your opportunity!' David's men whispered to him. 'Today the LORD is telling you, "I will certainly put your enemy into your power, to do with as you wish."' So David crept forward and cut off a piece of the hem of Saul's robe. But then David's conscience began bothering him because he had cut Saul's robe. 'The LORD knows I shouldn't have done that to my lord the king,' he said to his men. 'The LORD forbid that I should do this to my lord the king and attack the LORD's anointed one, for the LORD himself has chosen him.' So David restrained his men and did not let them kill Saul" (1 Samuel 24:4-7).

David knew what God expected of him in this situation, and he chose to go along with God's will. In trying to give our will to God, it is important to know what his will is in a given situation. When we aren't sure what to do, we can look to see if the Bible gives us any guidance on similar situations. Then we will have a clear view of what it means to turn our will over to God.

> When we've turned our lives over to God, we can
> rest assured that he is with us.

Day 19

Self-Control
Bible Reading: 2 Peter 1:2-9

> We made a decision to turn our wills and our lives
> over to the care of God.

We would love to have self-control! But trying to find it within ourselves can become as much of an obsession as our primary addiction.

According to Peter, self-control is one step in the middle of a larger progression. He said, "May God give you more and more grace and peace as you grow in your knowledge of God and Jesus our Lord. By his divine power, God has given us everything we need for living a godly life. We have received all of this by coming to know him, the one who called us to himself by means of his marvelous glory and excellence. And because of his glory and excellence, he has given us great and precious promises. These are the promises that enable you to share his divine nature and escape the world's corruption caused by human desires. In view of all this, make every effort to respond to God's promises. Supplement your faith with a generous provision of moral excellence, and moral excellence with knowledge, and knowledge with self-control, and self-control with patient endurance, and patient endurance with godliness, and godliness with brotherly affection, and brotherly affection with love for everyone. The more you grow like this, the more productive and useful you will be in your knowledge of our Lord Jesus Christ" (2 Peter 1:2-8).

Self-control is something that comes as we grow progressively closer to God. Taking one step at a time, one day at a time, God will give us his own character, including self-control.

> Our self-control increases as we give increasing
> control over to God.

Freedom in Forgiveness
Bible Reading: Matthew 6:9-15

> We made a decision to turn our wills and our lives
> over to the care of God.

We can sometimes get so focused on ourselves during recovery that we don't spend much time dealing with the way others have sinned against us. Or maybe we're totally focused on the way we've been mistreated, as an excuse for our behavior. This leaves us with emotional baggage that will hinder our progress. Forgiving others is an important key to turning our will over to God.

Jesus taught his disciples, "Pray like this: Our Father in heaven, may your name be kept holy. May your Kingdom come soon. May your will be done on earth, as it is in heaven. Give us today the food we need, and forgive us our sins, as we have forgiven those who sin against us. And don't let us yield to temptation, but rescue us from the evil one. If you forgive those who sin against you, your heavenly Father will forgive you. But if you refuse to forgive others, your Father will not forgive your sins" (Matthew 6:9-15).

Forgiveness is a choice of our will. Just as our forgiveness was not based on excusing the wrongs we've done, neither does our forgiveness of others call for us to excuse what they've done. We must first convict the offender in our minds, then turn the matter of vengeance over to God. This helps us face the truth about our own pain. It also frees us from any excuse to continue our compulsive behavior because of what's been done to us.

🌿

> Forgiveness begins as a choice but becomes a process
> that opens us to God's love and forgiveness.

Day 21

Learning to Trust
Bible Reading: Jeremiah 9:4-9

We made a decision to turn our wills and our lives over to the care of God.

Most of us know the pain caused by deceit, both for the deceiver and for the one who has been betrayed. We may be trying to learn to trust again after living in situations where we haven't been given any reason to trust.

David cried, "Help, O LORD, for the godly are fast disappearing! The faithful have vanished from the earth! Neighbors lie to each other, speaking with flattering lips and deceitful hearts. May the LORD cut off their flattering lips and silence their boastful tongues. They say, 'We will lie to our hearts' content. Our lips are our own—who can stop us?'" (Psalm 12:1-4).

Jeremiah prophesied, "'Beware of your neighbor! Don't even trust your brother! For brother takes advantage of brother, and friend slanders friend. They all fool and defraud each other; no one tells the truth. With practiced tongues they tell lies; they wear themselves out with all their sinning. They pile lie upon lie and utterly refuse to acknowledge me,' says the LORD. Therefore, this is what the LORD of Heaven's Armies says: 'See, I will melt them down in a crucible and test them like metal'" (Jeremiah 9:4-7).

When we turn our lives over to God, we should try to give him our trust as well. He understands that this will be hard. Our trust in God can be absolute. Trust in people should be cautious; it should only be placed in those who have proven themselves trustworthy.

Trust is only as worthy as its object; trust in God is always a wise bet.

84

Hope in God
Bible Reading: Jeremiah 17:5-8

We made a decision to turn our wills and our lives
over to the care of God.

We may have learned a long time ago that hoping only brings disappointment. Our hopes were dashed. The promises we believed were broken. We were left feeling like fools for ever hoping in the first place. But perhaps we were devastated because we put our hope in the wrong place.

"The LORD says: 'Cursed are those who put their trust in mere humans, who rely on human strength and turn their hearts away from the LORD. They are like stunted shrubs in the desert, with no hope for the future. They will live in the barren wilderness, in an uninhabited salty land. But blessed are those who trust in the LORD and have made the LORD their hope and confidence. They are like trees planted along a riverbank, with roots that reach deep into the water. Such trees are not bothered by the heat or worried by long months of drought. Their leaves stay green, and they never stop producing fruit'" (Jeremiah 17:5-8).

Turning our lives over to God includes placing our hope in him, even if people have disappointed us. When we place *all* of our hope in other people, it's like expecting a tree to flourish in a barren desert. Our thirst continues, and they are unable to satisfy our deepest needs. Placing our hope in God changes everything. Jesus said, "The water I give . . . becomes a fresh, bubbling spring within them, giving them eternal life" (John 4:14). When our hope is in God, and our lives in his care, we are sustained when we otherwise would be devastated.

If we put our trust and hope in God, we will never be let down.

God's Faithfulness
Bible Reading: Lamentations 3:17-26

> We made a decision to turn our wills and our lives
> over to the care of God.

Perhaps we're brokenhearted because of the bitter suffering in our family. Maybe our once-good reputations have been ruined and now we're ashamed. Our lives have been taken captive and destroyed before the watchful eyes of friend and foe alike.

Jeremiah watched this happen to his beloved nation, Israel. It's no wonder he's known as the weeping prophet. The people of God refused to listen to Jeremiah's warnings and were taken captive by a heathen nation as a result. Lamentations is a record of Jeremiah's lament over the shameful fate of God's people. He weeps, "Peace has been stripped away, and I have forgotten what prosperity is. I cry out, 'My splendor is gone! Everything I had hoped for from the LORD is lost!' The thought of my suffering and homelessness is bitter beyond words. I will never forget this awful time, as I grieve over my loss. Yet I still dare to hope when I remember this: The faithful love of the LORD never ends! His mercies never cease. Great is his faithfulness; his mercies begin afresh each morning. I say to myself, 'The LORD is my inheritance; therefore, I will hope in him!' The LORD is good to those who depend on him, to those who search for him. So it is good to wait quietly for salvation from the LORD" (Lamentations 3:17-26).

Turning our lives over to God includes giving him our pain and suffering. God is strong and loving enough to lift our burdens and mend our broken hearts.

> When all hope is gone, we can entrust ourselves to God,
> remembering his never-ending compassion.

Glorious Victory

Bible Reading: Zechariah 9:9-12

> We made a decision to turn our wills and our lives
> over to the care of God.

Our lives may be a battlefield. We may have been taken captive in the ongoing war between good and evil. When we turn our lives over to God, will he rescue us and keep us safe?

Five hundred years before the birth of Jesus, the prophet Zechariah wrote these words: "Rejoice, O people of Zion! Shout in triumph, O people of Jerusalem! Look, your king is coming to you. He is righteous and victorious, yet he is humble, riding on a donkey—riding on a donkey's colt. [This prophecy was fulfilled by the coming of Jesus (see Matthew 21:4-11).] I will remove the battle chariots from Israel and the warhorses from Jerusalem. I will destroy all the weapons used in battle, and your king will bring peace to the nations. His realm will stretch from sea to sea and from the Euphrates River to the ends of the earth. Because of the covenant I made with you, sealed with blood, I will free your prisoners from death in a waterless dungeon. Come back to the place of safety, all you prisoners who still have hope! I promise this very day that I will repay two blessings for each of your troubles" (Zechariah 9:9-12).

Jesus fulfilled part of these prophecies when he came the first time. He did deliver us from death by shedding his own blood to seal our pardon. When he comes again, as he promised, he will bring peace on earth. For now, we can take cover in Jesus as our refuge. When the war is over and Jesus is crowned King of kings, he will repay all those who are his, two blessings for every trouble suffered in the war! In the battles of life we can turn our lives over to God and have a strong, sure hope.

❧

> When we give ourselves to God, he always gives
> back more than we gave.

87

Day 25

Promised Joy
Bible Reading: 1 Peter 1:3-6

> We made a decision to turn our wills and our lives
> over to the care of God.

L ife is rough. We must constantly struggle against the sin inherent in our mortal bodies. We live with the realities of pain, sickness, and death. We live in a world that is constantly decaying. Even if we turn our lives over to God, what is there to look forward to?

Peter tells us, "Now we live with great expectation, and we have a priceless inheritance—an inheritance that is kept in heaven for you. . . . And through your faith, God is protecting you by his power until you receive this salvation, which is ready to be revealed on the last day for all to see. So be truly glad. There is wonderful joy ahead, even though you have to endure many trials for a little while" (1 Peter 1:3-6).

Paul encourages us with this: "And since we are his children, we are his heirs. In fact, together with Christ we are heirs of God's glory. But if we are to share his glory, we must also share his suffering. Yet what we suffer now is nothing compared to the glory he will reveal to us later. For all creation is waiting eagerly for that future day when God will reveal who his children really are. Against its will, all creation was subjected to God's curse. But with eager hope, the creation looks forward to the day when it will join God's children in glorious freedom from death and decay" (Romans 8:17-21). These promises are for us!

> Our trust in God's work on our behalf allows us
> to live in hope and joy.

Hungry Hearts
Bible Reading: Ruth 1–4

> We made a decision to turn our wills and our lives
> over to the care of God.

Please love me!" Isn't this the whispered cry of our hearts? We may be afraid to admit it for fear of rejection, but we are all hungry for love. Some of us are starving because of previous losses. We find ourselves gathering whatever crumbs we can find to fill that hunger deep inside.

Ruth was a young woman who had known loss and hunger. Her husband died, leaving her without any means of emotional or physical sustenance. She followed her mother-in-law, Naomi, to a foreign land and was forced to gather leftover grain from the harvested fields just to stay alive. The man who owned the fields was a relative who could, if he so chose, marry Ruth and fulfill her needs for love and protection. Naomi told her to go to the threshing floor where this man, Boaz, was sleeping and curl up at his feet. Culturally, this displayed a request to be taken care of. Boaz was quite happy to find Ruth there and married her, providing the love and provision she had lost and now longed for (Ruth 1–4).

In turning our lives over to God we need to venture toward developing healthy love relationships with people and with God. It's scary to say "please love me," but it's worth the risk. If we don't fill our hunger for love in a legitimate way, we'll be driven back toward our addictive/compulsive behaviors. We can be sure that when we "curl up" at the feet of Jesus, he will be glad to find us there. He will provide for us, protect us, and love us.

> When we risk reaching out to God, he fills the deep
> longings of our souls.

Day 27

Unconditional Love
Bible Reading: 1 John 4:7-10

> We made a decision to turn our wills and our lives
> over to the care of God.

Real love brings security into our lives. For many of us, feelings of insecurity contribute to the power of our addictions. Trusting that love can bring lasting security is hard for those of us who've been abandoned. Maybe someone we loved betrayed our trust. Perhaps someone turned away from us when we betrayed theirs. It could be that someone we needed died, leaving us permanently.

Jesus promised, "I will not abandon you as orphans—I will come to you" (John 14:18). We may ask, "How can I trust in God's love when it feels like all I've ever known is love that disappoints?" Here's the difference: Jesus is the only one who entered our lives through the "one way" door of death. "God showed how much he loved us by sending his one and only Son into the world so that we might have eternal life through him. This is real love—not that we loved God, but that he loved us and sent his Son as a sacrifice to take away our sins" (1 John 4:9-10). The psalmist wrote, "For he [God] knows we how weak we are; he remembers we are only dust. Our days on earth are like grass. . . . But the love of the LORD remains forever with those who fear him" (Psalm 103:14-17).

God's love is unconditional and always waiting for us. Turning our lives over to God involves opening the door of our hearts to his love. Filling up on God's love helps us to avoid relapse. It meets us at our deepest need and eases our most powerful insecurities.

❧

> As we give our lives over to God's care, he brings healing
> and love to our hurts and pain.

Day 28

Rest and Peace

Bible Reading: Philippians 4:4-7

> We made a decision to turn our wills and our lives
> over to the care of God.

T he world doesn't get any better just because we're in recovery! We still have to pay our bills, deal with people, and face the stressful changes that recovery can bring. There are pressures outside of our control that will tend to wear us down if we aren't careful to protect ourselves from the world's onslaught of anxiety.

The apostle Paul gave us a strategy to help guard against the troubles of daily life. He wrote, "Don't worry about anything; instead, pray about everything. Tell God what you need, and thank him for all he has done. Then you will experience God's peace, which exceeds anything we can understand. His peace will guard your hearts and minds as you live in Christ Jesus" (Philippians 4:6-7).

The word translated "guard" is a military term that means to protect with a sentry. The image is one of a guard marching around the border of our hearts and minds to keep out the pressing anxieties of life. This is only promised if we routinely turn every worry and need over to God and develop an attitude of gratitude. When we turn our worries over to the care of God, we will discover the protection of inner peace that exceeds our understanding.

> The key to God's peace is found in continually
> turning our lives over to him.

Day 29

Declared "Not Guilty"

Bible Reading: Romans 4:1-5

> We made a decision to turn our wills and our lives
> over to the care of God.

W hen our addictive patterns represent "sinful" behavior, it's common to feel awkward about getting close to God. We may feel ineligible to receive God's love; instead, we may expect anger. We might feel guilty and be afraid that God will reject us. Secretly, we may wish that we could have a loving relationship with God and the assurance of a place in heaven, but we feel that we will never be good enough.

The apostle Paul has shown us that we can have the love and acceptance we desire. He wrote, "For the Scriptures tell us, 'Abraham believed God, and God counted him as righteous.' . . . When people work, their wages are not a gift, but something they have earned. But people are counted as righteous, not because of their work, but because of their faith in God who forgives sinners. . . . God will also count us as righteous if we believe in him, the one who raised Jesus our Lord from the dead. He was handed over to die because of our sins, and he was raised to life to make us right with God" (Romans 4:3-5, 24-25).

There's a free gift waiting for us that could help in our recovery. It's God's forgiveness, acceptance, and support. It's a notice that we're "righteous." It's a special home in heaven with our name on it. There's no need for us to do anything but accept this free gift. This is the best reward of turning our lives over to God!

❧

> We begin our recovery burdened with guilt and shame; God
> encourages our recovery with the burden's release.

True Wisdom
Bible Reading: Matthew 7:24-27

> We made a decision to turn our wills and our lives
> over to the care of God.

W hen we lack wisdom, the storms of life can be devastating. After our lives are in pieces, we may realize that we have acted unwisely and want to change, but where do we start?

"How can men be wise?" the psalmist asks. "Fear of the LORD is the foundation of true wisdom. All who obey his commandments will grow in wisdom. Praise him forever!" (Psalm 111:10). God has given clear instructions for life. When we have enough reverence for God that we are willing to accept his instructions as the basis for all of our decisions, we have a good starting point.

Jesus said, "Anyone who listens to my teaching and follows it is wise, like a person who builds a house on solid rock. Though the rain comes in torrents and the floodwaters rise and the winds beat against that house, it won't collapse because it is built on bedrock" (Matthew 7:24-25). Listening to what the Bible says is the next step toward walking in wisdom. Filling our minds with God's teaching will lead us to follow them. This will also help us turn away from those things God says are wrong. Job tells us, "This is what he says to all humanity: 'The fear of the Lord is true wisdom; to forsake evil is real understanding'" (Job 28:28).

Turning our lives over to God is a wise move! Like most aspects of recovery, walking in wisdom is a process that we grow into. These three elements are the groundwork: fear of the Lord, listening to his teaching, and following them.

> True wisdom begins as we stand in awe of God's
> love and care for us.

STEP FOUR

We made a searching and fearless moral inventory of ourselves.

*Jesus said, "Why worry about a speck in your friend's eye
when you have a log in your own? . . . First get rid of the log
in your own eye; then you will see well enough to deal with the
speck in your friend's eye"*
(Matthew 7:3-5).

Facing the Sadness
Bible Reading: Nehemiah 8:7-10

We made a searching and fearless moral inventory of ourselves.

M ost of us falter at the prospect of making an honest personal inventory. The rationalizations and excuses abound for avoiding this step. The bottom line is, we know that there is an enormous amount of sadness awaiting us. And we fear the pain that facing the sadness will bring.

The Jewish exiles who returned to Jerusalem after captivity in Babylon had lost touch with God. During the exile, they hadn't been taught his laws; so naturally, they hadn't practiced them either. After rebuilding the city walls and the temple, the priests gathered the people together to read the Book of the Law. The people were overwhelmed with grief and began sobbing, because their lives in no way measured up. The priests said to them, "Don't mourn or weep on such a day as this! For today is a sacred day before the LORD your God. . . . Go and celebrate with a feast of rich foods and sweet drinks, and share gifts of food with people who have nothing prepared . . . for the joy of the LORD is your strength!" (Nehemiah 8:9-10).

That day marked the beginning of the Festival of Tabernacles, a required Jewish feast which celebrated their escape from bondage in Egypt and God's care for them while they wandered in the wilderness.

When we set out to face the pain and sadness of making a moral inventory, we will need the "joy of the Lord" to give us strength. This joy comes from recognizing, even celebrating, God's ability to bring us out of bondage and to care for us as we pass through the sadness toward a new way of life.

🌱

Our joy in the Lord helps us to face the sadness within ourselves.

Day 2

God's Standard
Bible Reading: James 1:21-25

We made a searching and fearless moral inventory of ourselves.

W hen making an inventory, some kind of list is usually used to help take stock of what's on hand. If we've lived our lives with dysfunctional influences, our idea of what's "normal" probably won't be a very good measuring stick for evaluating our lives. We'll need another standard to help us take account of where we are.

The Jewish exiles who returned to Jerusalem had grown up in captivity. They started their inventory by finding a new standard. "They remained standing in place for three hours while the Book of the Law of the LORD their God was read aloud to them. Then for three more hours they confessed their sins" (Nehemiah 9:3).

The apostle Paul ridiculed the idea that we could measure our lives by the people around us. He said this of the Corinthian believers: "They are only comparing themselves with each other, using themselves as the standard of measurement. How ignorant! . . . We will boast only about what has happened within the boundaries of the work God has given us" (2 Corinthians 10:12-13).

James wrote, "Humbly accept the word God has planted in your hearts, for it has the power to save your souls. . . . But if you look carefully into the perfect law that sets you free, and if you do what it says and don't forget what you heard, then God will bless you for doing it" (James 1:21, 25).

In doing our moral inventory, we will get better results if we use God's Word as a measuring stick. This should give us the perspective we need as we seek to sort out our lives.

Our recovery involves coming to terms with
ourselves as we really are.

Confession
Bible Reading: Nehemiah 9:1-3

We made a searching and fearless moral inventory of ourselves.

The heart of our moral inventory will probably deal with our destructive habits, defects of character, the wrongs we've done, the consequences that we now live with, and the hurt we've caused others. It's like sifting through all the garbage. This part is painful, but a necessary part of throwing away those rotten habits and behaviors that are spoiling the rest of our lives.

The returned Jewish exiles "confessed their own sins" (Nehemiah 9:2); this phrase speaks volumes. The word *confess* means "to bemoan something by wringing of the hands" and also "to throw away." The word *sins* means "offenses and their occasions"; it can also refer to habitual sinfulness and the consequences of such behavior.

This can serve as a model for us to follow. We can list the occasions of our offenses, our destructive habits, and the consequences we've brought into our lives and the lives of others. Let's also look at what was done as they "confessed their own sins." They owned each part; they bemoaned each part; and then they threw it all away. Their inventory was a time of cleaning out the garbage. After this they were better able to make a new start.

In dealing with the garbage in our lives we can "own" it by taking personal responsibility for our choices and actions. We can "bemoan" it by allowing ourselves to grieve. We can "throw it away" by leaving it behind and turning toward the future.

Our time of confession should be a time of celebration.

Day 4

Family Influence

Bible Reading: Nehemiah 9:34-38

We made a searching and fearless moral inventory of ourselves.

O ur family of origin has had an influence on who we are today. Some of us want to pretend that our families were, or are, nearly perfect. Others of us may tend to avoid responsibility for our actions by blaming our families. Whatever the case, when we think about our own lives, we also need to deal with our families and the effects they have had on who we are today.

We're told that the returned Jewish exiles "confessed their own sins and the sins of their ancestors" (Nehemiah 9:2). They blamed their ancestors for their captivity and the difficult situation they were facing. They said, "They [our ancestors] refused to turn from their wickedness. So now today we are slaves in the land of plenty that you gave our ancestors for their enjoyment! . . . We serve them [conquering kings] at their pleasure, and we are in great misery" (Nehemiah 9:35-37).

It's all right to admit the truth about what brought us into bondage. This might very well involve the wrongs committed by our parents and family. It's all right to express our anger and regret over what's been done to us. We have a right to hold others accountable and grieve over the negative effects they've had on our lives. That is part of the real picture. It's not all right to use this as an excuse for our wrong choices or for staying in bondage. They may be partly responsible for bringing us to this place. We're responsible for moving on to a better place for ourselves and our children.

Past generations helped create our present circumstances; our confessions can free us for a better future.

Day 5

Constructive Sorrow
Bible Reading: 2 Corinthians 7:8-11

We made a searching and fearless moral inventory of ourselves.

We all have to deal with sorrow. We may try to stuff it down and ignore it. We may try to drown it or avoid feeling it by intellectualizing. But sorrow doesn't go away. We need to accept the sorrow that will be a part of the inventory process.

Not all sorrow is bad for us. The apostle Paul had written a letter to the church in Corinth. It made them very sad because Paul was confronting them about something that they were doing wrong. At first he was sorry that he had hurt them. But later he said, "Now I am glad I sent it, not because it hurt you, but because the pain caused you to repent and change your ways. It was the kind of sorrow God wants his people to have. . . . For the kind of sorrow God wants us to experience leads us away from sin and results in salvation. There's no regret for that kind of sorrow. . . . Just see what this godly sorrow produced in you! Such earnestness, such concern to clear yourselves, . . . such zeal, and such a readiness to punish wrong" (2 Corinthians 7:9-11).

Jeremiah said, "Though he brings grief, he also shows compassion because of the greatness of his unfailing love. For he does not enjoy hurting people or causing them sorrow" (Lamentations 3:32-33).

This grief was good, for it came from honest self-evaluation, not morbid self-condemnation. We can learn to accept our sorrow as a positive part of our recovery, not just as punishment.

Honest self-examination can lead us to a sorrow
that inspires our growth.

Day 6

Coming out of Hiding
Bible Reading: Genesis 3:6-13

We made a searching and fearless moral inventory of ourselves.

Many of us have spent our lives in a state of hiding, ashamed of who we are inside. We may hide by living double lives, using our drug of choice to make us feel like someone else, or by self-righteously setting ourselves above others. Step Four involves uncovering the things we've been hiding, even from ourselves.

After Adam and Eve disobeyed God, "They suddenly felt shame at their nakedness. So they sewed fig leaves together to cover themselves. . . . The LORD God called to the man, 'Where are you?' He replied, 'I heard you walking in the garden, so I hid. I was afraid because I was naked'" (Genesis 3:7-10). Human beings have been covering up and hiding ever since!

Jesus consistently confronted the religious leaders for their hypocrisy. The word *hypocrite* describes a person who pretends to have virtues or qualities that he really doesn't have. One time Jesus said to them, "Hypocrites! For you are so careful to clean the outside of the cup and the dish, but inside you are filthy—full of greed and self-indulgence! . . . First wash the inside of the cup and the dish, and then the outside will become clean, too" (Matthew 23:25-26).

When the real person inside comes out of hiding, we'll have to deal with some dirt! Making this inventory is a good way to "wash the inside"; and some of that washing may involve bathing our lives with tears. It is only by uncovering the hidden parts of ourselves that we'll be able to change the outer person, including our addictive/compulsive behaviors.

Confessing our hidden parts brings healing and restoration.

Finger-Pointing
Bible Reading: Matthew 7:1-5

We made a searching and fearless moral inventory of ourselves.

There have probably been times when we've avoided our own wrongs and problems by pointing the finger at someone else. We may be out of touch with our internal affairs because we are still blaming others for our moral choices. Or perhaps we avoid examining ourselves by making moral inventory of the people all around us.

When God asked Adam and Eve about their sin, they both pointed the finger at someone else. "'Have you eaten from the tree whose fruit I commanded you not to eat?' The man replied, 'It was the woman you gave me who gave me the fruit, and I ate it.' Then the LORD God asked the woman, 'What have you done?' 'The serpent deceived me,' she replied" (Genesis 3:11-13). It seems to be human nature to blame others as our first line of defense.

We also may avoid our own problems by evaluating and criticizing the lives of others. Jesus tells us, "And why worry about a speck in your friend's eye when you have a log in your own? . . . Hypocrite! First get rid of the log in your own eye; then you will see well enough to deal with the speck in your friend's eye" (Matthew 7:3, 5).

While doing this step, we must constantly remind ourselves that this is a season of *self-examination*. We must guard against drifting off into blaming and examining the lives of others. There will be time in the future for helping others after we've taken responsibility for our own lives.

❦

Our inventory should turn our focus from what
others have done to what we can do.

Love Overcomes Fear

Bible Reading: 1 John 4:16-19

We made a searching and fearless moral inventory of ourselves.

The thought of making a fearless moral inventory may sound like an impossible task. Looking at our lives on a moral basis can be very frightening. How can we get to the place where the word *fearless* can actually describe the moral inventory we make?

The apostle John said, "As we live in God, our love grows more perfect. So we will not be afraid on the day of judgment, but we can face him with confidence because we live like Jesus here in this world. Such love has no fear, because perfect love expels all fear. If we are afraid, it is for fear of punishment, and this shows that we have not fully experienced his perfect love" (1 John 4:17-18).

Love is the key. God, who is the final judge of all morality, loves us perfectly. He doesn't just love us if we're perfect. Perhaps we've had people withhold love and shame us for our faults and failures. If we've only known love to be conditional, it only makes sense that admitting our faults causes us to be afraid of losing the love and acceptance we all need.

To eliminate the fear, we need to surround ourselves with unconditional love from God and other people. Only unconditional love will cover our shame and give us confidence that no matter what we find when we look at ourselves, we will always be loved. The apostle Peter affirmed this by saying, "Most important of all, continue to show deep love for each other, for love covers a multitude of sins" (1 Peter 4:8).

Our moral inventory needs a constant review from the perspective of God's love.

Day 9

A Searching Examination
Bible Reading: 2 Timothy 1:9-11

We made a searching and fearless moral inventory of ourselves.

Searching is more than just casually looking around; it implies an intense desire to discover what we're looking for. What could motivate us to make a *searching* moral inventory, especially since we know we'll be uncovering our inadequacies?

God is not looking for people good enough to deserve his love. Instead, God wants to find people who will identify their inadequacies as a place for his love and kindness to fit into their lives. If this is true, why shouldn't we be enthusiastic about searching, even for our failures? Every deficiency, every need, every shortcoming can make room for the love of God to be displayed prominently in our lives. The apostle Paul wrote to Timothy, saying, "God saved us and called us to live a holy life. He did this, not because we deserved it, but because that was his plan from before the beginning of time—to show us his grace through Christ Jesus" (2 Timothy 1:9).

If we approach our inventory with the intention of looking for places in our lives where God's mercy and love have the chance to make up for our failings, we can be enthusiastic about both the good and bad that we find there. Jude tells us, "Keep yourselves in the love of God, *looking* for the mercy of our Lord Jesus Christ unto eternal life" (Jude 1:21, NKJV, emphasis added). Knowing that God is looking for places to display his love in our lives, we can make an intense, yet fearless, search.

Our fearless internal search brings to light areas of our lives desperate for God's love and mercy.

Day 10

God's Mercy
Bible Reading: Revelation 20:11-15

We made a searching and fearless moral inventory of ourselves.

We may wish we could avoid making a moral inventory; it's normal to want to hide from examination. But in our hearts, we probably sense that a day will come when we'll have to look carefully at our lives.

The Bible tells us there's a day coming when an inventory will be made of every life. No one will be able to hide. In John's vision he saw "a great white throne and the one sitting on it. The earth and sky fled from his presence, but they found no place to hide. I saw the dead, both great and small, standing before God's throne. And the books were opened, including the Book of Life. And the dead were judged according to what they had done as recorded in the books. . . . And anyone whose name was not found recorded in the Book of Life was thrown into the lake of fire" (Revelation 20:11-12, 15).

It's best to do our own moral inventory now to make sure we're ready for the one to come. Anyone whose name is in the Book of Life is saved. This includes all whose sins have been atoned for by the death of Jesus. Those who refuse God's offer of mercy are left to be judged on the basis of their own deeds recorded in "the books." No one will pass that test! Perhaps now is a good time to make sure our names are in the right book. And when we know our lives are covered with God's forgiveness, we will be able to examine them fearlessly.

❧

We can be fearless in our inventory because we have
been loved and accepted by God.

Day 11

Understanding the Past

Bible Reading: 1 Corinthians 3:10-15

We made a searching and fearless moral inventory of ourselves.

Our addictions may already have destroyed everything we've worked for—our family, friendships, finances—everything may be lost. Beginning recovery is like starting back at the foundation and building a whole new life. Making an inventory should help us consider what caused our losses in the first place. That way, we'll be able to rebuild with materials that will hold up under fire.

The apostle Paul wrote, "But whoever is building on this foundation must be very careful. For no one can lay any foundation other than the one we already have—Jesus Christ. . . . Fire will reveal what kind of work each builder has done. The fire will show if a person's work has any value. If the work survives, that builder will receive a reward. But if the work is burned up, the builder will suffer great loss. The builder will be saved, but like someone barely escaping through a wall of flames (1 Corinthians 3:10-11, 13-15).

Even though Paul was referring to the final judgment, this also applies to recovery. We know that what we used in building our old way of life didn't hold up. By doing our inventory, we can make sure that we don't experience further loss by repeating our past patterns, which are vulnerable to destruction. When future tests come, the lasting effects of our recovery and the rewards of our new way of life will be evident to all.

Since we have turned our lives over to God, he is the foundation on whom we must build.

Wonderfully Made

Bible Reading: Psalm 139:13-18

We made a searching and fearless moral inventory of ourselves.

Growing up, we may have been led to believe that we just weren't "good enough." We probably tried to become "good enough" by *doing*, since we weren't acceptable just as we were. We need to be careful as we make a moral inventory not to replay in our own minds all the old lies about our lack of value as human beings. This is not the purpose of the inventory! Using it this way can be detrimental to our recovery.

We need to replace the misconceptions about our self-worth with the truth. David reflected on God's view of us when he wrote: "You made all the delicate, inner parts of my body and knit me together in my mother's womb. Thank you for making me so wonderfully complex! Your workmanship is marvelous—how well I know it. You watched me as I was being formed in utter seclusion, as I was woven together in the dark of the womb. You saw me before I was born. Every day of my life was recorded in your book. Every moment was laid out before a single day had passed. How precious are your thoughts about me, O God. They cannot be numbered! I can't even count them; they outnumber the grains of sand!" (Psalm 139:13-18).

David's glimpse of the high value God places on our lives, even before we are born, shows that our value precedes *doing*. By faith we need to accept this foundational truth about our basic value as human beings. We must accept that our lives are worth the pain of working through recovery.

❧

Aspects of God's perfect character are reflected in the lives of each and every person.

God's Likeness

Bible Reading: Genesis 1:25-31

We made a searching and fearless moral inventory of ourselves.

For most of us who have lived in bondage to our addictions, it's probably very easy for us to see the bad lurking within. It's much harder to see the qualities we have that are good or excellent. We may tend to see life in terms of all or nothing, good or bad. But we need to recognize that along with our shortcomings, we have also been made with an incredible potential for good.

At the end of the fifth day of creation, God had made everything except man and woman. "And God saw that it was good" (Genesis 1:25). Then God created man and woman. "In the image of God he created them; male and female he created them. Then God blessed them and said, 'Be fruitful and multiply. Fill the earth and govern it. Reign over the fish in the sea, the birds in the sky, and all the animals.' . . . Then God looked over all he had made, and he saw that it was very good!" (Genesis 1:27-28, 31).

God made a distinction between his estimation of mankind and the rest of creation. He saw us as *very good!* We were made in the image of God, with capacities far beyond mere animals. God was, and is, excited about us! He gave us abilities and responsibilities to reflect his own nature in all of creation.

Although we have a sin nature that came after the Fall, we are still created in the likeness of God. In doing our inventory, we need to see the good as well as the bad. Let's remind ourselves of the goodness and dignity inherent in being human as we honestly look at those things which miss the mark.

We are made to be like God and therefore share
many of his characteristics and feelings.

Day 14

Discovering Wisdom
Bible Reading: Proverbs 2:6-22

We made a searching and fearless moral inventory of ourselves.

I n recovery we come to realize that we're influenced by the
people we're around. We welcome the support of those who are
farther along on the road to recovery. We may rely heavily on
the encouragement of our sponsor or others who are supportive of
our new way of life. We will also come to see the negative influence
of associating with people who are still living the kind of life from
which we're trying to escape. Part of our inventory may include
considering whom we choose to spend our time with and whether
these decisions contribute to our recovery.

In Proverbs we are told, "Wisdom will enter your heart, and
knowledge will fill you with joy. Wise choices will watch over you.
Understanding will keep you safe. Wisdom will save you from evil
people, from those whose words are twisted. These men turn from
the right way to walk down dark paths. They take pleasure in doing
wrong, and they enjoy the twisted ways of evil" (Proverbs 2:10-14).
We are encouraged to "follow the steps of good men instead, and
stay on the paths of the righteous. For only the godly will live in
the land, and those with integrity will remain in it. But the wicked
will be removed from the land, and the treacherous will be uprooted" (Proverbs 2:20-22).

Are we exercising wisdom by following the steps of those
who are living the kind of life we truly desire? If we do this, we will
find our lives to be filled with joy. We will also be spared the loss
and destruction that await those who do not enter into recovery
and continue down darkened pathways.

Even if we've made bad choices in the past, we can reclaim the
lost parts of our lives by turning to choose the good.

Recognizing Strengths

Bible Reading: Judges 6:1-16

We made a searching and fearless moral inventory of ourselves.

For those of us who have lived in bondage to addictive/compulsive behaviors, loss of self-respect is a familiar feeling. It is easy to begin to see ourselves as chronically weak, small, even hopeless. We often fall into the rut of believing we're destined to bondage, poverty, and failure. When this view of ourselves and our lives persists, we give up the possibility of change. We settle for just trying to survive. We live in fear and shame, filling up with resentment as our lives remain in the pit. As we make our inventory, we should take time to test these kinds of assumptions about ourselves.

When we first meet Gideon, he is discouraged; he's a young man with little self-respect. His family was the poorest in a small tribe, and he was the least in his family. We first see him threshing wheat in a winepress, to hide the wheat from the enemy who would steal what little food he had. An angel appeared and called to him, "Mighty hero, the LORD is with you!" (Judges 6:12). Gideon didn't look or feel like a mighty soldier, but God could see his potential. By the end of the story, Gideon had become the deliverer of his people (Judges 6–8). His first step toward success was to see himself as God saw him—as a "mighty hero." Then he was able to hope in the possibility of freedom.

We can use our inventory to help us see ourselves in a new light and summon up the hope for a better life. Then, as God gives us the strength, we can pursue freedom from the bondage that surrounds us and our families.

We need to discover our special gifts and learn to focus them on the problems we face.

Seeking Truth

Bible Reading: Philippians 3:12-14

We made a searching and fearless moral inventory of ourselves.

T hose of us in recovery all struggle to move out of a difficult past and into a healthier future. We can't change our past, yet it's hard to accept the truth about it. It's hard to face the things that others have done to us and all the mistakes we have made. Our energy can easily be spent trying to rewrite the past, a task at which we can never succeed. In Step Four we are simply trying to honestly evaluate our lives, including everything in our past.

Jesus said, "You will know the truth, and the truth will set you free" (John 8:32). The path to freedom always leads through the truth, even the truth about our past. The apostle Paul once wrote to young Timothy: "Alexander the coppersmith did me much harm, but the Lord will judge him" (2 Timothy 4:14). Paul states the truth about someone who had hurt him but leaves the matter in God's hands. We, too, should honestly accept what has been done to us and then let it go, leaving it in God's hands.

Elsewhere, Paul examined his past, making an honest review of his earthly accomplishments, his wrongs, his mistakes, his family, his gains, and his losses. It was from this broad perspective that he could write these words: "I don't mean to say that I have already achieved these things or that I have already reached perfection. But I press on to possess that perfection for which Christ Jesus first possessed me" (Philippians 3:12). When we face the truth about our past, we can finally let go of it. Then we can journey on into a healthier future.

We can be fearless in our inventory, knowing that
the truth can only set us free.

Day 17

Buried Pain
Bible Reading: Philippians 4:10-14

We made a searching and fearless moral inventory of ourselves.

Some of us have never accepted the hurtful circumstances of our lives. We may be living in denial to avoid the pain. We continue to struggle against the painful realities, to rebel against who we are or what has happened to us. There are others of us who have accepted the bad, even to the point where it feels normal and comfortable. Therefore, we repeat cycles of behavior that are destructive; but we can't receive the good.

The apostle Paul wrote, "I have learned how to be content with whatever I have. I know how to live on almost nothing or with everything. I have learned the secret of living in every situation, whether it is with a full stomach or empty, with plenty or little" (Philippians 4:11-12). When Paul wrote these words he was in a Roman prison waiting to hear if he would be executed. And yet, we hear no whining or complaining. Instead, he learned to accept the circumstances he could not change.

Working Step Four should be a time of learning to find serenity while also accepting ourselves and our lives as they are. Life isn't fair. It isn't predictable or controllable. It can be wonderfully rich in some ways and terribly difficult in others. We must be willing to face the hurt in our lives and consider how we have reacted to it. Then our discomfort can lead us to break the destructive cycles. And then we can learn to be content with the things we cannot change.

Contentment lies in knowing and accepting ourselves,
while also trusting in Christ and his power.

Filling the Gaps
Bible Reading: Judges 4:1-21

We made a searching and fearless moral inventory of ourselves.

T here are times when chaos reigns in our lives because others are not willing or able to fulfill the role they should play. When this happens we may suffer from the lack of leadership and protection.

The time of the judges was a time of confusion for Israel. Each person did what was right in his own eyes instead of obeying the law. They were oppressed by tyrants, one of whom was General Sisera, who "ruthlessly oppressed the Israelites for twenty years" (Judges 4:3). At this time God chose Deborah to be a judge. Her job was to decide the disputes of the people.

One day Deborah summoned a man named Barak and told him that God would use him to defeat the army of Sisera. "Barak told her, 'I will go, but only if you go with me'" (Judges 4:8). So, Deborah agreed to go along, but she said, "You will receive no honor in this venture, for the LORD's victory over Sisera will be at the hands of a woman." (4:9). Barak lacked the faith to take on the responsibilities God had chosen him for. In the end, General Sisera did die at the hands of a woman. In the victory song, Deborah was honored. They sang, "There were few people left in the villages of Israel—until Deborah arose as a mother for Israel" (5:7).

When others don't fulfill their rightful duty and role, we have the option of finding a way to cope, with God's help. Deborah compensated for Barak's lack of faith. We don't have to endure the ongoing effects of other people's limitations. And we don't have to accept the painful circumstances that their weaknesses create.

❧

Staying in daily contact with God will help eliminate some of the painful circumstances we might otherwise create.

Day 19

Healthy Acceptance
Bible Reading: 1 Samuel 25:1-34

We made a searching and fearless moral inventory of ourselves.

When other people put us at risk or cause us pain, we may feel like there's nothing we can do. We may feel very comfortable in the role of victim and give in to our feelings of helplessness.

Abigail is a good example of someone who didn't give in to helplessness but had the wisdom to know what she could and couldn't change. Her husband, Nabal (which means "fool"), was "crude and mean in all his dealings" (1 Samuel 25:3). Before David became king, Nabal insulted his troops to the point that David and his men were on their way to kill him and anyone who got in their way. Through some fast thinking and some even faster talking, Abigail protected her family. She convinced David not to take vengeance into his own hands. A few weeks later Nabal was dead of natural, or perhaps supernatural, causes and Abigail became David's wife.

As part of our inventory, we might examine how we deal with other people who endanger us. Do we fall into the victim role and do nothing to protect ourselves from the results of their actions? Do we accept that we can't change them, or just resolve to try harder in our crusade? Acceptance of another's addiction or personality doesn't mean that we have to accept being the victim of their wrongs. We can give up our crusade to change them, without giving up our right to be treated with dignity.

❦

We can improve our circumstances in life without demanding radical changes in the people close to us.

Day 20

All or Nothing
Bible Reading: 1 Kings 19:3-18

We made a searching and fearless moral inventory of ourselves.

Perfectionists see the world in black and white. We may feel like we're superhuman, able to take on anything, until we discover a flaw. Then we come crashing down and consider ourselves to be worthless failures.

The prophet Elijah is one of the great heroes of the Bible. If anyone had reason to feel superhuman, it was he. He could pray and stop the rain for years. He commanded fire to come down from heaven and destroy his enemies. But even he could have a bad day. Let's consider his reaction after being threatened by Queen Jezebel. "'I have had enough, LORD,' he said. 'Take my life. . . . I have zealously served the LORD God Almighty. But the people of Israel have broken their covenant with you, torn down your altars, and killed every one of your prophets. I am the only one left, and now they are trying to kill me, too'" (1 Kings 19:4, 10). The Lord replied, "Yet I will preserve 7,000 others in Israel who have never bowed down to Baal" (19:18).

Like Elijah, if we're perfectionists, we may think of ourselves as being above everyone else. We work very hard to please God and other people. But we can grow dangerously discouraged if it doesn't seem to work. This "all or nothing" way of thinking is something to watch for while working Step Four. If we don't allow ourselves to be less than perfect, we may find ourselves at great risk during the times when life reminds us that we are only human after all.

Often periods of failure follow our successes; we need
to humbly recognize our limitations.

No Other Gods
Bible Reading: Exodus 20:1-17

We made a searching and fearless moral inventory of ourselves.

E ven if we don't practice a particular religion, we do worship something. Our hearts, souls, and minds can't exist in a vacuum. We're all under allegiance to some set of beliefs. Our love and need to be loved drive us to the feet of some god. Part of our inventory needs to include looking to see who or what brings us to our knees.

The first commandment God gave says, "You must not have any other god but me" (Exodus 20:3). He repeated the same command after the children of Israel had wandered forty years in the wilderness, adding some explanations: "I am the LORD your God, who rescued you from the land of Egypt, the place of your slavery. You must not have any other god but me" (Deuteronomy 5:6-7). Once when Jesus was talking with some people, "An expert in religious law tried to trap him with this question: 'Teacher, which is the most important commandment in the law of Moses?' Jesus replied, "'You must love the LORD your God with all your heart, all your soul, and all your mind." This is the first and greatest commandment'" (Matthew 22:35-38).

If we want to reorder our lives according to God's design, it is helpful to start with the standard he set up—the Ten Commandments. He begins by simply asking that we recognize him as God. Are we willing to admit that our Creator and Rescuer is fully deserving of our wholehearted love and commitment? Are we willing to turn away from our other gods to worship him alone?

If we give God the proper place in our lives, all of his commandments should follow naturally.

Day 22

False Images

Bible Reading: 1 Corinthians 10:12-14

We made a searching and fearless moral inventory of ourselves.

W e may find that our imaginations are held captive by an image or ideal that makes demands of us. We may be focused on the image of "the perfect body" and find ourselves swept into compulsive eating disorders, depression, or sexual addictions. We may be focused on the image of "the good life" and find ourselves swept into workaholism, stealing, or lying to try to appease the image we worship. We may have an image of ourselves as "the black sheep of the family" and slavishly live our lives playing out that role.

We don't talk much about idol worship in our culture, except perhaps when we talk of celebrities. Idolatry can be defined as image worship; it may involve becoming a slave to the ideas an image represents. This is the second commandment: "You must not make for yourself an idol of any kind or an image of anything in the heavens or on the earth or in the sea. You must not bow down to them or worship them, for I, the LORD your God, am a jealous God who will not tolerate your affection for any other gods" (Exodus 20:4-5). The apostle Paul warned, "So, my dear friends, flee from the worship of idols" (1 Corinthians 10:14).

In his protective love, God warns us not to let devotion to an image enslave our lives. The images we worship are more likely to come through television or other media than from an idol carved from stone. But we need to ask ourselves, What are the images and ideas that drive our compulsive behaviors?

☘

Taking inventory of the things we consider important may
alert us to the false gods in our lives.

Integrity
Bible Reading: Matthew 5:33-37

We made a searching and fearless moral inventory of ourselves.

W hen we live in a world where we need to pretend in order to cope, it's hard to maintain integrity. We learn to lie to cover up our shameful circumstances. We may lie to ourselves by escaping into another world through our addictions. When we don't feel sure of ourselves, some of us even hide behind religious words and experiences. We might say things like "The Lord told me this . . ." or "I swear to God . . ." in order to validate our actions.

The third commandment says, "You must not misuse the name of the LORD your God. The LORD will not let you go unpunished if you misuse his name" (Exodus 20:7; see also Deuteronomy 5:11). Jesus went further: "Our ancestors were told, 'You must not break your vows; you must carry out the vows you make to the LORD.' But I say, do not make any vows! . . . Do not even say, 'By my head!' for you can't turn one hair white or black. Just say a simple, 'Yes, I will,' or 'No, I won't.' Anything beyond this is from the evil one" (Matthew 5:33-34, 36-37).

Integrity is a key issue to consider while making our inventory. We need to ask ourselves where we are still in hiding. If we are making renewed vows, saying God ordained a specific course, perhaps we would do well to ask ourselves why we need all the extra endorsements.

🌿

Integrity will be the natural result of making an
honest inventory of ourselves.

Being, Not Doing

Bible Reading: Exodus 20:8-11

We made a searching and fearless moral inventory of ourselves.

S ome of us become addicted to our work and our accomplishments. It's not that we're just hardworking people; we use our activities to help us feel worthwhile. It's as though we believe deep inside that we are worthless, so we work and take care of others to earn the right to be loved. When our work is at the heart of our self-esteem, we have a hard time stopping whatever it is that gives us a feeling of value. We become slaves to what we do and can never do enough.

The fourth commandment says, "Remember to observe the Sabbath day by keeping it holy. You have six days each week for your ordinary work, but the seventh day is a Sabbath day of rest dedicated to the LORD your God. On that day no one in your household may do any work. This includes you, your sons and daughters, your male and female servants, your livestock, and any foreigners living among you. For in six days the LORD made the heavens, the earth, the sea, and everything in them; but on the seventh day he rested. That is why the LORD blessed the Sabbath day and set it apart as holy" (Exodus 20:8-11).

God gave the Hebrews this command when he brought them out of Egypt after four hundred years of slavery. The only value they had known had been measured by constant work. God reminds us with this command that he cares about who we are as well as about what we do.

❧

God's command that we spend a day resting is clear
evidence that he loves us.

Honoring Our Parents
Bible Reading: Deuteronomy 5:16

We made a searching and fearless moral inventory of ourselves.

We may feel a confusion of emotions as we relate to our parents. This is true especially if we've been abused during our childhood and bear the scars of that abuse. We may have been taught that failing to honor our parents is a sin. This raises some disturbing questions. How can we honor someone whose actions have been anything but honorable? Does this mean that we stay under their control and yield to their manipulations in order to please God?

The Bible does say, "Honor your father and mother, as the LORD your God commanded you. Then you will live a long, full life in the land the LORD your God is giving you" (Deuteronomy 5:16). The word *honor* comes from a root word meaning "heavy"; it implies fixing weighty value on the relationship. We are to place high value on our parents' role in our lives.

This does not mean, however, that they have the right to destroy our lives just because they brought us into the world. Even Jesus said, "I have come to set a man against his father, [and] a daughter against her mother. . . . Your enemies will be right in your own household!" (Matthew 10:35-36).

As we evaluate our lives, we can honor our parents by realizing the heavy impact they have had on us. We don't have to let them manipulate and abuse us in order to please God. But we can still choose to love them, even though we may need to set up boundaries in the relationship.

We can best honor our parents by the way we live our lives.

Day 26

A Debt of Love

Bible Reading: Romans 13:8-10

We made a searching and fearless moral inventory of ourselves.

While under the influence of an addiction, we end up hurting ourselves, others we don't know, and those we love the most. We may be horrified at how we could have done such things to the people we love. Does that mean we don't love them? Or how could the people we love have done such things to us? Does that mean that they don't love us? What conclusions are we to draw from the sin that stabs at our lives?

"Owe nothing to anyone—except for your obligation to love one another. If you love your neighbor, you will fulfill the requirements of God's law. For the commandments say, 'You must not commit adultery. You must not murder. You must not steal. You must not covet.' These—and other such commandments— are summed up in this one commandment: 'Love your neighbor as yourself.' Love does no wrong to others, so love fulfills the requirements of God's law" (Romans 13:8-10).

At first glance we may conclude from this passage that anyone who practices the evils warned against in the Ten Commandments couldn't have love for others. But it may actually show us that when we hurt the ones we love, maybe we are loving them the way we love ourselves—very poorly. May God help us to love ourselves, so that we may learn to love others also.

❧

It is our calling in life to love others and ourselves
as God has loved us.

Handling Anger
Bible Reading: Matthew 5:20-22

We made a searching and fearless moral inventory of ourselves.

S ome of us realize that all that's kept us from committing murder was the lack of opportunity at the moment we were in touch with the depth of our rage. Maybe we can stuff our ugly emotions down deep most of the time, only venting them when we're caught off guard or under the influence.

The law of Moses clearly says, "You must not murder" (Exodus 20:13). Moses went on to explain, "If someone hates another person and pushes him or throws a dangerous object at him and he dies, it is murder. Or if someone hates another person and hits him with a fist and he dies, it is murder. . . . But suppose someone pushes another person without having shown previous hostility, or throws something that unintentionally hits another person, or accidentally drops a huge stone on someone, though they were not enemies, and the person dies. If this should happen, the community must follow these regulations in making a judgment" (Numbers 35:20-24). Jesus taught, "You have heard that our ancestors were told, 'You must not murder. If you commit murder, you are subject to judgment.' But I say, if you are even angry with someone, you are subject to judgment" (Matthew 5:21-22).

If we took the time to think about it, we may realize that we're still in danger because of the rage burning beneath the surface. In order for our recovery to be complete, we must dig up the anger, vent it appropriately, and let it go. This is a vital part of our recovery process, which we dare not neglect.

Unresolved anger becomes a violation of God's command to love.

Day 28

Sexual Inventory
Bible Reading: Matthew 5:27-30

We made a searching and fearless moral inventory of ourselves.

W e're all sexual beings. For some of us sex becomes an addiction, used to medicate our pain. Instead of staying within the committed safety of marriage, as God prescribes, we overdose on sex, emotionally or physically. Any time the marriage bond is violated, deep wounds are created which damage our sense of security. This is true whether the damaged marriage involves our parents, ourselves, or both. Dealing properly with our sexuality is a vital part of our recovery.

Jesus taught us, "You have heard the commandment that says, 'You must not commit adultery.' But I say, anyone who even looks at a woman with lust has already committed adultery with her in his heart" (Matthew 5:27-28). One day, a group of lawyers brought a woman who had been caught in the act of adultery to Jesus and asked him to pass judgment. Jesus told them that they could stone her to death in accordance with the law, but only if a person without sin threw the first stone. "[The Jewish leaders] slipped away one by one, beginning with the oldest, until only Jesus was left in the middle of the crowd with the woman. Then Jesus stood up again and said to the woman, 'Where are your accusers? Didn't even one of them condemn you?' 'No, Lord,' she said. And Jesus said, 'Neither do I. Go and sin no more'" (John 8:9-11).

The point of making an inventory of our sexuality is not to bring condemnation upon ourselves or others. It is to see where the wounds are and to move toward healing the devastation.

🌱

Left unchecked, wrong desires lead to wrong actions, which will lead us away from God and from our recovery.

Day 29

Facing Loss
Bible Reading: John 10:1-13

We made a searching and fearless moral inventory of ourselves.

Addiction and stealing usually go hand in hand. Stealing is one way to fill our desperate needs when we have no other ways of getting them met. We may have been robbed ourselves and we feel violated, left with a deficit of our own. Somehow, in either case, we have to get to the point of being filled up. Both stealing and feeling ripped off are signs of a need that should be addressed.

Jesus told a story describing himself as a shepherd who has great love for us, his sheep. He also said, "I am the gate for the sheep. All who came before me were thieves and robbers. . . . The thief's purpose is to steal and kill and destroy. My purpose is to give them a rich and satisfying life" (John 10:7-8, 10). The apostle Paul warned, "If you are a thief, quit stealing. Instead, use your hands for good hard work, and then give generously to others in need" (Ephesians 4:28).

In our inventory we will easily spot the obvious things we've stolen or had stolen from us. But we also need to look further. We need to look deeply to find the areas where we feel deprived. We need to discover the places where we want more than what others might consider our fair share. We need to uncover the empty places carved out by our previous losses. As we inventory our deficits, we can bring all of the sins and the deprivations beneath them to Jesus so that he can fill them. It will be out of this sense of fullness that we can begin to give.

❧

Our inventory will uncover the empty places in our lives
so God can fill them with his love and care.

Day 30

Overcoming Envy
Bible Reading: Hebrews 13:5-6

We made a searching and fearless moral inventory of ourselves.

A major part of recovery deals with our tendency to create and live in a fantasy world. We escape the painful realities of our lives momentarily and trade them in for experiences that feel good. The pathway that leads to our addiction is paved with desires for the things, relationships, and experiences that we see in the lives of others and don't have ourselves.

One of the lesser known of the Ten Commandments says, "You must not covet your neighbor's house. You must not covet your neighbor's wife, male or female servant, ox or donkey, or anything else that belongs to your neighbor" (Exodus 20:17; see also Deuteronomy 5:21). Jesus also warned, "Beware! Guard against every kind of greed. Life is not measured by how much you own" (Luke 12:15). The writer of Hebrews said, "Don't love money; be satisfied with what you have. For God has said, 'I will never fail you. I will never abandon you'" (Hebrews 13:5).

Modern society and commercial advertising are designed to breed discontent. This is a threat to our recovery because it leads us into an emotional fantasy world. We need to make an inventory of the greed and covetousness lodged in our hearts and minds. Then we must treat these problems like a poison that will hurt us if allowed to remain in our lives.

Since only God can meet all our needs, true contentment can only be found in him.

STEP FIVE

We admitted to God, to ourselves, and to another human being the exact nature of our wrongs.

"If we confess our sins to him [God], he is faithful and just to forgive us our sins and to cleanse us from all wickedness"
(1 John 1:9).

Day 1

Freedom through Confession
Bible Reading: Romans 2:14-15

> We admitted to God, to ourselves, and to another human
> being the exact nature of our wrongs.

All of us struggle with our conscience, trying to make peace within ourselves. We may try to deny what we've done, find excuses, try to squirm out from beneath the full weight of our conduct. We may work hard to be "good," trying to counter-act our wrongs. We do everything we can to even out the internal score. In order to put the past to rest, we must stop rationalizing and admit the truth.

We are all born with a built-in buzzer that alerts us to what is wrong. God holds everyone accountable. "They know his law when they instinctively obey it, even without having heard it. They demonstrate that God's law is written in their hearts, for their own conscience and thoughts either accuse them or tell them they are doing right" (Romans 2:14-15).

Part of Step Five is to stop this internal struggle and admit that wrong is wrong. It's a time to agree with God and our own conscience about our cover-up and the exact nature of our wrongs. We're like people who have been accused of crimes which they actually committed. We may have spent years constructing alibis, coming up with excuses, and trying to plea-bargain. It's time to come clean. It's time to admit what we know deep down inside to be true: "Yes, I'm guilty as charged."

There is no real freedom without confession. What a relief it is to finally give up the weight of our lies and excuses. When we do confess, we will find the internal peace that we lost so long ago. We will also be one step closer to full recovery.

Admitting our failures is an essential step to
forgiveness and healing.

God, Our Friend

Bible Reading: Hebrews 4:14-16

> We admitted to God, to ourselves, and to another human
> being the exact nature of our wrongs.

Going to God can be scary. We may associate God with a condemning judge, a brutal father, or some other frightful image. Before we will be able to admit our wrongs to God, we'll need to feel confident that he is on our side.

In ancient times, people could not approach God on their own. The high priest would offer a sacrifice to cover their sin and then bring them before God. The high priest was on their side, even though he had to acknowledge and deal with their sins. We have someone on our side, too. "Since we have a great High Priest who has entered heaven, Jesus the Son of God, let us hold firmly to what we believe. This High Priest of ours understands our weaknesses, for he faced all of the same testings we do, yet he did not sin. So let us come boldly to the throne of our gracious God. There we will receive his mercy, and we will find grace to help us when we need it most" (Hebrews 4:14-16). "Since he himself has gone through suffering and testing, he is able to help us when we are being tested" (Hebrews 2:18).

We don't have to fear admitting our wrongs to God. In him we have a friend who understands our struggles and our suffering. When we go to him we won't have to flee from his condemnation. We will be welcome to stay at the throne of God to receive mercy. He will give us the grace we need in our struggle to recover.

❧

> When we face our wrongs, God understands and is
> able to help us.

Day 3

Overcoming Denial
Bible Reading: Genesis 38:1-30

We admitted to God, to ourselves, and to another human
being the exact nature of our wrongs.

Admitting our wrongs to ourselves can be the most difficult part of Step Five. Denial can be blinding! How can we be expected to admit to ourselves those things we are blind to? Here's a clue that can help us. We will often condemn in others the wrongs most deeply hidden within ourselves.

According to ancient Jewish law, a widow was entitled to marry the surviving brother of her husband in order to produce children. Tamar had been married successively to two brothers who died without giving her children. Her father-in-law, Judah, promised to give her his younger son also, but he never did. This left her alone and destitute. In an effort to protect herself, she disguised herself as a prostitute and became pregnant by Judah himself. And she kept his identification seal (Genesis 38:1-23).

When Judah heard that Tamar was pregnant and unmarried, he demanded her execution. "But as they were taking her out to kill her, she sent this message to her father-in-law: 'The man who owns these things made me pregnant. . . . Whose seal and cord and walking stick are these?' Judah recognized them immediately and said, 'She is more righteous than I am'" (Genesis 38:25-26).

It won't be easy to be honest with ourselves. "The human heart is the most deceitful of all things, and desperately wicked" (Jeremiah 17:9). However, we can look at those things we condemn in others as a clue to what may be lurking within ourselves.

It takes great courage to be honest with ourselves
about ourselves.

Healing through Confession
Bible Reading: James 5:16-18

> We admitted to God, to ourselves, and to another human
> being the exact nature of our wrongs.

Most of us resist the thought of admitting our wrongs to
another person. We may think, *Isn't it enough to admit my
faults to myself and to God? Why should I humiliate myself
before another person who is no better than I am?*

It seems that there is healing power in the act of telling
another person. James wrote, "Confess your sins to each other and
pray for each other so that you may be healed. The earnest prayer
of a righteous person has great power and produces wonderful
results" (James 5:16). The apostle Paul also commented on this:
"Share each other's burdens, and in this way obey the law of Christ.
If you think you are too important to help someone, you are only
fooling yourself" (Galatians 6:2-3).

We may laugh at the thought of finding a "righteous person"
to confide in. We needn't worry; the word James uses doesn't mean
self-righteous. He is referring to someone who is right in fulfilling
duties both with God and man. This kind of person will be just and
without prejudice, already made right with God through personal
confession. Someone with this kind of righteousness won't be prej-
udiced against us.

When we find someone who has already dealt honestly with
his struggle, our burden can be made lighter by sharing our own.
Our confessor will also be able to pray for us in an understanding
way. Such prayer can really make a positive impact on our recovery.

Confessing our faults opens up our lives to God's healing power.

Day 5

Escaping Self-Deception

Bible Reading: Galatians 6:7-10

> We admitted to God, to ourselves, and to another human
> being the exact nature of our wrongs.

We may fool ourselves into believing that we can simply bury our wrongs and go on, without ever having to admit them. In time, we all discover that those deeds we thought were buried once and for all were actually seeds. They grow and bear fruit. Eventually we have to deal with a crop of consequences and face the fact that self-deception doesn't work to our advantage.

"You will always harvest what you plant. Those who live only to satisfy their own sinful nature will harvest decay and death from that sinful nature. But those who live to please the Spirit will harvest everlasting life from the Spirit" (Galatians 6:7-8). "If we claim we have no sin, we are only fooling ourselves and not living in the truth. But if we confess our sins to him [God], he is faithful and just to forgive us our sins and to cleanse us from all wickedness" (1 John 1:8-9).

Step Five says good-bye to self-deception and hello to forgiveness and cleansing. We should note that there is cleansing from every wrong, not from "wrongdoing" in a general sense. Admitting the exact nature of our wrongs includes giving an account in exact and specific terms. It is only when we get specific that we will no longer be able to fool ourselves about the nature of our wrongs. Since we can't ignore God and get away with it anyway, we might as well come clean and be forgiven.

✣

> In recovery, planting our confessions will yield
> a harvest of forgiveness.

Fear of Rejection
Bible Reading: Hebrews 4:12-16

> We admitted to God, to ourselves, and to another human
> being the exact nature of our wrongs.

The thought of being totally honest about the exact nature of our wrongs causes us to hesitate for fear of rejection. How many times have we thought to ourselves, *If anyone ever knew the real me they wouldn't love me; they would probably leave me?*

Whether we like it or not, the Bible tells us that everyone will have to give an account of his life before God. "Yes, each of us will give a personal account to God" (Romans 14:12). But, we don't have to worry about surprising him with any of the hidden details. "Nothing in all creation is hidden from God. Everything is naked and exposed before his eyes, and he is the one to whom we are accountable" (Hebrews 4:13).

This can be encouraging if we think about it. The very fact that he already knows all about us and still requires us to give an account must mean that there is some value for us in the experience. Since he already knows every detail of our thoughts and actions and hasn't rejected us, we don't have to fear his rejection. "But if we confess our sins to him, he is faithful and just to forgive us our sins and to cleanse us from all wickedness" (1 John 1:9).

We don't go through the process of admitting our wrongs to God for his information, but for our transformation. Once we find the courage to work through this step with God, we will find more courage to help us risk telling another human being.

❧

> God knows all our secrets, but he lovingly waits
> for us to reveal them to him.

Feelings of Shame

Bible Reading: John 8:3-11

> We admitted to God, to ourselves, and to another human being the exact nature of our wrongs.

Shame has kept many of us in hiding. The thought of revealing ourselves to another human being stirs up feelings of shame and the fear of being publicly exposed.

"The teachers of religious law and the Pharisees brought a woman who had been caught in the act of adultery. They put her in front of the crowd. 'Teacher,' they said to Jesus, . . . 'The law of Moses says to stone her. What do you say?' . . . Jesus stooped down and wrote in the dust with his finger. They kept demanding an answer, so he stood up again and said, 'All right, but let the one who has never sinned throw the first stone!' Then he stooped down again and wrote in the dust. When the accusers heard this, they slipped away one by one . . . until only Jesus was left in the middle of the crowd with the woman" (John 8:3-9).

Many believe that it was Jesus' writing in the dust that caused the accusers to leave. Perhaps he was listing the secret sins of the Jewish leaders. If this is true, it gives us a beautiful picture of the kind of person Jesus is—a person with whom we can safely expose our secrets. Our confessor needs to be someone who is not surprised by sin and will not be waiting to condemn us. Such a person needs to take private note of our wrongs, writing them in the soft dust, not etching them in stone and posting them in public. Since shame can be a trigger for addictive behavior, we need to be careful about whom we choose.

> With God's help we can accept his forgiveness and be released from our shame.

Restoring Relationships

Bible Reading: Matthew 18:15-18

We admitted to God, to ourselves, and to another human being the exact nature of our wrongs.

When we're grappling with addictions in our family, we are likely to draw away from people and from honest communication about our problems. Step Five is the place where we can return to the relationships that will help us face the truth. Paul spoke of the value of honesty, saying, "So stop telling lies. Let us tell our neighbors the truth, for we are all parts of the same body" (Ephesians 4:25).

Jesus even laid out specific instructions for dealing with people who have done wrong but are persisting in denial. He said, "If another believer sins against you, go privately and point out the offense. If the other person listens and confesses it, you have won that person back. But if you are unsuccessful, take one or two others with you and go back again, so that everything you say may be confirmed by two or three witnesses. If the person still refuses to listen, take your case to the church. Then if he or she won't accept the church's decision, treat that person as a pagan or a corrupt tax collector" (Matthew 18:15-17).

Accountability and honesty in our relationships are essential to successful recovery. When we make ourselves accountable to others, the caring influence of the group can help to keep us on the right track. They can provide us with an objective perspective, helping us to admit the truth. We often find ourselves isolated as a result of our shame or our fear that we will be rejected if we ever reveal who we really are. Admitting our wrongs to a trustworthy person always helps to break down the isolation.

❧

Lies destroy our relationships; the truth restores them.

133

Relief from Dishonesty

Bible Reading: Psalm 32:1-6

> We admitted to God, to ourselves, and to another human being the exact nature of our wrongs.

Living a lie is miserable. Perhaps we carry the heavy burden of hiding our secret lives. Maybe we're avoiding God and withdrawing from people because of our fear of being found out.

Moses understood the price to be paid for trying to live a lie. He prayed, "We wither beneath your anger; we are overwhelmed by your fury. You spread out our sins before you—our secret sins—and you see them all. We live our lives beneath your wrath, ending our years with a groan" (Psalm 90:7-9). David showed us the other side. "Oh, what joy for those whose disobedience is forgiven! . . . What joy for those whose record the LORD has cleared of guilt, whose lives are lived in complete honesty! When I refused to confess my sin, my body wasted away, and I groaned all day long. Day and night your hand of discipline was heavy on me. My strength evaporated like water in the summer heat. Finally, I confessed all my sins to you and stopped trying to hide my guilt. I said to myself, 'I will confess my rebellion to the LORD.' And you forgave me! All my guilt is gone. Therefore, let all the godly pray to you while there is still time, that they may not drown in the floodwaters of judgment" (Psalm 32:1-6).

Why should we live with the weight of dishonesty when relief is available to us? God already knows our secret sins anyway. Why continue to suffer needless agony when we can be relieved?

God wants to forgive; it has always been a part of his loving nature.

Both Good and Bad

Bible Reading: Romans 3:10-12

> We admitted to God, to ourselves, and to another human
> being the exact nature of our wrongs.

We may see ourselves as different from other people—either much worse or much better. We may look down on ourselves and continually compare ourselves with "good" people. Or perhaps our addiction is more socially acceptable. We may console ourselves by placing ourselves above others whose sins seem worse than ours.

"As the Scriptures say, 'No one is righteous—not even one. No one is truly wise; no one is seeking God. All have turned away; all have become useless. No one does good, not a single one'" (Romans 3:10-12).

The first chapter of Romans is often used to condemn sexual sins, or sexual addictions. People often skip over the last few verses, which condemn the more acceptable sins such as backstabbing, disobedience to parents, or being a proud braggart. Right after this chapter, the apostle Paul speaks to people who see themselves as better than others: "You may think you can condemn such people, but you are just as bad, and you have no excuse! When you say they are wicked and should be punished, you are condemning yourself, for you who judge others do these very same things" (Romans 2:1).

Every one of us is made of the same stuff, both good and bad. We may act out in different ways; but in God's eyes, we're the same. When we focus on admitting our wrongs, it helps us remember that we're not so different from others after all.

❧

> We are all sinful, but we are also loved by God
> and valuable in his eyes.

Day 11

Good Counselors
Bible Reading: Proverbs 15:22-33

> We admitted to God, to ourselves, and to another human
> being the exact nature of our wrongs.

In recovery, we learn new ways of seeing things, new ways of responding, and new guidelines for making decisions. Our old patterns of thinking and living didn't work very well. Now that we're establishing new patterns, we'll need counselors. They will supply the support we need and will listen as we share our story.

King Solomon gives this advice: "Plans go wrong for lack of advice; many advisers bring success" (Proverbs 15:22). "There is safety in having many advisers" (Proverbs 11:14). King David looked to God's word for counsel, saying, "Your laws please me; they give me wise advice" (Psalm 119:24). Isaiah prophesied of the Messiah (Jesus), saying, "For a child is born to us, a son is given to us. The government will rest on his shoulders. And he will be called: Wonderful Counselor, Mighty God, Everlasting Father, Prince of Peace" (Isaiah 9:6).

When we surround ourselves with dependable counselors, we are developing a safety net. Good counsel can come from the Bible and from people. When we admit our wrongs to other people they can also become a source of counsel for our lives. They may be professionals who understand addiction and recovery. They might be people who know us and measure their advice by godly wisdom. Or perhaps they are people who have experienced what we're now going through. Find someone!

❧

> We need the help of those who can enlarge our vision
> and broaden our perspective.

Day 12

Unending Love
Bible Reading: Hosea 11:8-11

We admitted to God, to ourselves, and to another human being the exact nature of our wrongs.

We may be sorely aware of the deep shame, trouble, and pain inflicted on our families because someone (ourselves or someone we love) is acting out his addictions. We may be afraid of admitting the exact nature of our wrongs, because we don't understand how God could love someone who is so bad.

Hosea was a prophet to the rebellious nation of Israel. God used his life to demonstrate God's unconditional love for us. The Lord told Hosea to marry a prostitute. He married her, loved her, and devoted himself to her. She relapsed into her old ways, broke Hosea's heart, and brought shame on their family. She ended up falling into slavery. God then baffled Hosea by telling him, "Go and love your wife again, even though she commits adultery with another lover. This will illustrate that the LORD still loves Israel, even though the people have turned to other gods" (Hosea 3:1).

We may be asking, *How could God (or anyone) still love me?* But God asks, "Oh, how can I give you up? . . . How can I let you go? How can I destroy you? . . . My heart is torn within me, and my compassion overflows. . . . For I am God and not a mere mortal. I am the Holy One living among you, and I will not come to destroy" (Hosea 11:8-9). There is absolutely nothing we can do or admit that would cause God to stop loving us! (See Romans 8:38-39.)

God is committed to us and our recovery even when we want to quit and run away.

Day 13

Facing Consequences

Bible Reading: 1 Samuel 15:10-23

We admitted to God, to ourselves, and to another human being the exact nature of our wrongs.

Part of admitting our wrongs involves having to consider and to accept the consequences of our actions. We may want to deny our wrongs and try to justify them. We may feel wrongly accused and defensive as we try to escape the accountability we must surely face some day.

Saul was the first king of Israel. At his coronation the people were told, "Now if you fear and worship the LORD and listen to his voice, and if you do not rebel against the LORD's commands, then both you and your king will show that you recognize the LORD as your God" (1 Samuel 12:14). But Saul disobeyed the Lord. "Then the LORD said to Samuel, 'I am sorry that I ever made Saul king, for he has not been loyal to me and has refused to obey my command'" (15:10-11). When Samuel confronted Saul, he denied doing any wrong and put up his defenses. So Samuel replied, "Rebellion is as sinful as witchcraft, and stubbornness as bad as worshiping idols. So because you have rejected the command of the LORD, he has rejected you as king" (15:23). Saul then led his entire family and country into years of civil war, as he fought to remain king. He finally died at his own hand, surrounded by enemy troops. His three sons died with him.

There's no escaping the consequences of our actions. But, when we admit our wrongs and face the consequences, we may spare ourselves and our loved ones years of additional pain.

Though we may not escape the consequences of our actions, we can experience God's forgiveness.

Denial Leads to Bondage

Bible Reading: John 8:30-36

We admitted to God, to ourselves, and to another human
being the exact nature of our wrongs.

L iving in denial is living dishonestly. How many times have
we lied to ourselves and others, saying, "I can stop any time
I want!" Or "I have the right to choose how I live my own
life!" Or "My behavior doesn't affect anyone but me!" Ironically,
as we asserted our freedom to live as we chose, we soon lost the
freedom to choose anything other than our addiction; we became
enslaved to it.

Jesus said to some would-be disciples, "'You are truly my
disciples if you remain faithful to my teachings. And you will
know the truth, and the truth will set you free'. . . . 'A slave is not
a permanent member of the family, but a son is part of the family
forever. So if the Son sets you free, you are truly free'. . . . 'Why
can't you understand what I am saying? It's because you can't even
hear me! For you are the children of your father the devil. . . . He
was a murderer from the beginning. He has always hated the truth,
because there is no truth in him. When he lies, it is consistent
with his character; for he is a liar and the father of lies'" (John
8:31-36, 43-44).

Spiritual forces swaying our lives have their roots in either
truth or deceit. Truth leads to freedom; deceit to bondage and
death. Denial is a lie that keeps us in slavery. When we're slaves to
our addictions we lose the right to choose any other way of life. It's
only when we break the denial, when we become brutally honest
about our bondage, that there's any chance for real freedom.

❦

Denial keeps us in bondage to our vices; confession
leads us to recovery and freedom.

Aiming at Truth

Bible Reading: Ephesians 4:12-16

We admitted to God, to ourselves, and to another human
being the exact nature of our wrongs.

W e probably grew up believing lies about life, about ourselves, about our families. We may still experience confusion and uncertainty because we don't have a strong
sense of what's true. The lies we believe about ourselves can play
into our addictive ways. So we need to reexamine our lives in the
light of what's true.

The apostle Paul talked about how the people who believed
in Christ were to function like a single body. Each member is to be
"measuring up to the full and complete standard of Christ" (Ephesians 4:13), offering the gifts they have to help the whole body
grow up into maturity. Since Jesus described himself as "the truth"
(John 14:6), and we are to be filled with him, our recovery process
involves becoming "truth-full." Paul continued, "Then we will no
longer be immature like children. We won't be tossed and blown
about by every wind of new teaching. We will not be influenced
when people try to trick us with lies so clever they sound like the
truth. Instead, we will speak the truth in love" (Ephesians 4:14-15).

Recovery can be like growing up all over again. As we grow,
we need to continue to aim ourselves in the direction of what is
true. In the past we measured truth against whatever sounded right
to us at the time. Now we can have the sure measurement of God's
Word and Jesus Christ himself. From this perspective we need to
reevaluate our beliefs. What is true about God? What is true about
me? What is right? What is wrong?

Commitment to the truth involves both our words
and our actions.

Cleaning the Inside
Bible Reading: Luke 11:39-44

We admitted to God, to ourselves, and to another human
being the exact nature of our wrongs.

We often protect ourselves by focusing our attention on other people and their behaviors. That way we don't have to examine our own. We often stay in relationships where we seem powerless, for in doing so, we maintain built-in excuses for failure. We may also spend time looking down on others who are "worse" than we are, thus avoiding an examination of our own corruption. But in doing these things, we fail to take responsibility for our own recovery by honest self-examination.

Jesus confronted the Pharisees, saying, "You Pharisees are so careful to clean the outside of the cup and the dish, but inside you are filthy—full of greed and wickedness!" (Luke 11:39). Can you imagine polishing the outside of a cup, which is moldy on the inside, and then drinking from it? Of course not! But we do this in a spiritual sense because it's hard to deal with the "filth" inside our hearts.

Step Five is all about cleaning the inside of our cup. We must begin by turning our eyes away from everyone else around us. This may include those we blame for our condition in life or those we condemn to make our wrongs seem less in comparison. Then we can get back to looking within ourselves. Every one of us has some residue of wrongdoing in our lives. When we admit this to God, to ourselves, and to another human being, we will experience the cleansing of humility and forgiveness. Then we'll have lives that can bring refreshment to others.

Our recovery not only requires that we look inward; it also
demands that we confess what we find inside.

Receiving Forgiveness
Bible Reading: Acts 26:12-18

> We admitted to God, to ourselves, and to another human
> being the exact nature of our wrongs.

As we work our recovery program, we go through a process of accepting the truth about our lives and the consequences of our choices. We may feel like we have to earn forgiveness instead of just receiving it. We may find it easier to forgive others who have hurt us than to forgive ourselves for the hurt we have caused.

When Jesus confronted the apostle Paul, he gave him this mission: "Now get to your feet! For I have appeared to you to appoint you as my servant and witness. . . . Yes, I am sending you to the Gentiles to open their eyes, so they may turn from darkness to light and from the power of Satan to God. Then they will receive forgiveness for their sins and be given a place among God's people, who are set apart by faith in me" (Acts 26:16-18).

God's goal in sending his Word to us is that we may receive forgiveness and a place among his people, like anyone else who turns to him. The process involves first opening our eyes to our true condition, which happens in Steps One, Two, and Four. This allows us the opportunity to repent, changing our minds so that we're in agreement with God and ready to admit our wrongs. God wants us to receive immediate forgiveness, based on the finished work of Christ. We're not second-class citizens in the Kingdom of God. We don't have to work the rest of the Twelve Steps as a form of penance. Forgiveness awaits us right now, if we will only receive it.

> We all share equally in God's promise of forgiveness
> as we confess our wrongs before him.

The Plumb Line

Bible Reading: Amos 7:7-8

> We admitted to God, to ourselves, and to another human
> being the exact nature of our wrongs.

The kind of instrument we use to measure our lives will often determine the kinds of problems we uncover. If we use a faulty guideline, we won't be able to make an accurate assessment. We may wonder why we aren't progressing in our recovery programs. It may be that we need to look closely at the measuring stick we are using to uncover our problem areas.

The prophet Amos recorded this vision: "I saw the Lord standing beside a wall that had been built using a plumb line. He was using a plumb line to see if it was still straight. And the LORD said, . . . 'I will test my people with this plumb line'" (Amos 7:7-8).

A plumb line is a length of string that has a weight tied to one end. When you hold the string up, letting the weighted end hang down, gravity ensures that the string is perfectly vertical. When held next to a building structure, the plumb line provides something sure by which to check whether the building is "in line" with the physical universe or not. If a building is built in line with the plumb line, the structure will be sturdy and function well.

The same holds true in the spiritual realm. God's Word is our spiritual plumb line. Just as we can't argue with the law of gravity, we can't change the spiritual laws revealed in the Bible. It is to our advantage to measure our lives by that divine plumb line. And when things don't measure up, it is important that we admit there is a problem and start rebuilding accordingly.

🌿

> God's Word is our plumb line, keeping us in line with
> his loving plans for us.

Admitting Hypocrisy
Bible Reading: Amos 5:21-24

We admitted to God, to ourselves, and to another human
being the exact nature of our wrongs.

Many of us live two lives, one ruled by our addictions and
passions, the other governed by the laws of religion or
social respectability. We probably know the pain of living
in both worlds and the fear of being found out.

During a period of peace and prosperity, Israel's upper class
was living in luxury. Much of their wealth, however, was gained
by exploiting the poor. They violated God's laws and worshiped
idols, while still keeping up their "proper" religious duties. God
said to them, "I hate all your show and pretense—the hypocrisy
of your religious festivals and solemn assemblies. I will not accept
your burnt offerings and grain offerings. I won't even notice all
your choice peace offerings. . . . I want to see a mighty flood of
justice, an endless river of righteous living" (Amos 5:21-22, 24).

God sees through the external images we present and looks
upon the heart. He understands the pain and bondage of living
in hiding; he hates the pretending. Step Five is the time to face
our hypocrisy. We need to stop trying to make up for the darkness
inside by going overboard with religious displays. Let's stop singing
louder to drown out the cry of our guilty conscience. We need to
let God's justice convict us of every sin and let Jesus' blood cover it.
Then we'll be able to honestly sing praises, move toward a whole,
integrated life, and be free from pretending.

God wants us to have honest hearts, willing to show
others who we really are.

Marking Off Boundaries

Bible Reading: Ephesians 4:17-19

> We admitted to God, to ourselves, and to another human
> being the exact nature of our wrongs.

We may feel that we are somehow above the rules everyone else needs to live by. We may have grown so proud of ourselves and our power to "handle" our addiction that we've completely lost sight of right and wrong. At this point we have become slaves to our lusts. This is a time of great danger.

The apostle Paul warned, "Live no longer as the Gentiles do, for they are hopelessly confused. Their minds are full of darkness; they wander far from the life God gives because they have closed their minds and hardened their hearts against him. They have no sense of shame. They live for lustful pleasure and eagerly practice every kind of impurity" (Ephesians 4:17-19).

The Lord spoke through the prophet Amos: "Can horses gallop over boulders? Can oxen be used to plow them? But that's how foolish you are when . . . . You boast, 'Didn't we take Karnaim by our own strength?' 'O people of Israel, I am about to bring an enemy nation against you'" (Amos 6:12-14).

We may be deluded into believing that we can break all the rules and make a mockery out of what God says is right and good, but this isn't true. If this is what we believe, we may need the help of someone else to even determine what is wrong. Then we will be able to turn from it and be protected from the consequences.

❧

We discover true freedom when we seek to become
what God has designed us to be.

Filling the Empty Places
Bible Reading: 2 Timothy 3:14-17

> We admitted to God, to ourselves, and to another human
> being the exact nature of our wrongs.

W e may feel like we have to live with a deficiency. It seems that somehow something inside is missing, something we really needed in order to be complete. This feeling of being "less than" others can fuel our need for our addictions, to make us feel good or "normal."

The apostle Paul said, "All Scripture is inspired by God and is useful to teach us what is true and to make us realize what is wrong in our lives. It corrects us when we are wrong and teaches us to do what is right. God uses it to prepare and equip his people to do every good work" (2 Timothy 3:16-17).

God has a plan to deal with that sense of lack in our lives. He wants to fill up that "something" that is missing that makes us feel like we need our addiction to be normal. He knows that we need help to be complete and fully "equipped." His Word is there to give us the tools we need to compensate for our lack. God's Word is also given for correction, to restore us to an upright state.

When we let addictions become the focal point of our lives, we're always off balance. We need to align our lives to the Word of God, admitting our wrongs and needs to God. This will allow us to be fully restored and to find what we need to balance our lives.

🌿

Confession opens us to God's equipping power,
filling the empty places inside us.

Gods That Can't Satisfy

Bible Reading: Jeremiah 2:10-26

> We admitted to God, to ourselves, and to another human
> being the exact nature of our wrongs.

We've all become slaves to gods that cannot satisfy. We run after that elusive "high" that only heightens our thirst for more. In the process, we lose our sense of appropriate guilt. We regret getting caught, but fail to mourn the deeper tragedy of repeatedly returning to the wrong well to satisfy our thirst.

God spoke through Jeremiah: "For my people have . . . abandoned me—the fountain of living water. And they have dug for themselves cracked cisterns that can hold no water at all! Why has Israel become a slave? . . . When will you stop running? When will you stop panting after other gods? But you say, 'Save your breath. I'm in love with these foreign gods, and I can't stop loving them now!' Israel is like a thief who feels shame only when he gets caught" (Jeremiah 2:13-14, 25-26).

God knows how thirsty we are. He's the fountain that gushes with the water that can truly satisfy. A cistern is a man-made holding tank. Our addictions are like "cracked cisterns" that don't stay full. The fundamental mistake being pointed out here is that we're running repeatedly to the wrong source for our satisfaction. Instead of just being sorry that we "get caught," God wants us to realize the deeper wrong. He wants us to return to him, find true satisfaction, and eliminate our need to keep going back to our addictions. Admitting our wrongs should include the sources we've turned to that don't fully satisfy.

> We can replace the cracked cisterns of our addictions
> with the life-giving fountain that God promises.

Joyful Confession
Bible Reading: Isaiah 43:25–44:5

We admitted to God, to ourselves, and to another human
being the exact nature of our wrongs.

Our wrongs may have been left unattended for a long time.
Our lives may seem like parched fields where good things
just don't grow anymore. Years of denial have left the
stubble of pain on the landscape of our lives. We look at the lives
of our children and feel ashamed. We see the desolation they suffer
because we didn't have the means to meet even our own needs, let
alone theirs.

The Lord wants our wrongs brought before him so that he
can flood them with forgiveness. He spoke through Isaiah: "I—yes,
I alone—will blot out your sins for my own sake and will never
think of them again. Let us review the situation together, and you
can present your case to prove your innocence. . . . I will pour out
water to quench your thirst and to irrigate your parched fields. And
I will pour out my Spirit on your descendants, and my blessing on
your children. They will thrive like watered grass, like willows on a
riverbank" (Isaiah 43:25-26; 44:3-4).

We don't have to leave our wrongs scattered over the landscape of our past. The Lord longs to overcome them with loving
forgiveness, so that we can spring to life once again. The forgiveness is instantaneous, erasing all the wrongs in our past. God
longs to replenish the landscapes of our lives and our children's
lives so that we will be beautiful to behold. When we admit our
wrongs to God we can do so joyfully, reminding him of his wonderful promises!

When God forgives us, we don't have to worry that he
might remind us later of our past offenses.

Blinding Rationalization

Bible Reading: Hosea 12:6-7

> We admitted to God, to ourselves, and to another human
> being the exact nature of our wrongs.

When we constantly have to rationalize our behavior to get around a guilty conscience or to cover up for something, we begin to lose sight of how to accurately measure our lives. We may have cheated for so long that we now find it difficult to measure out the "exact nature of our wrongs." At this point, we may need an objective person to help us. We may have lost the ability to be impartial in our judgment.

God says, "Do not use dishonest standards when measuring length, weight, or volume" (Leviticus 19:35). The Lord demands fairness in every business deal. The book of Proverbs says, "The LORD demands accurate scales and balances; he sets the standards for fairness" (Proverbs 16:11). "So now, come back to your God. Act with love and justice, and always depend on him. But no, the people are like crafty merchants selling from dishonest scales—they love to cheat" (Hosea 12:6-7).

We should never underestimate the power of rationalization to warp our perspective on our sins. God requires impartial judgment, a task we may not be able to manage on our own. It is helpful and crucial to admit the exact nature of our wrongs to another human being. He should be able to see the blind spots in our lives better than we can. His perspective will help us adjust our understanding so that it better matches reality.

❧

God's measure of success is different than ours;
he calls us to honest confession.

Day 25

Confession Brings Mercy
Bible Reading: Psalm 51:1-6

> We admitted to God, to ourselves, and to another human
> being the exact nature of our wrongs.

M any of the wrongs we need to confess are shameful. They are kept in the dark because we can't bear to look at what they reflect about our human condition. We somehow know deep in our being that we have violated the way things "should have been." It sometimes takes the reflection of another person to help us see the truth about our actions.

Before the prophet Nathan confronted King David about his sins, David had gone on with his life as if nothing were wrong. After Nathan informed David of God's judgment because of his adultery with Bathsheba and his murder of her husband, Uriah, David responded by writing this psalm. "Have mercy on me, O God, because of your unfailing love. Because of your great compassion, blot out the stain of my sins. Wash me clean from my guilt. Purify me from my sin. For I recognize my rebellion; it haunts me day and night. Against you, and you alone, have I sinned; I have done what is evil in your sight. You will be proved right in what you say, and your judgment against me is just" (Psalm 51:1-4).

It is human nature to want to cover our shameful deeds and to hide from God. When we are forced to face the reality of the situation, we can follow David's example. We can recall God's nature, which is full of love, kindness, and compassion. Then we should realize that we have sinned against God, not just another person, and we should recognize that God saw it all. After this, we must confess accordingly, accepting his verdict and sentence.

No sin is too great to be forgiven!

Day 26

Joy Restored

Bible Reading: Psalm 51:7-15

> We admitted to God, to ourselves, and to another human
> being the exact nature of our wrongs.

W hen we admit that we're sinners, like everyone else, we may assume that we're disqualified from being used by God to lead others. We may look up to those who seem so proud that God has kept them from sin and feel worthless in comparison.

In his confession of adultery and murder, David prays, "Do not banish me from your presence, and don't take your Holy Spirit from me. Restore to me the joy of your salvation, and make me willing to obey you. Then I will teach your ways to rebels, and they will return to you" (Psalm 51:11-13). David understood that admitting his wrongs would provide a bridge to other hurting souls.

This is quite different from the prayer he prayed as a young man, who had yet to realize that he was a sinner like the rest of us. Here's part of that prayer: "I hate the gatherings of those who do evil, and I refuse to join in with the wicked. . . . Don't let me suffer the fate of sinners. Don't condemn me along with murderers. Their hands are dirty with evil schemes, and they constantly take bribes. But I am not like that; I live with integrity. So redeem me and show me mercy" (Psalm 26:5, 9-11).

Admitting our sins doesn't disqualify us from being used of God. Recognizing the sin in our lives can only make us more useful to him. It allows us to glorify God for his grace and it removes any reasons we might have for exalting ourselves.

❦

> The more we've experienced God's forgiveness, the more
> we desire his presence and his joy.

Crying to God
Bible Reading: Psalm 38:9-16

> We admitted to God, to ourselves, and to another human
> being the exact nature of our wrongs.

We may need to pay the price for our wrongs in order to wake up and admit them. And as we suffer those consequences, the pain may be increased by seeing our loved ones and friends draw back from us, while our enemies close in for the kill. Those we love may withdraw in order to deal with their own pain, leaving us feeling abandoned. Those we wish would leave us alone prepare to attack and destroy us.

David knew what this was like. He prayed this prayer when experiencing the consequences of his wrongs: "My loved ones and friends stay away, fearing my disease. Even my own family stands at a distance. Meanwhile, my enemies lay traps to kill me. Those who wish me harm make plans to ruin me. All day long they plan their treachery. But I am deaf to all their threats. I am silent before them as one who cannot speak. I choose to hear nothing, and I make no reply. For I am waiting for you, O LORD. You must answer for me, O Lord my God. I prayed, 'Don't let my enemies gloat over me or rejoice at my downfall'" (Psalm 38:11-16).

Sometimes there's nothing we can say that will make up for what we've done. Instead, it's a time to call out to God for his protection. God can help us to deal with our wrongs. He can draw our loved ones back to us and put an end to the arrogance of those who gloat over our downfall. God is not one of our enemies. He doesn't enjoy our pain. But, he will often use the natural consequences of our actions to get our attention.

*As we confess to others, we need to be silent as they respond,
and depend on God for protection.*

Day 28

Stop and Listen
Bible Reading: Isaiah 28:16-22

We admitted to God, to ourselves, and to another human
being the exact nature of our wrongs.

W e've tried time and again to take care of ourselves.
Maybe we learned early on that no one else would; at
least that's the belief we've built our lives on. Time and
again we find that life tends to overwhelm us, especially when we
turn to our addictions to try to meet our needs. It just doesn't work.

"This is what the Sovereign LORD says: 'Look! I am placing a foundation stone in Jerusalem, a firm and tested stone. It is
a precious cornerstone that is safe to build on. Whoever believes
need never be shaken. I will test you with the measuring line of
justice and the plumb line of righteousness. Since your refuge is
made of lies, a hailstorm will knock it down. Since it is made of
deception, a flood will sweep it away. . . . Again and again that
flood will come, morning after morning, day and night, until you
are carried away.' This message will bring terror to your people"
(Isaiah 28:16-17, 19).

When life comes crashing in, and we realize that our
attempts to take care of ourselves don't quite make it, we have a
choice. We can run away again, or we can stop and get the message God is sending. The pain God allows in our lives and the dis-
satisfactions we feel are meant to wake us up to the dangers of our
chosen lifestyles. This will help us transfer our dependence to God,
who can provide us with a solid foundation for living.

In the midst of our confessions, we need to continue to
listen to what God may be saying to us.

God Understands
Bible Reading: Psalm 38:1-22

We admitted to God, to ourselves, and to another human
being the exact nature of our wrongs.

We may know the anguish of feeling like we deserve the
suffering in our life. Sins carry their own painful consequences, many of them in the form of physical disease
and discomfort. It's a terrible thing to realize that our pain may be
discounted by others because we brought it upon ourselves. We
may have encountered self-righteous people who look down on us
in our pain, as if to say, "Well, that should teach you! I bet you'll
never do that again!" They don't seem to understand the power
the addiction holds over us.

David prayed, "O LORD, don't rebuke me in your anger or
discipline me in your rage! Your arrows have struck deep, and your
blows are crushing me. Because of your anger, my whole body is
sick; my health is broken because of my sins. My guilt overwhelms
me—it is a burden too heavy to bear. My wounds fester and stink
because of my foolish sins. I am bent over and racked with pain.
All day long I walk around filled with grief. . . . I am on the verge
of collapse, facing constant pain. But I confess my sins; I am deeply
sorry for what I have done" (Psalm 38:1-6, 17-18).

We can call out to God in the midst of our pain. He has
compassion on us, even if we brought the pain upon ourselves. We
can admit that we're still on the verge of sin in the same prayer
that says how truly sorry we are. Such is the nature of addiction.
People may never understand, but God does.

As we confess, we need to admit that we are always
on the verge of falling.

154

Confession versus Guilt

Bible Reading: Genesis 42:1-26

We admitted to God, to ourselves, and to another human
being the exact nature of our wrongs.

S ometimes we've lived a lie for so long, and built so much of
our lives on a false foundation, that we're afraid to admit the
truth. It would mean dismantling much of the good we've
worked for in order to go back and explain. But we're plagued with
guilt and fear of exposure, constantly looking over our shoulder.
We may fear divine judgment and human vengeance, forfeiting
years of peace. We may interpret everything that goes wrong in
our lives as just punishment for the lie we're living.

This was the case for the brothers of Joseph, who sold him
into slavery and told their father he was dead. Their story is told
in Genesis 37–50. We see later that they interpreted their trouble
with the Egyptian officials as God's punishment for their hidden
sins. When they tried to explain why they couldn't leave their
young brother Benjamin, they had to repeat the lie that Joseph
was dead. They didn't realize that the man they were addressing
was their brother Joseph. They were snared in their own lies and
tormented by fears of retribution. When Joseph finally revealed
himself and offered forgiveness, they found it hard to believe and
receive.

When we refuse to take the risk of uncovering lies, we're
condemning ourselves to a life of guilt. It may be hard to face the
truth, but it isn't as bad as living with the heavy burden of the lies.
With a clean conscience, there is freedom and hope for a good life.

🌿

It may be hard to admit the truth, but that's the path
to our recovery.

STEP SIX

We were entirely ready to have God remove these
defects of character.

*"And so, dear brothers and sisters, I plead with you to
give your bodies to God because of all he has done for you.
Let them be a living and holy sacrifice—
the kind he will find acceptable"*
(Romans 12:1).

Discovering Hope

Bible Reading: John 5:1-9

> We were entirely ready to have God remove these
> defects of character.

H ow can we honestly say that we're *entirely* ready for God to remove our defects of character? If we think in terms of all or nothing, we may get stuck here because we will never feel entirely ready. It's important to keep in mind that the Twelve Steps are guiding ideals. No one can work them perfectly. Our part is to keep moving, to get as close as we can to being ready.

In Jesus' day there was a pool where people came in hope of finding miraculous healing. "One of the men lying there had been sick for thirty-eight years. When Jesus saw him and knew he had been ill for a long time, he asked him, 'Would you like to get well?' 'I can't, sir,' the sick man said, 'for I have no one to put me into the pool when the water bubbles up. Someone else always gets there ahead of me.' Jesus told him, 'Stand up, pick up your mat, and walk!' Instantly, the man was healed! He rolled up his sleeping mat and began walking!" (John 5:5-9).

This man was so crippled that he couldn't go any farther on his own. He camped as near as he could to a place where there was the hope of recovery. God met him there and brought him the rest of the way. For us, "entirely ready" may mean getting as close to the hope of healing as we can in our crippled condition, using the support available to us. When we do, God will meet us there and take us the rest of the way.

> Our confession readies us for God's work of
> cleansing and releasing.

God's Abundant Pardon

Bible Reading: Isaiah 55:1-9

> We were entirely ready to have God remove these
> defects of character.

P eople tell us to repent and stop thinking the way we do. Most of us would give anything to do this. If it were only that simple to put a stop to our obsessive thoughts! When we're starving emotionally, it's almost impossible to stop thinking about what has fed that hunger, even when we realize it doesn't satisfy.

People don't seem to understand. They may quote a verse like, "Let the wicked change their ways and banish the very thought of doing wrong" (Isaiah 55:7). But we think, *How? My thoughts seem to be out of my control.*

God does understand. He put that verse into the larger context of dealing with the hunger within our soul. He said, "Why spend your money on food that does not give you strength? Why pay for food that does you no good? Listen to me, and you will eat what is good. You will enjoy the finest food. Come to me with your ears wide open. Listen, and you will find life. . . . Let them turn to the LORD that he may have mercy on them. Yes, turn to our God, for he will forgive generously" (Isaiah 55:2-3, 7). The word translated *generously* can be understood to mean "in progressively increasing measure each time we come."

We need to fight our addictions on two fronts: dealing with the hunger deep inside us, and changing our thoughts of doing wrong. Neither battle is easily won; each requires our daily readiness for God to satisfy our hunger and remove our defects of character.

❧

> God not only forgives us, but also promises to satisfy
> the hunger we feel deep inside.

158

Healing the Brokenness
Bible Reading: Psalm 51:16-19

> We were entirely ready to have God remove these
> defects of character.

I f we have sincerely practiced the previous steps, we have probably found enough pain inside to break our hearts. Facing the
fact that brokenness is part of the human condition can be
crushing. But if we've arrived at this point, it is probably a sign that
we are ready for God to change us.

King David, as a young man, wasn't ready for God to change
his defects of character because he didn't recognize that they were
there. He prays, "Don't let me suffer the fate of sinners. . . . But I
am not like that; I live with integrity. So redeem me and show me
mercy" (Psalm 26:9, 11). He approached God on the basis of his
own merit.

It wasn't until later in his life when he was confronted with
his sins of adultery and murder that he was able to say, "I was born
a sinner—yes, from the moment my mother conceived me" (Psalm
51:5). He also said, "You do not desire a sacrifice, or I would offer
one . . . The sacrifice you desire is a broken spirit. You will not
reject a broken and repentant heart, O God" (Psalm 51:16-17).

Jesus taught, "God blesses those who mourn, for they will be
comforted" (Matthew 5:4). God isn't looking for evidence of how
good we are or how hard we try. He only wants us to mourn over
our brokenness. Then he will not ignore our needs, but will forgive
us, comfort us, and cleanse us.

> We can't please God by what we do; he looks at the
> attitudes of our hearts.

Day 4

Crossing the Barriers
Bible Reading: Joshua 3:1-17

> We were entirely ready to have God remove these
> defects of character.

For those of us who've used dysfunctional patterns to govern our lives, crossing over into an entirely new way of living takes some preparation. We may see where we're supposed to end up, but we don't know how to get there.

Israel had wandered for forty years in the wilderness. Finally they arrived at the Jordan River and were able to see the Promised Land. But still, there was no way for them to cross the river. They were instructed, "When you see the Levitical priests carrying the Ark of the Covenant of the LORD your God, move out from your positions and follow them. Since you have never traveled this way before, they will guide you" (Joshua 3:3-4). God miraculously stopped the flow of the river, and the people focused their attention on the Ark of God as they crossed on dry ground.

We, too, have never traveled this way before, where we are now going. We can be guided by focusing on what the Ark represents. "Inside the Ark were a gold jar containing manna, Aaron's staff that sprouted leaves, and the stone tablets of the covenant" (Hebrews 9:4). These represented God's presence, his law, his promised provision, and a warning against rebellion to "prevent any further deaths" (Numbers 17:10).

As God helps us cross the final barriers we need to remember that his law is there to guide us and he will provide our daily bread. We also need to bear in mind the dangers of rebellion. With this focus and preparation, we will be ready to move ahead.

We can move ahead with confidence when our eyes are on God.

Attitudes and Actions
Bible Reading: Philippians 3:12-14

> We were entirely ready to have God remove these
> defects of character.

Getting "entirely ready" to have God remove "all" our defects of character sounds impossible. In reality we know that such perfection is out of reach. This is another way of saying that we're going to do our best to approach a lifelong goal, which no one ever completes this side of eternity.

The apostle Paul expressed a similar thought. He said, "I don't mean to say that I have already achieved these things or that I have already reached perfection. But I press on to possess that perfection for which Christ Jesus first possessed me. . . . Forgetting the past and looking forward to what lies ahead, I press on to reach the end of the race and receive the heavenly prize for which God, through Christ Jesus, is calling us" (Philippians 3:12-14).

This combination of a positive attitude and energetic effort is a part of the mystery of our cooperation with God. Paul said, "Work hard to show the results of your salvation, obeying God with deep reverence and fear. For God is working in you, giving you the desire and the power to do what pleases him" (Philippians 2:12-13).

We'll need to practice these steps the rest of our lives. We don't have to demand perfection of ourselves. It is enough to keep moving ahead as best we can. We should look forward to our rewards, with hopes of becoming all God intends us to be.

🌱

> Hoping in Christ, we can let go of past guilt and look
> ahead to the good things God has planned for us.

Long-Lasting Change

Bible Reading: Matthew 15:16-20

We were entirely ready to have God remove these
defects of character.

W hen we were consumed with addictive/compulsive
behaviors, we considered the behaviors to be "the problem." When we are sober and not acting out our compulsions, we realize that "the problem" goes much deeper. We used
to think, *If I could only change my behavior, everything would be fine*.
Now that we're in recovery, and the behavior may be under control, it's time to look to the state of our innermost being to get to
the heart of the problem.

Early in his life King David prayed, "Declare me innocent"
(Psalm 26:1), focusing on his deeds. Later in life, he was able to
pray on a deeper level, "Create in me a clean heart, O God. Renew
a loyal spirit within me" (Psalm 51:10).

Jesus explained the true source of our problem: "But the
words you speak come from the heart—that's what defiles you.
For from the heart come evil thoughts, murder, adultery, all sexual
immorality, theft, lying, and slander" (Matthew 15:18-19). We
needn't worry, though. God is in the business of heart transplants.
He promised Israel, "I will take away their stony, stubborn heart
and give them a tender, responsive heart, so they will obey my
decrees and regulations. Then they will truly be my people, and
I will be their God" (Ezekiel 11:19-20).

Being entirely ready means that we want God to go deeper
than dealing with our destructive behaviors. We want him to
change our motives and create a new, clean heart within us.

❧

Who we are deep down matters more to God than
who we may appear to be on the surface.

Removed, Not Improved

Bible Reading: Romans 6:5-11

We were entirely ready to have God remove these
defects of character.

Most of us have made numerous attempts at self-improvement. Perhaps, we've consciously tried to improve our attitudes, our education, our appearance, or our habits. We probably have had some success in self-improvement on some level. However, when it comes to our struggles with defects of character, chances are we've only experienced deep frustration.

There is a reason for our frustration. These character defects can only be removed, never improved! The illustration given us in the Bible is that these defects of character must be put to death, as Jesus was, with the hope of new life to follow. The apostle Paul wrote, "Our old sinful selves were crucified with Christ so that sin might lose its power in our lives. We are no longer slaves to sin" (Romans 6:6). "Those who belong to Christ Jesus have nailed the passions and desires of their sinful nature to his cross and crucified them there" (Galatians 5:24).

There is no Band-Aid cure for these defects of character. They have been crucified and must die their death on the cross. This process is never easy. Who goes to a crucifixion without some measure of anxiety? But when we accept this and allow God to remove our defects, we will be surprised by the new life that greets us on the other side.

Before, we were slaves to our addictions; now, we can choose
to have God remove all the old, destructive patterns.

Day 8

Telling the Truth
Bible Reading: Colossians 3:9-11

> We were entirely ready to have God remove these
> defects of character.

L ying can be habitual. We may even have lied to ourselves, pretending we don't have a problem with lying. We may have learned to cover up our problems by becoming excellent liars. We can see the unhappiness caused by our lies, how they've hurt us and our loved ones. And lying is one of the defects we can give up with many promised benefits.

Think about these promises: "Does anyone want to live a life that is long and prosperous? Then keep your tongue from speaking evil and your lips from telling lies!" (Psalm 34:12-13). "Don't lie to each other, for you have stripped off your old sinful nature and all its wicked deeds. Put on your new nature, and be renewed as you learn to know your Creator and become like him" (Colossians 3:9-10). "Stop telling lies. Let us tell our neighbors the truth, for we are all parts of the same body" (Ephesians 4:25).

There are great benefits to truthfulness. What other virtue is accompanied by such promises? Honesty is vital to recovery. Since lying may be second nature to us, it may be difficult to change. Part of any successful recovery involves guarding our lips and our thoughts, to rid ourselves of the lies that hurt us and others. Since this may have been a lifelong way of coping, we must accept that learning to tell the truth is a gradual process.

> Telling the truth is an excellent way to build bridges
> and break down barriers.

Results Reveal Value
Bible Reading: Hebrews 12:5-11

We were entirely ready to have God remove these
defects of character.

S ome phases of our recovery may be very painful; it may feel
to us like we're being punished. We may assume that the bad
things happening are because we are bad. And we may begin
to believe that God doesn't love us.

It may hurt when God removes these defects, but this in
itself is a display of love. The Bible says, "Don't give up when
he corrects you. For the LORD disciplines those he loves, and he
punishes each one he accepts as his child. As you endure this
divine discipline, remember that God is treating you as his own
children. Who ever heard of a child who is never disciplined by
its father? . . . God's discipline is always good for us, so that we
might share in his holiness. No discipline is enjoyable while it is
happening—it's painful! But afterward there will be a peaceful
harvest of right living" (Hebrews 12:5-7, 10-11).

Our recovery is a time of discipline; it's a time of facing
problems and character flaws, and changing incorrect beliefs. There
may be seasons when we do have to pay for our past. God will use
this time to redirect our lives toward a better life. His correction
isn't arbitrary or abusive, but it's still painful. Knowing that God's
discipline demonstrates his love for us can be comforting in the
midst of the pain. It helps to remember that his love will only allow
that which is for our ultimate good.

When God corrects us, he proves his loving concern for us.

A New Identity

Bible Reading: 1 Corinthians 6:9-11

> We were entirely ready to have God remove these
> defects of character.

Our addictions may be so ingrained in us that we define our identity by them. It may feel like we are predisposed to behave as we do. And yet we're condemned for our behavior that feels out of our control! How can we let go of seeing ourselves primarily in terms of the kinds of addictions that dominate our lives?

One passage in Scripture seems to identify people by their behavior. It says, "Those who indulge in sexual sin, or who worship idols, or commit adultery, or are male prostitutes, or practice homosexuality, or are thieves, or greedy people, or drunkards, or are abusive, or cheat people—none of these will inherit the Kingdom of God." This doesn't seem fair. We feel like we'll never be able to escape our addictive nature. But the passage goes on: "Some of you were once like that. But you were cleansed; you were made holy; you were made right with God by calling on the name of the Lord Jesus Christ and by the Spirit of our God" (1 Corinthians 6:9-11). "Anyone who belongs to Christ has become a new person. The old life is gone; a new life has begun!" (2 Corinthians 5:17).

God doesn't just erase the behavior. When we identify ourselves with Christ, he wants to give us a new identity. We'll always remember what we were and realize that our sin nature and our body may always be predisposed to a particular addiction. We'll still slip up, but we should no longer see our addiction as the definition of who we are.

God accepts us because our identity is found in Christ.

Day 11

Transformed from the Inside
Bible Reading: Romans 12:1-2

> We were entirely ready to have God remove these
> defects of character.

How many times have we wished that we could be someone else? Perhaps part of the reason we act out our addictions is because we can't stand ourselves. Self-hatred is often associated with addictive/compulsive personalities. If we don't like who we are, it's reassuring to know that we can change dramatically.

The apostle Paul wrote, "Present your bodies a living sacrifice, holy, acceptable to God, which is your reasonable service. And do not be conformed to this world, but be transformed by the renewing of your mind, that you may prove what is that good and acceptable and perfect will of God" (Romans 12:1-2, NKJV).

The words *conformed* and *transformed* describe processes that happen to things that are changeable or unstable. In this case, we are the changeable things in mind. *Conformed* refers to an outward change to make one thing appear like another. *Transformed* describes a change from the inside out. It comes from the same word that describes a caterpillar changing into a butterfly.

We all have great potential for change. We've tried to change our outward behavior and found that it doesn't last. As we yield ourselves to God in the cocoon of the recovery process, he will renew our minds. He will begin to remove our defects of character, transforming us inwardly so that it affects both our character and our behavior.

God has good, pleasing, and perfect plans for us, his children.

Day 12

Seeking Wisdom
Bible Reading: Proverbs 3:13-23

> We were entirely ready to have God remove these
> defects of character.

N one of us set out with the goal of becoming addicted. We
were seeking something else—escape from the pain, perhaps something to make up for our losses and brokenness
or maybe an inner desire to self-destruct. Unfortunately, the things
we seek are not able to satisfy our deepest needs and desires.

Our needs are legitimate. The defect that needs to be
changed is our tendency to go the wrong way to try to meet them.
The Bible says, "Don't lose sight of common sense and discern-
ment. Hang on to them, for they will refresh your soul. They are
like jewels on a necklace. They keep you safe on your way, and
your feet will not stumble" (Proverbs 3:21-23).

Wisdom leads to the benefits most of us want out of life.
When we seek wisdom, as if it were a hidden treasure, we'll find the
other things we desire. "Joyful is the person who finds wisdom, the
one who gains understanding. For wisdom is more profitable than
silver, and her wages are better than gold. Wisdom is more precious
than rubies; nothing you desire can compare with her. She offers
you long life in her right hand, and riches and honor in her left"
(Proverbs 3:13-16). As we change our focus and begin to seek after
wisdom, we will find our lives more fulfilled and secure. This may
also help us avoid the destructive paths we've previously taken as
we have tried to fulfill our own unmet needs and desires.

> Common sense is given to everyone; wisdom is
> given only to those who follow God.

Day 13

Repairing Our Boundaries

Bible Reading: 2 Chronicles 32:5-9

> We were entirely ready to have God remove these
> defects of character.

Recovery involves repairing or building healthy boundaries in the places where our boundaries are weak or defective. Boundaries are the limits set in our lives for our protection. Perhaps boundaries have been violently trampled down through abuse, or they may have grown weaker as we lost our ability to maintain limits. We let people walk all over us or let down our guard against our own destructive behavior.

In Bible times each city was fortified by boundary walls that served as protection from outside enemies. If these walls were weak or broken there was grave danger of an invasion and destruction. At one point in Israel's history an enemy was threatening to attack Jerusalem. The king "worked hard at repairing all the broken sections of the wall, erecting towers, and constructing a second wall outside the first. He . . . encouraged them by saying: 'Be strong and courageous! . . . We have the LORD our God to help us and to fight our battles for us!' Hezekiah's words greatly encouraged the people" (2 Chronicles 32:5-8).

Part of the recovery process involves repairing our boundaries. We can also construct a second wall of defense by developing a strong support network around us. We will still need to be brave and remember that whatever enemies we face in the form of destructive behaviors, there is someone with us who is far greater. We, too, can let this greatly encourage us!

> Looking through the eyes of faith helps us to see the
> support that God provides around us.

Day 14

Courage to Change

Bible Reading: 2 Chronicles 15:1-16

We were entirely ready to have God remove these
defects of character.

There comes a point in recovery when we need to face ourselves. We need to acknowledge the wrongs we've committed and the harm we've brought because of our slavery. It takes courage to make the preparations necessary to allow God to change our lives and relationships in ways supporting our recovery.

King Asa was a man who lived at a time when the people of Israel had given themselves over to the worship of idols. They had turned away from God and the way of life they knew to be right. A messenger of God told the king: "'The LORD will stay with you as long as you stay with him! Whenever you seek him, you will find him. But if you abandon him, he will abandon you.' . . . When Asa heard this message . . . he took courage and removed all the detestable idols from the land . . . and he repaired the altar of the LORD" (2 Chronicles 15:2, 8). Asa even removed his mother from her position of power because she had been influential in Israel's idolatry.

Allowing God to remove all our defects of character takes courage, because the changes he makes in us will affect every part of our lives. The time will come when we need to crush and burn the "idols" we've served, to go against the crowd, to make a commitment to God, and even to separate ourselves from those people who do not contribute to our recovery. When we do these things, we will find that the Lord will be there for us, encouraging us as we set things straight.

Stay in contact with people who love God and you
will find the courage to change.

Leaving the Familiar
Bible Reading: Matthew 14:23-33

> We were entirely ready to have God remove these
> defects of character.

Having God remove our defects can be frightening. No
matter how bad life gets we tend to feel at home with
what's familiar. We may stay trapped in destructive life
patterns because we fear change. But if we wait for all the fear
to go away before we take courageous steps, we'll never make
significant progress.

Courage isn't the absence of fear. Courage means to seize the
strength you find within you, to encourage yourself, to be obstinate
or steadfastly minded. It doesn't mean being free of fear. It means
finding enough strength to take the next step.

In the account where Jesus walks on the water, the disciples
are terrified when they see him. "Then Peter called to him, 'Lord,
if it's really you, tell me to come to you, walking on the water.'
'Yes, come,' Jesus said. So Peter went over the side of the boat and
walked on the water toward Jesus. But when he saw the strong
wind and the waves, he was terrified and began to sink. 'Save me,
Lord!' he shouted. Jesus immediately reached out and grabbed him"
(Matthew 14:28-31).

Peter gathered up enough courage to take one step. He ven-
tured out into a new experience. When he got in over his head,
he called out and found the help he needed. We, too, only need to
summon the courage to take the next step. This doesn't mean that
we won't feel fear or need help. It does mean that with God's help,
we'll make it. All we need is the courage to take just one more step.

We need to walk with our eyes on Jesus, not on the
situations we face.

Day 16

Removing Self-Hatred

Bible Reading: Psalm 139:13-18

We were entirely ready to have God remove these
defects of character.

M any of us have spent our lives trying to be someone we're
not. Our addictive/compulsive behaviors may revolve
around this desperate attempt to escape from ourselves.
Maybe we have difficulty accepting our personality, our appearance, our handicaps, even our talents. Perhaps we spend our lives
trying to be what someone else wants us to be because we feel that
who we are is not enough. We may do all we can to distance ourselves from our inner being because we are so deeply ashamed of
who we are.

Self-hatred is a defect of character that needs to be removed.
It breeds the sin of covetousness, that is, longing to be in someone else's situation or have what they have. The psalmist wrote,
"Thank you for making me so wonderfully complex! Your workmanship is marvelous—how well I know it" (Psalm 139:14). Saying
we are God's "workmanship" means that we're unique and beautiful
masterpieces, works of poetry. Beauty and value are designed into
our very fiber, by virtue of our Creator.

One important step in our recovery is to allow God to
remove self-hatred, helping us to value ourselves for who we are.
We have been miraculously created and we are treasured by God.
And this has been true since the time in our mother's womb, long
before we could *do* anything to earn it! As we begin to see how
unique and special we are—embraced and accepted by God himself—our strides toward recovery should grow faster and longer.

We need to see ourselves as God does—a creature, wonderfully
crafted, made by the very hands of God.

Removing Impatience

Bible Reading: James 1:1-4

> We were entirely ready to have God remove these
> defects of character.

We would all love to have an instant recovery. Many times our addictive behavior has its source in trying to fill an inner void with some form of immediate pleasure. When we enter into recovery, we have to admit that there is no immediate "fix" for the needs we have deep within. We need to prepare for God to remove our impatience. Recovery comes in seasons and takes time.

The Bible says, "When troubles come your way, consider it an opportunity for great joy. For you know that when your faith is tested, your endurance has a chance to grow. So let it grow, for when your endurance is fully developed, you will be perfect and complete, needing nothing" (James 1:2-4).

It's nice to know that the troubles of life have significant value. They are sent as our friends, to help us mature and develop the kind of character that isn't dependent on outside sources for fulfillment. The difficult seasons of life are like the fire that purifies precious metal. They are designed to burn away the impurities and leave us better than before. The process takes time, but it's worth it because of the strength, purity, and beauty that result.

When we finally accept that there's no shortcut on the way to wholeness, we will be able to find joy in each season of recovery. We will develop endurance, true maturity, and lasting fulfillment as God replaces our defects with his character.

❦

Our continued struggles are prime opportunities
for growth and healing.

God's Will, God's Way

Bible Reading: Matthew 26:36-39

> We were entirely ready to have God remove these
> defects of character.

As we work through the steps of recovery, we look up a long, difficult road toward a better life. And though we know the goal is worthy of our commitment, we often find the challenge of the process overwhelming. As God goes about removing our defects, we may wish there were some other way. We may feel fear, a lack of confidence, deep anguish, and a host of other emotions which threaten to stop us in our tracks.

Jesus understands how we feel. He had a similar experience the night he was arrested. His friends were nearby, but when he needed them they were asleep. He told his friends, "My soul is crushed with grief to the point of death" (Matthew 26:38). As he realized the enormity of the pain he would face, he looked for some other way. He was not immediately able to accept the path set before him. Instead, he struggled and prayed the same thing three times: "My Father! If it is possible, let this cup of suffering be taken away from me. Yet I want your will to be done, not mine" (26:39). Finally he found the grace to accept God's plan.

We may be overwhelmed as we face our own crosses on the way to a new life. But during such times of stress, we can look to Jesus for encouragement. As we look to him, we can express our deepest emotions. We can be honest about our struggle and cry out for help. We also can be confident that we'll be given the strength we need for the next step.

> Because of the anguish Jesus experienced, he can
> truly relate to our suffering.

Removing Hate
Bible Reading: Jonah 1–4

> We were entirely ready to have God remove these
> defects of character.

When people have hurt us deeply it is easy to hate and
wish for vengeance. But holding tightly to these feelings
can easily become a defect of character. The bitterness
threatens our recovery because it causes us to blame others for our
problems. It may scare us to think of forgiving those who have hurt
us. We may be afraid that releasing our hatred will require us to
condone the bad things people have done to us.

Jonah felt this way, too. He hated the people of Nineveh
for their cruelty toward Israel. God told Jonah to go and warn
them of the destruction planned for them. Instead, he tried to run
away by boarding a ship going the opposite direction. The Lord
caused a life-threatening storm, and Jonah ended up in the belly
of a great fish. Suddenly, the Lord had Jonah's attention and Jonah
reluctantly obeyed. Jonah preached to the people of Nineveh, they
changed their ways, and God put off his planned destruction. Jonah
complained, "Didn't I say before I left home that you would do this,
Lord? . . . I knew that you are a merciful and compassionate God,
slow to get angry and filled with unfailing love. You are eager to
turn back from destroying people" (Jonah 4:2).

We won't be able to remove our bitterness alone. And it will
never be easy to accept that God wants to rescue even the people
we hate. We'll need to allow God to change our hearts as we work
toward forgiving those who have hurt us. This will take time. God
only asks that we be willing to let him begin the work.

❧

> We can only become bitter after we've forgotten
> how much God has forgiven us.

Day 20

Taking Time to Trust
Bible Reading: 1 Samuel 13:6-14

> We were entirely ready to have God remove these
> defects of character.

We're all susceptible to the negative influences of others. We may get pushed into rushed decisions by peer pressure and find ourselves in trouble as a result. This weakness should alert us to a defect in our lives and our need for help.

Saul had this defect but refused God's help. Israel was at war. In the midst of battle it was required that a priest offer sacrifices. Samuel told Saul that he would come at an appointed time to offer a sacrifice. Saul waited and began to feel pressured because his troops were leaving him. He knew it was against God's law for anyone other than a priest to offer sacrifices, but he let the pressure get to him. Saul did it himself. As soon as he had finished, Samuel arrived. "'How foolish!' Samuel exclaimed. 'You have not kept the command the LORD your God gave you. Had you kept it, the LORD would have established your kingdom over Israel forever. But now your kingdom must end, for the LORD has sought out a man after his own heart'" (1 Samuel 13:13-14).

If Saul had waited one more hour he would have kept his kingdom. Our tendency to be unduly influenced by others needs to be replaced with strength from God and faith in his plan.

> When we take the time to wait for God, he will
> meet and bless us according to our needs.

Recovering Childhood
Bible Reading: 1 Corinthians 13:11-12

> We were entirely ready to have God remove these
> defects of character.

Many of us spend our lives trying to fill up the empty spaces. Perhaps, we missed out on a carefree childhood. We may have had to take care of our parents when they should have been taking care of us. Maybe our real needs were never met, leaving a deficit that prompts us to fulfill even our unhealthy desires. Our addictions are fed by the sense that we deserve some comfort in our pain-filled lives.

During childhood our needs should have been met—and immediately! But for many of us, they weren't. We may have learned to cope by giving ourselves what we wanted when we wanted it. Now we literally spoil ourselves to make up for the needs that weren't filled when they should have been.

The apostle Paul used this illustration: "When I was a child, I spoke and thought and reasoned as a child. But when I grew up, I put away childish things" (1 Corinthians 13:11). Children can only see the moment. As adults we can see a bigger picture and allow a long-range perspective to lend wisdom to our choices.

Some of us haven't yet put away childish things. We can't get back our lost childhood. Demanding immediate pleasure and relief from pain is a defect that ultimately brings unhappiness. We need to let it go and allow God to address the deep, unmet needs from childhood as we work through recovery.

🌿

> Our addictions have kept us from growing up; our
> recovery allows us to put away childish things.

Time to Change

Bible Reading: Deuteronomy 7:21-24

> We were entirely ready to have God remove these
> defects of character.

I f our inner selves were transformed overnight, major changes would take place in our lives and relationships. We may fear some of these changes. We may be afraid that God will thrust us into a new way of life that we won't be able to handle. We do want new lives, but we know how fierce and tenacious our character defects can be, making us pause at the thought of dealing with them.

As the people of Israel were about to conquer the Promised Land, Moses said to them, "No, do not be afraid of those nations, for the LORD your God is among you, and he is a great and awesome God. The LORD your God will drive those nations out ahead of you little by little. You will not clear them away all at once, otherwise the wild animals would multiply too quickly for you. But the LORD your God will hand them over to you. He will throw them into complete confusion until they are destroyed" (Deuteronomy 7:21-23).

Israel's entrance into the Promised Land parallels our journey into a new life. Their conquest and removal of the enemy nations is similar to the conquests we have over our character defects. God understands that sudden, dramatic changes would endanger us. He will never expect us to maintain a life completely different from what we know. But he wants us to remember that he is with us. And he will cast out our defects a little at a time so we can handle the changes. We'll then be able to gradually move into a new life, experiencing victory one step at a time.

❦

> God could change us in an instant, but often he chooses
> to change us slowly, one step at a time.

God Wants Our Recovery

Bible Reading: Isaiah 59:15-21

> We were entirely ready to have God remove these
> defects of character.

S ome of our families may attack us for trying to discover a better life. But despite their opposition, we know we can't go another step in the wrong direction. We're tired of being separated from God. We want more from life. Can God really step in and change the course of our lives?

"Listen! The LORD's arm is not too weak to save you, nor is his ear too deaf to hear you call. It's your sins that have cut you off from God" (Isaiah 59:1-2). God understands the obstacles we face. He said through Isaiah, "Yes, truth is gone, and anyone who renounces evil is attacked. The LORD looked and was displeased to find there was no justice. He was amazed to see that no one intervened to help the oppressed. So he himself stepped in to save them with his strong arm, and his justice sustained him" (59:15-16).

Our relationships with God really can be transformed, our defects removed, the future of our families, bright. "'The Redeemer will come to Jerusalem to buy back those in Israel who have turned from their sins,' says the LORD. 'And this is my covenant with them,' says the LORD. 'My Spirit will not leave them, and neither will these words I have given you. They will be on your lips and on the lips of your children and your children's children forever'" (59:20-21).

When we get tired of holding God off and allow him to come into our lives, he will fight for our recovery. He will send his Holy Spirit to stay with us and transform our affections. He will cause us to want the things that are good and to turn from the bad.

❧

When our recovery becomes overwhelming,
God personally steps in to help.

Day 24

Avoiding Rationalization
Bible Reading: 1 Samuel 15:7-23

We were entirely ready to have God remove these
defects of character.

W e may feel we are ready to have God remove *all* our
defects of character. At the same time, however, we
may have unwittingly organized our lives in a way that
preserves some of the defects that should be removed. We call this
rationalization, and sometimes we don't even know we're doing it!

King Saul claimed to be fully committed to obeying God's
will. He would have sworn that he was ready to have God remove
all his defects of character, but he had kept a few, rationalizing
them. Samuel confronted Saul about this: "'And the Lord sent you
on a mission and told you, "Go and completely destroy the sinners,
the Amalekites, until they are all dead." Why haven't you obeyed
the Lord? Why did you rush for the plunder and do what was evil
in the Lord's sight?' 'But I did obey the Lord,' Saul insisted. 'I carried out the mission he gave me. I brought back King Agag, but I
destroyed everyone else. Then my troops brought in the best of the
sheep, goats, cattle, and plunder to sacrifice to the Lord your God
in Gilgal.' But Samuel replied, 'What is more pleasing to the Lord:
your burnt offerings and sacrifices or your obedience to his voice?
Listen! Obedience is better than sacrifice'" (1 Samuel 15:18-22).

We need to ask God to show us the things we've rational-
ized into being acceptable. It is easy for us to overlook some of our
defects. It may be helpful at this point in recovery to have someone
else double-check our list.

Selective obedience is just another form of disobedience.

Day 25

Removing Deeper Hurts
Bible Reading: Jonah 4:4-8

We were entirely ready to have God remove these
defects of character.

When we are upset, we often depend on our addictions to
make us feel better. But as we get rid of our addictions,
we then face the deeper character defects that God
wants to heal. Our addictions function as places of "shelter" from
our pain. But when those "shelters" are removed, deep anger may
surface, exposing yet deeper character flaws that need healing.

Jonah had a glaring defect of character: he couldn't seem
to forgive and have compassion on the people he hated. When
God decided not to destroy them, Jonah threw a temper tantrum.
"The LORD replied, 'Is it right for you to be angry about this?' Then
Jonah went out to the east side of the city and made a shelter to
sit under. . . . And the LORD God arranged for a leafy plant to grow
there, and soon it spread its broad leaves over Jonah's head, shad-
ing him from the sun. . . . The next morning . . . [the plant] with-
ered away. And as the sun grew hot, God arranged for a scorching
east wind to blow on Jonah. The sun beat down on his head until
he grew faint and wished to die" (Jonah 4:4-8).

God did this to show Jonah that the real problem wasn't the
loss of his shelter. Hatred was the real problem. The removal of our
sheltering addictions may expose deeper problems. This may spark
defensive anger as God touches our deepest hurts. It's all right to
let the anger out. But it's also important to let God take the real
problem, too.

We can bring our anger to God; he's big enough
to handle it lovingly.

Taking Time to Grieve
Bible Reading: Genesis 23:1-4; 35:19-21

> We were entirely ready for God to remove these
> defects of character.

The pathway to recovery and finding new life also involves the death process. The different means we used to cope were "defective," but still, they did give us comfort or companionship. Giving them up is often like suffering the death of a loved one.

Abraham and his grandson, Jacob, both lost loved ones as they traveled to the Promised Land. "Sarah . . . died at Kiriath-arba (now called Hebron) in the land of Canaan. There Abraham mourned and wept for her. Then, leaving her body, he said . . . 'Here I am, a stranger and a foreigner among you. Please sell me a piece of land so I can give my wife a proper burial.' . . . Then Abraham buried his wife, Sarah, there" (Genesis 23:1-4, 19). A generation later, Jacob was given a new name, Israel, and the promise of a great heritage in the Promised Land. On his way there, he, too, lost his beloved wife. She died while giving birth to their son, Benjamin. "So Rachel died and was buried on the way to Ephrath (that is, Bethlehem). Jacob set up a stone monument over Rachel's grave, and it can be seen there to this day. Then Jacob traveled on" (Genesis 35:19-21).

As we travel toward our new lives, we will necessarily lose some of our defective ways of coping. When this happens, we need to stop and take time to give our losses a proper burial. We need to put them away, cover the shame, and allow ourselves to grieve the loss of something very familiar to us. When the time of grieving is over, we, too, can travel on.

> We need to grieve our loss of the familiar so we can
> be ready for the new to come.

Day 27

New for Old
Bible Reading: Matthew 26:17-28

> We were entirely ready to have God remove these defects of character.

There are many rituals involved in the addictive process. These bring comfort and a sense of security to our lives. When we give up the rituals associated with acting out our addictions, we have a real need to replace them with new ones.

The Jewish people celebrated Passover to commemorate how God had delivered them from the Angel of Death by commanding that they sprinkle a lamb's blood on their doorposts; this proved that the people inside the house belonged to God. Jesus became the Lamb of God to take away the sins of the world, thus abolishing the need to rely on the sacrificial lamb of Passover. But Jesus, in removing the need for this important ritual, replaced it with a new one. "On the first day of the Festival of Unleavened Bread . . . Jesus took some bread and blessed it. Then he broke it in pieces and gave it to the disciples, saying, 'Take this and eat it, for this is my body.' And he took a cup of wine and gave thanks to God for it. He gave it to them and said, 'Each of you drink from it, for this is my blood, which confirms the covenant between God and his people. It is poured out as a sacrifice to forgive the sins of many'" (Matthew 26:17, 26-28).

When preparing to have our defects removed, we need to anticipate the loss of rituals that made us feel safe. We need to find new rituals and ceremonies to celebrate the truth of our new promises without acting out our addictions.

> God wants to support us as we walk on the paths he's made for us.

Taking Our Time
Bible Reading: Esther 2:12-14

> We were entirely ready to have God remove these
> defects of character.

As we go about removing our defects, the pathway to recovery may seem very negative. It might be refreshing to discover that sometimes defects are removed as we lavish ourselves with good things.

The story of Esther is a kind of dream come true. The king needs a new queen. So he searches for the most beautiful girl in his kingdom. Esther is one of the girls selected as a candidate for this royal beauty contest. She was given a special menu of royal foods and was favored with beauty treatments. She was given a luxurious apartment with seven maids to take care of her. "Before each young woman was taken to the king's bed, she was given the prescribed twelve months of beauty treatments—six months with oil of myrrh, followed by six months with special perfumes and ointments. When it was time for her to go to the king's palace, she was given her choice of whatever clothing or jewelry she wanted to take from the harem" (Esther 2:12-13).

This sounds wonderful! Who wouldn't welcome getting the royal beauty treatment? Surely, all the girls were beautiful, but they all had defects. Notice that the beauty treatment took a whole year. They were also given choices of the items they wanted to enhance their natural beauty. When God sets out to remove our defects, he has plans to lavish us with good things. No matter how good we may look, all of us can use some help. And we need to realize that real transformations take time.

❦

> We gave time to our addictions; now we need
> to give time to our recovery.

Loving Support
Bible Reading: John 3:14-17

> We were entirely ready to have God remove these
> defects of character.

We may find it hard to believe that anyone would want us—really want us—just as we are. It may be especially hard to believe that a holy God would consider us worthy of his love, and so much so that he would sacrifice the life of his Son to make us his own. That's the stuff of fairy tales; and we probably aren't used to thinking of our lives in terms of "happily ever after."

And yet, "God loved the world so much that he gave his one and only Son, so that everyone who believes in him will not perish but have eternal life" (John 3:16). The apostle Paul went on to describe a love story that has the power to cleanse and transform the beloved. (In this case, that's us!) He wrote, "For husbands, this means love your wives, just as Christ loved the church. He gave up his life for her to make her holy and clean, washed by the cleansing of God's word. He did this to present her to himself as a glorious church without a spot or wrinkle or any other blemish. Instead, she will be holy and without fault" (Ephesians 5:25-27).

When we are ready to have God remove all of our defects, our decision is welcomed by a loving God. He accepts us as we are, with nothing hidden from his all-seeing eyes. Baptism symbolizes the burial of our old life and a resurrection to a new one. He will continue his transforming work until every defect is wiped away.

❧

God's involvement with us is always based on his love for us.

Day 30

Our Promised Future
Bible Reading: Revelation 21:3-6

We were entirely ready to have God remove these
defects of character.

As we think about God removing our defects of character,
we probably find ourselves dwelling on the defects themselves. Removing them may seem to be an overwhelming
task—even if God has promised to do the work! We may have a
hard time visualizing the beautiful scene where all the defects are
gone from our lives. Perhaps, if we could catch a glimpse of life
beyond recovery, beyond the defects and the pain, we would shout
for joy. What hope is inspired when, by faith, we take hold of our
promised future!

The apostle Paul wrote, "And I am certain that God, who
began the good work within you, will continue his work until it
is finally finished" (Philippians 1:6). The apostle John wrote, "I
heard a loud shout from the throne saying, 'Look, God's home is
now among his people! He will live with them, and they will be
his people. God himself will be with them. He will wipe every
tear from their eyes, and there will be no more death or sorrow
or crying or pain. All these things are gone forever.' And the
one sitting on the throne said, 'Look, I am making everything
new!' And then he said. . . 'Write this down, for what I tell you
is trustworthy and true.' And he also said, 'It is finished! I am the
Alpha and the Omega—the Beginning and the End. To all who
are thirsty I will give freely from the springs of the water of life'"
(Revelation 21:3-6).

One day the defects will be gone and we will be satisfied!

No matter what we face today, God writes the last
chapter—there is still hope!

STEP SEVEN

We humbly asked God to remove our shortcomings.

God said, "Come now, let's settle this. . . . Though your sins are like scarlet, I will make them as white as snow"
(Isaiah 1:18).

Day 1

Made Right
Bible Reading: Romans 3:23-28

We humbly asked God to remove our shortcomings.

What are our shortcomings? We all realize that we have them. Is this just another way of saying that we've fallen short of our personal ideals? At some time, all of us have held high ideals; we've used them to define what we think life should be like. But most of us learned early on that we couldn't measure up to them. And worse yet, we have often fallen short of the expectations of others, and we certainly haven't fulfilled all that God desires of us. Oh, the weight of guilt we carry! Oh, the pain to think of how we've disappointed those we love! Oh, the longing for some way to make up the difference between what we are and what we should be!

The apostle Paul once wrote, "For everyone has sinned; we all fall short of God's glorious standard. Yet God, with undeserved kindness, declares that we are righteous. He did this through Christ Jesus when he freed us from the penalty for our sins" (Romans 3:23-24). Paul goes on to ask, "Can we boast, then, that we have done anything to be accepted by God? No, because our acquittal is not based on obeying the law. It is based on faith. So we are made right with God through faith and not by obeying the law" (3:27-28).

When God removes our shortcomings, he does a great job! "He has removed our sins as far from us as the east is from the west" (Psalm 103:12). We can trust God to remove our shortcomings, moment by moment, if we humble ourselves to accept his way. That means having faith in Jesus Christ to make up for our lack in both character and action.

❦

No matter how great our sins, God's grace is greater.

Pride Born of Hurt

Bible Reading: Luke 11:5-13

We humbly asked God to remove our shortcomings.

Our pride can keep us from asking for what we need. We may have grown up in families or relationships where we were consistently refused, ignored, or disappointed. No one listened when we asked that our needs be met. Some of us may have reacted by determining to become self-sufficient. We were not going to ask for help. In fact, we were going to strive to never need anyone's help ever again!

It is this type of pride, born of hurt, that will hold us back from asking God to remove our shortcomings. Jesus said, "Keep on asking, and you will receive what you ask for. Keep on seeking, and you will find. Keep on knocking, and the door will be opened to you. For everyone who asks, receives. Everyone who seeks, finds. And to everyone who knocks, the door will be opened" (Luke 11:9-10). "If your children ask for a loaf of bread, do you give them a stone instead? Or if they ask for a fish, do you give them a snake? Of course not! So if you sinful people know how to give good gifts to your children, how much more will your heavenly Father give good gifts to those who ask him" (Matthew 7:9-11).

We must come to the place of giving up our prideful self-sufficiency; we must be willing to ask for help. And we can't ask for help just once and be done with it. We must be persistent and ask repeatedly as the needs arise. When we practice Step Seven in this way, we can be assured that our loving heavenly Father will respond by giving us good gifts and by removing our shortcomings.

❧

God promises to lovingly respond when we ask him for help.

Day 3

Becoming like Clay
Bible Reading: Jeremiah 18:1-6

We humbly asked God to remove our shortcomings.

Giving up control may be difficult for us. When we get ready for God to remove our shortcomings, we still may want to control how he does it. We're so used to calling the shots that we'll ask for God's help as long as he does it on our terms. We may demand that the changes happen on our timetable, or in the order we feel ready to give them up, or at a speed convenient to us.

God doesn't work that way. That is why humility is such an important part of this step. God told Jeremiah to go to the house of the potter to learn a lesson. Jeremiah said, "I did as he told me and found the potter working at his wheel. But the jar he was making did not turn out as he had hoped, so he crushed it into a lump of clay again and started over. Then the LORD gave me this message: . . . Can I not do to you as this potter has done to his clay? As the clay is in the potter's hand, so are you in my hand" (Jeremiah 18:3-6). God told Isaiah, "What sorrow awaits those who argue with their Creator. Does a clay pot argue with its maker? Does the clay dispute with the one who shapes it, saying, 'Stop, you're doing it wrong!' Does the pot exclaim, 'How clumsy can you be?'?" (Isaiah 45:9).

When we put our lives in God's hands he will reshape them as he sees fit. It is our attitude of humility that allows us to accept the fact that he is the Creator. Our new life may be similar to the one we left behind, or entirely different. God is the master craftsman. Whatever he does, we can trust that he will recreate our lives beautifully once we get out of his way!

When we ask him to, God reshapes our lives into
something wonderful.

Day 4

Humility versus Humiliation
Bible Reading: Luke 14:8-14

We humbly asked God to remove our shortcomings.

No one wants to be disgraced. Maybe one reason we hesitate to ask God to remove our shortcomings is for fear of being humiliated. Perhaps people have put us down or publicly embarrassed us in an attempt to turn us away from our addiction. We wonder if God will do the same if we ask him to change us.

God's goal is not to put us down, but rather to lift us up. He wants us to be spared embarrassment. Jesus showed this when he taught, "When you are invited to a wedding feast, don't sit in the seat of honor. What if someone who is more distinguished than you has also been invited? The host will come and say, 'Give this person your seat.' Then you will be embarrassed, and you will have to take whatever seat is left at the foot of the table! Instead, take the lowest place at the foot of the table. Then when your host sees you, he will come and say, 'Friend, we have a better place for you!' Then you will be honored in front of all the other guests. For those who exalt themselves will be humbled, and those who humble themselves will be exalted" (Luke 14:8-11). We are promised, "Humble yourselves under the mighty power of God, and at the right time he will lift you up in honor" (1 Peter 5:6).

God's goal is to spare us further humiliation and to lift us up once again to a position of respectability. This will happen at the time he knows is good for us, not necessarily when we feel ready. Our attitude of humility will help us wait for God to restore us in his good time.

❧

Humility is not self-degradation; it is realistic affirmation.

Day 5

Into the Open
Bible Reading: Philippians 2:5-9

We humbly asked God to remove our shortcomings.

Our pride often causes us to hide behind defenses during the recovery process. We may hide behind our good reputation, our position, or delusions of superiority. We may feel such inner shame that we go overboard to cover up with a self-righteous public identity. Those of us who have tried to protect ourselves in this way will need a dramatic change of attitude.

The apostle Paul wrote, "You must have the same attitude that Christ Jesus had. Though he was God, he did not think of equality with God as something to cling to. Instead, he gave up his divine privileges; he took the humble position of a slave and was born as a human being. When he appeared in human form, he humbled himself in obedience to God and died a criminal's death on a cross. Therefore, God elevated him to the place of highest honor and gave him the name above all other names" (Philippians 2:5-9). The author of Hebrews encouraged us to keep "our eyes on Jesus, the champion who initiates and perfects our faith. Because of the joy awaiting him, he endured the cross, disregarding its shame. Now he is seated in the place of honor beside God's throne" (Hebrews 12:2).

We can ask God to change our attitudes. When he deals with our pride, we will be able to stop hiding behind our reputation. We will allow ourselves to become "anonymous," known as just another person struggling with addiction. When we humbly yield to God in recovery, he promises us future honor and the restoration of a good name.

The deeper our relationship with God, the deeper our humility.

Made of Gold

Bible Reading: 2 Timothy 2:20-22

We humbly asked God to remove our shortcomings.

Our shortcomings and character defects can interfere with our ability to make positive contributions. We probably wish God would make our problems disappear in an instant. Then, we think, we could find our purpose in life or be useful once again.

God wants our lives to be worthwhile, but we must remember that truly valuable things take time to purify. Peter reminds us that our faith (reliance upon God for complete recovery) "is being tested as fire tests and purifies gold" (1 Peter 1:7). When gold is purified it is melted by severe heat. In the molten state, the impurities rise to the surface where they can be skimmed off. The gold is then allowed to cool again and the process is repeated, over and over, until the gold is pure enough for its intended purpose. God will deal with us likewise, continually revealing and removing our shortcomings in an ongoing process.

God is moving us toward a goal. The apostle Paul told Timothy, "In a wealthy home some utensils are made of gold and silver, and some are made of wood and clay. The expensive utensils are used for special occasions, and the cheap ones are for everyday use. If you keep yourself pure, you will be a special utensil for honorable use. Your life will be clean, and you will be ready for the Master to use you for every good work" (2 Timothy 2:20-21).

His goal is to help us stay away from sin, one day at a time, as he continues to remove our shortcomings. This lifelong process will purify us and make us useful for God's highest purposes.

※

Our recovery is a refining process that burns away impurities.

Day 7

A Humble Heart
Bible Reading: Luke 18:10-14

> We humbly asked God to remove our shortcomings.

After examining ourselves closely (as we did in Steps Four, Five, and Six), we may feel cut off from God. Considering the scope of what we have done, we may feel unworthy to ask God for anything. Maybe our problem behaviors are despised as the lowest kind of evil by those whom we consider respectable. We may struggle with self-hatred. Our genuine remorse may cause us to wonder if we even dare approach God to ask for his help.

We are welcome to come to God, even when we feel this way. Jesus told this story: "Two men went to the Temple to pray. One was a Pharisee, and the other was a despised tax collector. The Pharisee stood by himself and prayed this prayer: 'I thank you, God, that I am not a sinner like everyone else. For I don't cheat, I don't sin, and I don't commit adultery. I'm certainly not like that tax collector! I fast twice a week, and I give you a tenth of my income.' But the tax collector stood at a distance and dared not even lift his eyes to heaven as he prayed. Instead, he beat his chest in sorrow, saying, 'O God, be merciful to me, for I am a sinner.' I tell you, this sinner, not the Pharisee, returned home justified before God" (Luke 18:10-14).

Tax collectors were among the most despised members of Jewish society. Pharisees, on the other hand, commanded the highest respect. Jesus purposely chose this illustration to show that it doesn't matter where we fit in society's hierarchy. It is the humble heart that opens the door to God's forgiveness.

As we humbly seek God each day, we will discover his mercy.

Day 8

A Forgiven Past

Bible Reading: Psalm 103:1-16

We humbly asked God to remove our shortcomings.

We may have a hard time believing in God's forgiveness. We may think, *After all I've done, I don't feel like I should expect anyone to completely forgive me.* Maybe we feel that we've done such horrible things, or hurt people so badly, that there's no way our sins could ever be erased entirely. Even if we could be forgiven, who could ever forget the things we've done?

When we think of people we know—the people we've hurt—perhaps these fears are well founded. But when it comes to forgiveness from God, we need to remember that his ways are higher than man's ways. The psalmist wrote, "He [God] does not punish us for all our sins; he does not deal harshly with us, as we deserve. For his unfailing love toward those who fear him is as great as the height of the heavens above the earth. He has removed our sins as far from us as the east is from the west" (Psalm 103:10-12). God has said, "Come now, let's settle this. . . . Though your sins are like scarlet, I will make them as white as snow. Though they are red like crimson, I will make them as white as wool" (Isaiah 1:18). "I—yes, I alone—will blot out your sins for my own sake and will never think of them again" (Isaiah 43:25).

Part of our recovery is to accept complete forgiveness from God. When we come to God through the atoning blood of Jesus Christ, his forgiveness is complete. We may keep track of our failures, adding every fall to the long list we carry against ourselves. But God doesn't keep lists of our past sins; in his eyes we are clean.

Because God forgives and forgets, we need never
wallow in the forgiven past.

Day 9

God's Sensitivity
Bible Reading: Isaiah 42:1-7

We humbly asked God to remove our shortcomings.

D ealing with our own failings and weaknesses can be discouraging. Sometimes it doesn't seem fair that we have to face life with the burdens and emptiness we feel. Some of the things we've experienced have left us bruised and broken. The flame of hope seems to be wavering. In times when we feel weak like this, we need someone else to encourage us that God can make up for the injustices we've endured and the shortcomings we have.

God sent Jesus to meet our needs: "Look at my servant, whom I strengthen. He is my chosen one, who pleases me. I have put my Spirit upon him. He will bring justice to the nations. He will not shout or raise his voice in public. He will not crush the weakest reed or put out a flickering candle. He will bring justice to all who have been wronged" (Isaiah 42:1-3).

When we humbly ask God to remove our shortcomings we can point out the areas where we are hurting: "Here's where I'm weakest. This is where the light is flickering and I can't see the way. Here's where I'm fainthearted and tempted to despair. This is where there has been a shortage of justice during the times I've been wronged and no one protected me." God gave this mission to Jesus: "You will open the eyes of the blind. You will free the captives from prison, releasing those who sit in dark dungeons" (Isaiah 42:7). This is what God longs to do for us.

When you feel broken, weak, or worthless, God gently picks you up and surrounds you with his care.

A New Freedom

Bible Reading: Isaiah 49:8-12

> We humbly asked God to remove our shortcomings.

Many of us have lived life with a recurrent sense of dissatisfaction. There's a hunger and thirst inside that just can't be filled. Our problems seem like mountains, far too big for us to scale. Our own shortcomings seem like deep, dark valleys; they lead us away from all the positive goals we've set. We set out to deal with the mountains in life and find ourselves going down into the deep valleys of old patterns and addictions. Will we ever break free and find a better way?

God has said, "I will say to the prisoners, 'Come out in freedom,' and to those in darkness, 'Come into the light.' They will be my sheep, grazing in green pastures and on hills that were previously bare. They will neither hunger nor thirst. The searing sun will not reach them anymore. For the LORD in his mercy will lead them; he will lead them beside cool waters. And I will make my mountains into level paths for them. The highways will be raised above the valleys" (Isaiah 49:9-11).

God can free us from the constant hunger and thirst by providing new sources of nourishment for our souls. In his mercy, he will provide refreshing streams to satisfy us deeply. With God's help, some of the problems that now seem insurmountable will become approachable. He will help us find alternate routes to our goals without having to go back down the paths of addiction. We still have to face life's ups and downs. We still have to take the steps forward. But he can show us a new highway, above the valleys, which will lead us to where we want to go.

> True freedom is discovered as God nourishes the
> hunger in our souls.

Irresistible Love
Bible Reading: Isaiah 53:1-6

We humbly asked God to remove our shortcomings.

Maybe we haven't given much thought to what it would take to remove our sins. It seems like once we've failed, or once our shortcomings have become evident, there is nothing that can really compensate for them. And yet we know the guilt and pain that come from continuing as we have in the past.

In God's eyes, our sins and shortcomings are very important. He can't just pretend that sin is all right. He knows the human suffering that results and longs to free us by removing the guilt and sin. Let's take a moment to consider what he went through in order to remove our shortcomings. "He was despised and rejected—a man of sorrows, acquainted with deepest grief. We turned our backs on him and looked the other way. He was despised, and we did not care. Yet it was our weaknesses he carried; it was our sorrows that weighed him down. And we thought his troubles were a punishment from God, a punishment for his own sins! But he was pierced for our rebellion, crushed for our sins. He was beaten so we could be whole. He was whipped so we could be healed. All of us, like sheep, have strayed away. We have left God's paths to follow our own. Yet the LORD laid on him the sins of us all" (Isaiah 53:3-6).

Removing our sins was, and still is, very important to God. It cost him a great deal to purchase the gift of forgiveness, which he offers freely to us. It is a humbling experience to ponder what it took for God to be able to remove our shortcomings. How can we resist such love?

❧

Since God has already overcome our shortcomings, we can approach him with both humility and confidence.

The Power of Asking

Bible Reading: Isaiah 53:10-12

We humbly asked God to remove our shortcomings.

Most of us probably feel that since we don't really have a great relationship with God, we don't really have the grounds to expect him to remove our shortcomings. We may still see ourselves in a negative light. We may wonder why in the world God would do this for us.

Here's why: "it was the LORD's good plan to crush him [Jesus] and cause him grief. Yet when his life is made an offering for sin, he will have many descendants. He will enjoy a long life, and the LORD's good plan will prosper in his hands. When he sees all that is accomplished by his anguish, he will be satisfied. And because of his experience, my righteous servant will make it possible for many to be counted righteous, for he will bear all their sins" (Isaiah 53:10-11). The apostle Paul said, "For his Spirit joins with our spirit to affirm that we are God's children" (Romans 8:16).

We can expect God to remove our shortcomings because of all Jesus went through to make us righteous. Upon receiving Christ, we become children of God and heirs to many privileges. If we don't have this affirmed as "his Spirit joins with our spirit," perhaps we should consider whether we've accepted God's gift of forgiveness (see John 1:12). We may not feel like children of God, especially after a fall, but we can be sure that his promises are true. He offers new life and the removal of shortcomings to everyone willing to accept his offer.

The removal of our shortcomings is God's work alone—we only need to ask.

Day 13

Clearing the Mess
Bible Reading: Isaiah 57:12-19

We humbly asked God to remove our shortcomings.

I n many ways Step Seven represents a turning point in our recovery. It forms a bridge between the inner work of the first six steps and the final steps, which emphasize outer work—changes in behavior. Our shortcomings may seem to clutter the road out of our past. Just because we're working the steps doesn't mean that our lives are as they should be. Will God really come into the mess and lead us out?

"God says, 'Rebuild the road! Clear away the rocks and stones so my people can return from captivity.' The high and lofty one who lives in eternity, the Holy One, says this: 'I live in the high and holy place with those whose spirits are contrite and humble. . . . I have seen what they do, but I will heal them anyway! I will lead them. I will comfort those who mourn" (Isaiah 57:14-15, 18).

God is a great help when it comes to clearing the way to a better future. He looks forward to removing our shortcomings so that we can better avoid being tripped up. When we come to him with humility, admitting that we still struggle with many of our shortcomings, he refreshes us and gives us the courage we need to go on. He isn't put off by the things we do. He sees what we do, but chooses to heal us anyway! He'll keep leading us toward recovery, one step at a time. He'll comfort us when we face sorrow and walk with us all the way.

God has seen the things we do, and he promises
to heal us anyway!

Day 14

God's Mercy

Bible Reading: Isaiah 64:5-9

We humbly asked God to remove our shortcomings.

When it comes to asking God to remove our shortcomings, we probably either feel like a professional sinner who is the scum of the earth and has no right to ask anything from him, or we feel like we're one of the godly ones, who sins occasionally (everybody does) but always tries to live a good life.

The prophet Isaiah said, "You [God] welcome those who gladly do good, who follow godly ways. But you have been very angry with us, for we are not godly. We are constant sinners; how can people like us be saved? We are all infected and impure with sin. When we display our righteous deeds, they are nothing but filthy rags. Like autumn leaves, we wither and fall, and our sins sweep us away like the wind. Yet no one calls on your name or pleads with you for mercy. Therefore, you have . . . turned us over to our sins. And yet, O LORD, you are our Father. We are the clay, and you are the potter. We all are formed by your hand" (Isaiah 64:5-8).

Those of us who feel like the "bad guys" may not call on God because we still feel disqualified. If we do call on God, we have the advantage of recognizing our need for God's mercy. Those of us who feel like a "good guy" probably call on God often, and pride ourselves for doing so. The obstacle for us is that we may not plead for God's mercy, because we're not convinced we really need it. We all need to humbly plead for God's mercy. When we do, he can reshape us, leaving our shortcomings out of the formula.

❧

God rejects us when we come brandishing our "good works";
he accepts us when we come seeking his mercy.

201

Knowing God
Bible Reading: 2 Peter 1:2-4

We humbly asked God to remove our shortcomings.

As we work through recovery, humility develops naturally as we realize our powerlessness over life, even over ourselves. We want a good life, and we want our character to change in ways that will make this possible. In asking God to remove our shortcomings, we dare to reach out to the one who has the power we need.

The apostle Peter was a man with many admitted character flaws. His relationship with Jesus brought him face-to-face with his own weaknesses. He found that he wasn't able to live up to his own values, let alone the values of Jesus. But God dramatically changed his character to the point that he began to reflect the very character of Jesus. He left us with this advice: "May God give you more and more grace and peace as you grow in your knowledge of God and Jesus our Lord. By his divine power, God has given us everything we need for living a godly life. We have received all of this by coming to know him, the one who called us to himself by means of his marvelous glory and excellence. And because of his glory and excellence, he has given us great and precious promises. These are the promises that enable you to share his divine nature and escape the world's corruption caused by human desires" (2 Peter 1:2-4).

This is Peter's secret for discovering the good life: Grow in your knowledge of God and Jesus our Lord. It is a growing love relationship with God that will open the door to a life untainted by our present character flaws. God has the mighty power to give us everything we need; and everything we need is found in him as he instills his character in us.

❧

The power of recovery doesn't come from within; it comes from knowing God better and better.

Eyes of Love
Bible Reading: Hebrews 12:10-13

We humbly asked God to remove our shortcomings.

M ost of us probably aren't used to getting the things we ask for. How can we have confidence that God will hear our prayers? How do we know he will answer when we ask him to remove our shortcomings?

The apostle Paul wrote, "Even before he made the world, God loved us and chose us in Christ to be holy and without fault in his eyes" (Ephesians 1:4). God's primary goal is to make us holy, that is, to paint his character into our lives. Looking through the eyes of love, he already sees us as we will look when his work is done. Then he works out his goals for us in the arena of everyday life. The Bible tells us: "God's discipline is always good for us, so that we might share in his holiness" (Hebrews 12:10). We can be sure that our holiness—the removal of our shortcomings—is God's will.

The apostle John wrote, "And we are confident that he hears us whenever we ask for anything that pleases him. And since we know he hears us when we make our requests, we also know that he will give us what we ask for" (1 John 5:14-15).

It is clearly God's will to have our shortcomings removed. And he has promised to give us anything we ask for within his will. Therefore, we can have full confidence that God will remove our shortcomings in his time.

We can ask with confidence because God looks
at us with eyes of love.

Day 17

In God's Time
Bible Reading: 2 Peter 3:8-9

We humbly asked God to remove our shortcomings.

W e may be impatient to have our weaknesses and short-comings removed immediately. It's hard to struggle along, feeling we don't have what it takes to live the life God wants for us. We may wish that he would just wave his magic wand, and *poof!* . . . a perfect person!

The Bible makes it clear that it is God's plan to perfect us. But it is also clear that God doesn't always work according to our timetable. Even the birth of the Messiah had to wait until "the right time." The apostle Paul wrote, "But when the right time came, God sent his Son, born of a woman, subject to the law. God sent him to buy freedom for us who were slaves to the law, so that he could adopt us as his very own children" (Galatians 4:4-5).

The apostle Peter left us another reminder: "But you must not forget this one thing, dear friends: A day is like a thousand years to the Lord, and a thousand years is like a day. The Lord isn't really being slow about his promise, as some people think. No, he is being patient for your sake. He does not want anyone to be destroyed, but wants everyone to repent" (2 Peter 3:8-9).

God has "the right time" planned for us, too. He takes everything into account when he decides how and when our prayers will be answered. It may seem like he's too slow in fulfill-ing his promises. But we can be sure that if he is slow in acting, it's for a good reason. In the meantime, he supplies the strength we need to continue in recovery, even with our shortcomings.

❦

However long our road to recovery, with God we're
always "right on time."

Day 18

A Thorough Washing
Bible Reading: 1 Peter 3:18-21

We humbly asked God to remove our shortcomings.

When we ask God to remove our shortcomings, we show that we want our sins to be washed away. We may be burdened by what we've learned about ourselves while working the previous steps. We may feel dirty, and trapped; unable to make a break from our old life.

God realizes our need to feel clean and new. He has given us the command to accomplish this through baptism. The ceremonial dipping in water symbolically demonstrates our desire to have our sins or shortcomings washed away. The apostle Peter explained it this way: "That water [Noah's flood] is a picture of baptism, which now saves you, not by removing dirt from your body, but as a response to God from [or as an appeal to God for] a clean conscience. It is effective because of the resurrection of Jesus Christ" (1 Peter 3:21).

In describing his own conversion, the apostle Paul said, "A man named Ananias . . . came and stood beside me and said, . . . 'The God of our ancestors has chosen you to know his will and to see the Righteous One and hear him speak. For you are to be his witness, telling everyone what you have seen and heard. What are you waiting for? Get up and be baptized. Have your sins washed away by calling on the name of the Lord'" (Acts 22:12-16).

Some of us may never have been baptized, but the Bible urges us to do so. God has prescribed this special act for our healing. Baptism demonstrates our exit from an old life and our entrance into a new one. Why delay?

As we humbly ask God to remove our sins, he promises to wash and cleanse our hearts.

Day 19

Breaking the Pattern
Bible Reading: Romans 6:1-4

We humbly asked God to remove our shortcomings.

W e want to believe that there's another kind of life available to us. We don't want to continue sinning, watching our lives being ruined. We vividly recall the baffling power sin has held over us in the past. Why should we believe that this power can be broken? How can we hope for freedom in the future?

As the apostle Paul taught about God's grace, some of his listeners asked this question: "Well then, should we keep on sinning so that God can show us more and more of his wonderful grace?" Paul replied like this: "Of course not! Since we have died to sin, how can we continue to live in it? Or have you forgotten that when we were joined with Christ Jesus in baptism, we joined him in his death? For we died and were buried with Christ by baptism. And just as Christ was raised from the dead by the glorious power of the Father, now we also may live new lives" (Romans 6:1-4).

When we choose to obey God by being baptized, we're symbolizing a spiritual truth. The nature inside us, which was bound to sin, has been united with Jesus at the Crucifixion. When he died, it died. When we're covered by water in baptism, that symbolizes the burial of our old sin nature. When we come up from the water, that symbolizes our resurrection to a new way of life. Being united with Christ in his death and resurrection gives us the opportunity to live free from bondage to sin.

When we become one with Jesus Christ, the power
of our past is broken.

A Major Miracle
Bible Reading: Joshua 10:5-15

We humbly asked God to remove our shortcomings.

At this point in recovery, we may feel that nothing short of a major miracle will win the battles we face. We may have been badly beaten as we tried to fight our addictions in the past. We probably concluded that we were too weak to win. What could be different now that will bring victory over our shortcomings?

When we fight alone, we are too weak to win. But if we call on the Lord to fight with us, it's a different story. Joshua was called upon to help an ally fight against several attacking enemies. "'Do not be afraid of them,' the LORD said to Joshua, 'for I have given you victory over them. Not a single one of them will be able to stand up to you'" (Joshua 10:8). Just as God promised, Israel won a decisive victory. "On the day the LORD gave the Israelites victory over the Amorites, Joshua prayed to the LORD in front of all the people of Israel. He said, 'Let the sun stand still over Gibeon, and the moon over the valley of Aijalon.' So the sun stood still and the moon stayed in place until the nation of Israel had defeated its enemies. . . . There has never been a day like this one before or since, when the LORD answered such a prayer. Surely the LORD fought for Israel that day!" (Joshua 10:12-14).

It may take a major miracle to overcome the foes we face; but God is in the miracle business! He declares that every shortcoming is already defeated and given to us to destroy. When we call out to God for help in the heat of battle, we can have confidence in receiving his help. When the Lord is fighting for us, he won't stop until all our shortcomings are wiped out!

☙

When we feel discouraged we must remember that
God has already won the battle.

207

Day 21

Supportive Friends
Bible Reading: Mark 2:1-12

We humbly asked God to remove our shortcomings.

Our personal weaknesses can cripple our lives, leaving us handicapped. Some of us have lived a long time in this condition. We've come to the point of not being able to go to God for help on our own. We may need to rely on the help and the faith of others who don't have the same handicaps we do. They may be able to take us to where we can receive God's healing touch.

Here's a relevant story: While Jesus was preaching at a crowded house, "four men arrived carrying a paralyzed man on a mat. They couldn't bring him to Jesus because of the crowd, so they dug a hole through the roof above his head. Then they lowered the man on his mat, right down in front of Jesus. Seeing their faith, Jesus said to the paralyzed man, 'My child, your sins are forgiven.' . . . Then Jesus turned to the paralyzed man and said, 'Stand up, pick up your mat, and go home!'" (Mark 2:3-5, 10-11).

This man faced what seemed like insurmountable obstacles in his hope for recovery. His friends risked embarrassment to carry him to the place where he could receive forgiveness and wholeness. If we are crippled by our addictions and personal "handicaps," the road to healing may be more difficult for us than for others who don't have the same shortcomings. We may have to rely on friends to carry us until we receive the healing that will make us able to move out on our own two feet.

While in recovery we often need the support and help from friends to bring about our healing.

A Singular Focus

Bible Reading: Mark 10:46-52

We humbly asked God to remove our shortcomings.

We may face a special challenge as we seek recovery: there may be people watching us who don't believe we'll ever make it. If this is so, we'll need the humility to aggressively seek help despite the added distraction of people looking on. They may treat us with disrespect and tell us to give up our hopes of healing. But we don't have to listen!

Think about this story: "As Jesus and his disciples left town, a large crowd followed him. A blind beggar named Bartimaeus . . . was sitting beside the road. When Bartimaeus heard that Jesus of Nazareth was nearby, he began to shout, 'Jesus, Son of David, have mercy on me!' 'Be quiet!' many of the people yelled at him. But he only shouted louder, 'Son of David, have mercy on me!' When Jesus heard him, he stopped and said, 'Tell him to come here.' So they called the blind man. 'Cheer up,' they said. 'Come on, he's calling you!' Bartimaeus threw aside his coat, jumped up, and came to Jesus. 'What do you want me to do for you?' Jesus asked. 'My rabbi,' the blind man said, 'I want to see!' And Jesus said to him, 'Go, for your faith has healed you.' Instantly the man could see, and he followed Jesus down the road" (Mark 10:46-52).

We, too, need to keep calling out for God's help regardless of the negative responses of those around us. He'll hear our earnest cry and heal us, to the astonishment of those who say it'll never happen!

Recovery and healing is our primary task; let no one distract us from it!

Day 23

New Hearts
Bible Reading: Ezekiel 36:22-27

We humbly asked God to remove our shortcomings.

We may feel like we don't deserve God's help because of the way our behavior has tarnished his reputation. These feelings may be especially strong if we were Christians while we were acting out our addictions. Can we really expect God's help again after we've let him down?

The people of Israel were created to represent the Lord to the rest of the world. But instead of obeying him and making him proud of them, they embarrassed him by worshiping idols and behaving in sinful ways. But the Lord didn't give up on them. He spoke through the prophet Ezekiel: "Therefore, give the people of Israel this message from the Sovereign LORD: I am bringing you back, but not because you deserve it. I am doing it to protect my holy name, on which you brought shame while you were scattered among the nations. . . . Your filth will be washed away, and you will no longer worship idols. And I will give you a new heart, and I will put a new spirit in you. I will take out your stony, stubborn heart and give you a tender, responsive heart. And I will put my Spirit in you so that you will follow my decrees and be careful to obey my regulations" (Ezekiel 36:22, 25-27).

God will deliver us from our shortcomings to bring glory to his name, not because we deserve it. When people see how much God does for us, they may believe that he can help them, too. If we've tarnished his reputation, he has the power to restore us in a way that will make up for the damage and bring glory to himself.

Our continued recovery, even when we've suffered a relapse, brings great honor to God.

A Good Future

Bible Reading: Titus 2:11-14

We humbly asked God to remove our shortcomings.

We can hope for recovery in spirit, mind, and body. In the past we may have concluded that we just couldn't change. But by now, our attitude may be changing; we may have come to believe there is a way out. This hopeful disposition will help us to turn to God and begin again. Perhaps for the first time, we can now look forward to a future filled with promised blessings.

"May the God of peace make you holy in every way, and may your whole spirit and soul and body be kept blameless until our Lord Jesus Christ comes again. God will make this happen, for he who calls you is faithful" (1 Thessalonians 5:23-24).

"For the grace of God has been revealed, bringing salvation to all people. And we are instructed to turn from godless living and sinful pleasures. We should live in this evil world with wisdom, righteousness, and devotion to God, while we look forward with hope to that wonderful day when the glory of our great God and Savior, Jesus Christ, will be revealed. He gave his life to free us from every kind of sin, to cleanse us, and to make us his very own people, totally committed to doing good deeds" (Titus 2:11-14).

God has promised us a wonderful future. In the present, he's in the process of rescuing us from constantly falling into sin. Our willingness to let go of the past and our expectations for good things in the future will help in our recovery.

We have great hope, because the power we need to recover comes from Jesus Christ, the greatest of healers.

Day 25

Filling Our Needs
Bible Reading: Ephesians 3:14-19

We humbly asked God to remove our shortcomings.

I dentifying our shortcomings should help to clarify our needs. We need resources, inner strength, love, direction, and power. And we don't just need these things once, we need them to be replenished constantly because it seems that we keep running out.

The apostle Paul prayed, "From his [God's] glorious, unlimited resources he will empower you with inner strength through his Spirit. Then Christ will make his home in your hearts as you trust in him. Your roots will grow down into God's love and keep you strong. And may you . . . experience the love of Christ, though it is too great to understand fully. Then you will be made complete with all the fullness of life and power that comes from God. . . . Don't act thoughtlessly, but understand what the Lord wants you to do. Don't be drunk with wine, because that will ruin your life. Instead, be filled with the Holy Spirit" (Ephesians 3:16-19; 5:17-18).

The words *made complete* and *filled* in these passages mean "to fill up completely" or "to make full." The verb tense used indicates that this is an ongoing process—we are to be made complete and filled up continually. True recovery only comes as we find a way to fill up the needs in our lives. Wherever we are short, God has the resources, love, direction, strength, and power to meet our needs. We can invite the Holy Spirit to fill us up every day.

God's love reaches into every corner of our experience.

Continuing Forward
Bible Reading: Colossians 1:9-14

We humbly asked God to remove our shortcomings.

E ven when our recovery is progressing and we're doing well, we will face difficulties that may upset us. If we come from a dysfunctional family, our loved ones who are not in recovery will continue to experience problems and crises that will touch our lives. We need to have a source of constant contact with God so that we can keep on going no matter what happens.

The apostle Paul wrote, "So we have not stopped praying for you since we first heard about you. We ask God to give you complete knowledge of his will and to give you spiritual wisdom and understanding. Then the way you live will always honor and please the Lord, and your lives will produce every kind of good fruit. All the while, you will grow as you learn to know God better and better. We also pray that you will be strengthened with all his glorious power so you will have all the endurance and patience you need. May you be filled with joy, always thanking the Father. He has enabled you to share in the inheritance that belongs to his people, who live in the light. For he has rescued us from the kingdom of darkness and transferred us into the Kingdom of his dear Son, who purchased our freedom and forgave our sins" (Colossians 1:9-14).

We need to be continually asking God to remove our shortcomings and fill us up. He can give us the joy, strength, thankfulness, wisdom, and spiritual understanding to handle whatever happens.

Strengthened with all his glorious power, we will have all the
endurance and patience we need.

A Healing Fire
Bible Reading: 1 Peter 4:12-13

We humbly asked God to remove our shortcomings.

We all know how deeply imbedded some of our shortcomings are. When we're ready to let God remove them, we must be willing to let him do whatever it takes to get the job done.

When we ask God to remove our shortcomings and purify us, we should be prepared to take some heat. The best way to purify something precious is to melt it down with fire. Even in the Old Testament God commanded that precious metals be passed through fire for ceremonial purification. "Anything made of gold, silver, bronze, iron, tin, or lead—that is, all metals that do not burn—must be passed through fire in order to be made ceremonially pure" (Numbers 31:22-23).

Throughout the Bible there are allusions to God using fire to purify us. The apostle Peter wrote, "Dear friends, don't be surprised at the fiery trials you are going through, as if something strange were happening to you. Instead, be very glad—for these trials make you partners with Christ in his suffering, so that you will have the wonderful joy of seeing his glory when it is revealed to all the world" (1 Peter 4:12-13). The author of Hebrews wrote, "No discipline is enjoyable while it is happening—it's painful! But afterward there will be a peaceful harvest of right living" (Hebrews 12:11).

God only uses fire on things that can take the heat and come out better in the end. He doesn't send trials to destroy us, but rather to purify us and develop our character. The fire hurts, but in the end it leaves something beautiful in our lives.

God can create something beautiful out of the ruined past.

STEP SEVEN

Day 28

God Our Helper
Bible Reading: Exodus 3:1-12

We humbly asked God to remove our shortcomings.

The thought of facing life without an addictive "crutch" may be frightening. Most of us have suffered from feelings of inadequacy for most of our lives. Our addictions have helped us to deal with our inadequacies.

Even Moses felt inadequate at times. When God called him to free the Israelites from slavery in Egypt, he felt incompetent for the task. "'Who am I to appear before Pharaoh?'. . . 'O Lord, I'm not very good with words. . . . I get tongue-tied, and my words get tangled.' Then the LORD asked Moses, 'Who makes a person's mouth? Who decides whether people speak or do not speak, hear or do not hear, see or do not see? Is it not I, the LORD? Now go! I will be with you as you speak, and I will instruct you in what to say.' But Moses again pleaded, 'Lord, please! Send anyone else.' Then the LORD became angry with Moses. 'All right,' he said. 'What about your brother, Aaron the Levite? I know he speaks well. . . . Talk to him, and put the words in his mouth. I will be with both of you as you speak, and I will instruct you both in what to do'" (Exodus 3:11; 4:10-15).

God has the power to make up for any inadequacies we might have. He has the power to heal and transform our abilities. He can give us confidence in situations that are intimidating. If we still feel inadequate, even with God's promised presence and help, he is willing to give us someone to go with us and help us. That companion may be the Holy Spirit or a person who has what it takes to compensate for our shortcomings.

❦

When God is with us, no situation is too difficult
or too frightening.

215

Day 29

Strength from Humility
Bible Reading: Isaiah 6:1-7

We humbly asked God to remove our shortcomings.

I f we want to experience humility and have a sincere desire to have our shortcomings removed, we need to seek after God. When we catch a glimpse of his holiness, we will be humbled and transformed.

The prophet Isaiah shares this experience: "It was in the year King Uzziah died that I saw the Lord. He was sitting on a lofty throne, and the train of his robe filled the Temple. Attending him were mighty seraphim, each having six wings. . . . They were calling out to each other, 'Holy, holy, holy is the LORD of Heaven's Armies! The whole earth is filled with his glory!' Their voices shook the Temple to its foundations, and the entire building was filled with smoke. Then I said, 'It's all over! I am doomed, for I am a sinful man. I have filthy lips, and I live among a people with filthy lips. Yet I have seen the King, the LORD of Heaven's Armies.' Then one of the seraphim flew to me with a burning coal he had taken from the altar with a pair of tongs. He touched my lips with it and said, 'See, this coal has touched your lips. Now your guilt is removed, and your sins are forgiven'" (Isaiah 6:1-7).

Isaiah's experience took the form of a supernatural vision. At just a glimpse of God's holiness, he became acutely aware of his own deep need for cleansing. We may never see God as Isaiah did, but we can experience God's presence in a place of worship. As we develop the habit of worshiping God, we will find growing humility in our lives and a growing desire to have him purify us fully.

How amazing that we can see God's greatness and our contrasting sinfulness, yet still experience his forgiveness!

Weakness Transformed
Bible Reading: 1 Samuel 17:17-51

We humbly asked God to remove our shortcomings.

A s we look at ourselves, we may see more shortcomings than we really have. And we may be underestimating the unique gifts God has given us. Some of the things we beg God to remove may have a good side to them that we just haven't grown to appreciate yet.

Young David went to visit his older brothers at the battlefield. When he heard the taunts of the giant, Goliath, he was ready for a fight. When David asked to be sent out to fight the giant, King Saul said, "Don't be ridiculous! . . . You're only a boy" (1 Samuel 17:33). Saul finally gave in to David's requests. "Then Saul gave David his own armor. . . . David put it on, strapped the sword over it, and took a step or two to see what it was like. . . . 'I can't go in these,' he protested to Saul. 'I'm not used to them.' So David took them off again. He picked up five smooth stones from a stream and put them into his shepherd's bag. Then, armed only with his shepherd's staff and sling, he started across the valley to fight the Philistine" (17:38-40). David used the stones and sling to kill the giant.

The things that appeared to be David's shortcomings were actually strengths. While growing up, David learned to compensate for his small stature by learning to use the slingshot to protect the flocks. Some of our apparent shortcomings may have taught us to compensate in positive ways. They may work for us and don't need to be removed. They just need to be reframed in our thinking and handed over to God for his purposes.

🌿

When seen from God's perspective, even some of our
shortcomings can become strengths.

STEP EIGHT

We made a list of all persons we had harmed and became willing to make amends to them all.

Jesus taught, "If you are presenting a sacrifice at the altar in the Temple and you suddenly remember that someone has something against you, . . . go and be reconciled to that person"
(Matthew 5:23-24).

Forgiven to Forgive

Bible Reading: Matthew 18:23-35

> We made a list of all persons we had harmed and became
> willing to make amends to them all.

L isting all the people we've harmed will probably trigger a natural defensiveness. With each name we put on our list, another mental list may begin to form—a list of the wrongs that have been done against us. How can we deal with the resentment we hold toward others, so we can move toward making amends?

Jesus told a story: "A king . . . decided to bring his accounts up to date with servants who had borrowed money from him. In the process, one of his debtors was brought in who owed him millions of dollars" (Matthew 18:23-24). The man begged for forgiveness. "Then his master was filled with pity for him, and he released him and forgave his debt. But when the man left the king, he went to a fellow servant who owed him a few thousand dollars. He grabbed him by the throat and demanded instant payment" (18:27-28). This was reported to the king. "Then the king called in the man he had forgiven and said, 'You evil servant! I forgave you that tremendous debt because you pleaded with me. Shouldn't you have mercy on your fellow servant, just as I had mercy on you?' Then the angry king sent the man to prison to be tortured until he had paid his entire debt. That's what my heavenly Father will do to you if you refuse to forgive your brothers and sisters from your heart" (18:32-35).

When we look at all that God has forgiven us, it makes sense to choose to forgive others. This also frees us from the torture of festering resentment. We can't change what they did to us, but we can write off their debt and become willing to make amends.

The value we place on God's forgiveness is best measured
by our willingness to forgive others.

219

Day 2

Grace-Filled Living
Bible Reading: Romans 12:17-21

> We made a list of all persons we had harmed and became
> willing to make amends to them all.

Most of us probably have relationships in which we are
holding grudges. Sure, we've hurt them, but they've hurt
us, too. We become like children quarreling back and
forth: "You hit me first!" "I did not!" Somehow, it just doesn't seem
fair to let them off the hook! Now, we're supposed to become willing to make amends to everyone? Even those who have wronged
us? How?

The apostle Paul left us this advice: "Never pay back evil
with more evil. Do things in such a way that everyone can see you
are honorable. Do all that you can to live in peace with everyone.
Dear friends, never take revenge. Leave that to the righteous anger
of God. . . . Instead, 'If your enemies are hungry, feed them. If they
are thirsty, give them something to drink.' . . . Don't let evil conquer you, but conquer evil by doing good" (Romans 12:17-21).

This is not impossible. We are not called to create peace,
only to "do all that [we] can" to be at peace. We are not required to
say that others don't deserve punishment, only to turn the job over
to God. We don't give up a quarrel because someone else is necessarily right, but for the sake of our recovery. We can't change other
people, but we can ask God for the courage to change ourselves.

This may seem all backwards, but God's ways are not our
ways. As we turn our will and our lives over to God, we will learn
that his ways do work.

❧

If we've really experienced God's grace, we'll want
to pass it on to others.

Overcoming Loneliness
Bible Reading: Ecclesiastes 4:9-12

We made a list of all persons we had harmed and became willing to make amends to them all.

Feelings of loneliness and isolation go along with the guilt and shame we feel about who we are or what we've done. We may feel so cut off from others that we feel lonely even when we're around other people. Our fear of being hurt, our guilt and self-hatred can make us unable to believe in the love others have for us. We can feel all alone in the struggle even when there are people beside us who love us and want to help. Being willing to let their love in is part of our preparation for making amends.

Wise King Solomon observed, "Two people are better off than one, for they can help each other succeed. If one person falls, the other can reach out and help. But someone who falls alone is in real trouble. Likewise, two people lying close together can keep each other warm. But how can one be warm alone? A person standing alone can be attacked and defeated, but two can stand back-to-back and conquer. Three are even better, for a triple-braided cord is not easily broken" (Ecclesiastes 4:9-12).

Loneliness can break us and defeat our recovery process. When we prepare to make amends, we also need to prepare our hearts to accept whatever love, support, or friendship is offered in return. These supportive relationships, along with the third "strand" of God's supporting hand, will strengthen our lives considerably.

❧

Making amends builds relationships, releasing the healing power of human companionship.

221

Day 4

Scapegoats
Bible Reading: Leviticus 16:20-22

> We made a list of all persons we had harmed and became
> willing to make amends to them all.

I t's natural to hope that the people we've hurt will think better of us once we've sought to make amends. We may fear that
there are some who will never upgrade their opinions about us,
no matter what we do. In reality they may not, especially if they
have chosen to use us as a scapegoat.

Before the coming of Jesus, the Jews were instructed to
select a live goat which would carry away their sins. (When Jesus
came, he became our scapegoat and took our sins upon himself.)
The priest was to place his hands on this goat and confess over it
all the sins of the people. "He [the priest] will transfer the people's
sins to the head of the goat. Then a man specially chosen for the
task will drive the goat into the wilderness. As the goat goes into
the wilderness, it will carry all the people's sins upon itself into a
desolate land" (Leviticus 16:21-22).

Some of the people we've hurt will use us as their scapegoat. Since we have hurt them, they feel justified in sending us
away with more than our share of the burden. They unconsciously
place the blame for their pain on us, so we can carry it away. As
their scapegoat, we play the role of removing something they were
unable to deal with in any other way. Because of this, they may
never welcome us back. We should prepare for this kind of response
and realize that it says more about them than it says about us.

> At times we will be forced to carry the pain of another; be
> thankful that God has agreed to do the same for us.

222

Day 5

A Forgiving God
Bible Reading: Matthew 6:9-15

We made a list of all persons we had harmed and became
willing to make amends to them all.

One motivation for preparing our list and making amends
with the people we've hurt is the hope of having a clear
conscience. We have lived with self-condemnation and
probably hope that making amends will help us find forgiveness.
Looking for forgiveness in the wrong places, however, may bring
disappointment and give others unwarranted power over us.

The Bible doesn't teach us to go to people to find forgiveness. God is the one who grants forgiveness: "If we confess our
sins to him [God], he is faithful and just to forgive us our sins and
to cleanse us from all wickedness" (1 John 1:9). Jesus taught us
to pray: "Forgive us our sins, as we have forgiven those who sin
against us" (Matthew 6:12). He went on to explain, "If you forgive
those who sin against you, your heavenly Father will forgive you.
But if you refuse to forgive others, your Father will not forgive your
sins" (6:14-15).

The purpose for making amends is to take personal responsibility for our behavior and the effect it has had on others. If those
people respond by offering forgiveness, that is a nice bonus. Our
forgiveness, however, is not in their hands. Forgiveness is with God
in Jesus Christ. "For he [God] forgave all our sins. He canceled the
record of the charges against us and took it away by nailing it to
the cross. In this way, he disarmed the spiritual rulers and authorities" (Colossians 2:13-15).

❧

By refusing to make amends, we deny our own sinfulness
and our need of God's forgiveness.

The Fruit of Forgiveness

Bible Reading: 2 Corinthians 2:5-8

> We made a list of all persons we had harmed and became
> willing to make amends to them all.

Some of the things we've done have earned us disapproval
and possibly a loss of love. We have found that some people
in our lives only love us if they can approve of our behavior.
We may have struggled with bitterness toward them because we
feel like they have been trying to punish us. If our "sins" have been
made public, we may assume that we've lost the love of everyone
who disapproves of our actions. This fear of rejection might deter
us from reaching out to make amends.

In the young Corinthian church, a man was cut off from
church fellowship when his sins were made public. After he turned
around and tried to make amends, some people refused to welcome
him back into the church. The apostle Paul told them, "[Remember] the man who caused all the trouble. . . . Most of you opposed
him, and that was punishment enough. Now, however, it is time
to forgive and comfort him. Otherwise he may be overcome by
discouragement. So I urge you now to reaffirm your love for him"
(2 Corinthians 2:5-8). Some people will follow this advice and
reaffirm their love for you when you go to them.

There will be some people who will respond with forgiveness, comfort, acceptance, and love. This will help us overcome
the grief, the bitterness, and the discouragement we may feel.
Their forgiveness will help us to move on with our recovery.

*When we seek to make amends, we risk rejection; when
we fail to do so, we risk losing the joy of forgiveness.*

Day 7

Unintentional Sins
Bible Reading: Leviticus 4:1-28

> We made a list of all persons we had harmed and became
> willing to make amends to them all.

As we allowed our lives to get out of control, we probably hurt people without even realizing it. Many of the people on our list were hurt by our mistakes, not by something we did intentionally. We may not remember hurting some of them, and only realize it when someone points it out. Nevertheless, we still need to take responsibility for our actions by making amends.

When God gave the commandments, he included instructions for handling mistakes as well as intentional sins. He said, "This is how you are to deal with those who sin unintentionally by doing anything that violates one of the LORD's commands. . . . If any of the common people sin . . . but they don't realize it, they are still guilty. When they become aware of their sin, they must bring as an offering for their sin a female goat with no defects" (Leviticus 4:2, 27-28). "But suppose you unintentionally fail to carry out all these commands that the LORD has given you. . . . If the mistake was made unintentionally, and the community was unaware of it, the whole community must present a young bull for a burnt offering. . . . They will be forgiven. For it was an unintentional sin, and they have corrected it with their offerings to the LORD" (Numbers 15:22-25).

We are responsible for the way our behavior has affected others. This is true even when we didn't realize we were hurting them. These unintentional sins need to be acknowledged and corrected as soon as we discover them. God forgives all our sins. In the recovery process, however, the unintentional sins need to be accounted for along with the more glaring ones.

❧

*Forgiveness from unintentional sins can be a source
of unintentional joy.*

Reaping Goodness
Bible Reading: Galatians 6:7-10

> We made a list of all persons we had harmed and became
> willing to make amends to them all.

While in recovery, we learn to accept responsibility for our actions, even when we're powerless over our addictions. We come to realize that all our actions yield consequences. Some of us may have deceived ourselves into thinking we could escape the consequences of the things we did. But with time, it becomes clear that God has made accountability a necessary element of healthy human living.

"You will always harvest what you plant. Those who live only to satisfy their own sinful nature will harvest decay and death from that sinful nature. But those who live to please the Spirit will harvest everlasting life from the Spirit" (Galatians 6:7-8).

The law of sowing and reaping can also work for us. God spoke through the prophet Hosea: "Plant the good seeds of righteousness, and you will harvest a crop of love. Plow up the hard ground of your hearts, for now is the time to seek the LORD, that he may come and shower righteousness upon you" (Hosea 10:12).

God says we *always* harvest what we've planted. Even after we've been forgiven, we must deal with the consequences of our actions. It may take a season of time to finish harvesting the negative consequences from our past, but we shouldn't let this discourage us. Making our list of those we've harmed is a step toward planting good seeds. In time we'll see a good crop begin to grow.

❧

> Our small, everyday actions can produce long-term
> consequences for good.

Day 9

Becoming Responsible
Bible Reading: 1 Thessalonians 4:9-12

> We made a list of all persons we had harmed and became willing to make amends to them all.

M any of us know what it is like to be a burden on others. It is a common side effect of being controlled by an addictive/compulsive behavior. Sometimes our behaviors have caused us to lose our jobs or have made us unable to hold one down. As a result, we've found ourselves in financial need. This humiliation can affect our families in many ways. We may have caused loved ones great stress and shame because we haven't provided for their needs.

The apostle Paul taught us to follow this standard: "For you know that you ought to imitate us. We were not idle when we were with you. We never accepted food from anyone without paying for it. We worked hard day and night" (2 Thessalonians 3:7-8). "Make it your goal to live a quiet life, minding your own business and working with your hands. . . . People . . . will respect the way you live, and you will not need to depend on others" (1 Thessalonians 4:11-12).

It is important for us to think about how our irresponsibility has affected others. Much pain may have been caused by our failure to provide for our families' needs. We need to reflect on how this failure has caused us to lose their respect and trust. The shame of not facing this aspect of our lives can be terribly discouraging. Once we face this and become willing to make amends, our self-respect will get quite a boost. This step will help us get rid of some of our daily stress, freeing us up to proceed with recovery.

Making amends is a sure way to rediscover our
ability to be responsible.

Day 10

A New Outlook

Bible Reading: Acts 10:10-17

> We made a list of all persons we had harmed and became
> willing to make amends to them all.

Some of the hurt we've caused has resulted from wrong behaviors that can be changed. Some of it, however, has been caused by attitudes and characteristics that are deeply ingrained. They are so much a part of us that we're not sure where they end and where we begin. Can we change these deeply ingrained characteristics?

The apostle Peter was a devout Jew, even after he became a follower of Jesus. One day, as he was praying, "he fell into a trance. He saw the sky open, and something like a large sheet. . . . In the sheet were all sorts of animals, reptiles, and birds [forbidden to the Jews for food]. Then a voice said to him, 'Get up, Peter; kill and eat them.' 'No, Lord,' Peter declared. 'I have never eaten anything that our Jewish laws have declared impure and unclean.' But the voice spoke again: 'Do not call something unclean if God has made it clean.' . . . Peter was very perplexed" (Acts 10:10-17). Immediately after this vision passed, a group of non-Jews came and asked him to come and tell them about God. Peter agreed to go to the home of a Gentile, something that just wasn't done by a devout Jew. But the vision had shown him that his old way of life needed to change.

We're free to change by the power of God. We may look at some area of our life and say, "There's no way! I've never been able to do that, and I can't imagine that I ever will." Get ready! If God says we can, there's a whole new world out there.

❧

> As we continue in recovery, God is allowed to create
> something new out of our past.

Day 11

Our Comforter
Bible Reading: John 16:8-15

> We made a list of all persons we had harmed and became
> willing to make amends to them all.

We may wonder whether a particular name belongs on the list of those we've hurt. We may worry that we won't be able to determine whom we've hurt. Or we may hesitate, fearing that our introspection will cause us to condemn ourselves too strongly. But we need not worry; we have a helper to help us handle these problems.

Jesus said, "If you love me, obey my commandments. And I will ask the Father, and he will give you another Advocate, who will never leave you. He is the Holy Spirit, who leads into all truth" (John 14:15-17). "And when he comes, he will convict the world of its sin, and of God's righteousness, and of the coming judgment. . . . When the Spirit of truth comes, he will guide you into all truth. He will not speak on his own but will tell you what he has heard. He will tell you about the future" (John 16:8, 13).

The Holy Spirit is "God with us." We can ask the Holy Spirit to reveal to us all the names of those we have hurt. He will reveal them to us. The Holy Spirit comes to convict us of sin and remind us of God's goodness and deliverance from judgment. He is not there just to condemn us. Each pang of guilt can be given over to God for forgiveness the moment it arises. We don't need to worry about leaving someone off the list. The Holy Spirit can remind us about them later. Just write down everyone who comes to mind, asking God to give you the willingness to make amends.

❧

> As we face each new step, God will help us do and
> understand everything necessary to continue.

Our Debt of Love
Bible Reading: Luke 10:30-37

We made a list of all persons we had harmed and became
willing to make amends to them all.

When we're self-consumed or consumed by someone else's
addiction, we may hurt others by ignoring their needs.
Jesus told this story: "A Jewish man was traveling
from Jerusalem down to Jericho, and he was attacked by bandits.
They stripped him of his clothes, beat him up, and left him half
dead beside the road. By chance a priest came along. But when he
saw the man lying there, he crossed to the other side of the road
and passed him by. A Temple assistant walked over and looked at
him lying there, but he also passed by on the other side. Then a
despised Samaritan came along, and when he saw the man, he felt
compassion for him. Going over to him, the Samaritan soothed
his wounds with olive oil and wine and bandaged them. Then he
. . . took him to an inn, where he took care of him" (Luke 10:30-
34). Jesus was making the point that it can be hurtful to ignore the
needs we see around us. One of the laws of Moses said, "If you see
that the donkey of someone who hates you has collapsed under its
load, do not walk by. Instead, stop and help" (Exodus 23:5).

We owe love to one another. Those who depend on us for the
love they need can be deeply hurt by our neglect. There are people
who need us to "walk along beside" them when they're hurting.
Whom have we ignored when we were so focused on ourselves,
or on the addict in the family? Whose cries and needs have gone
untended? Who has been harmed by our neglect?

Love demands that we act to meet the needs around us;
that's how God loves us.

Giving Our Best
Bible Reading: Colossians 3:22-25

> We made a list of all persons we had harmed and became
> willing to make amends to them all.

T hough we've sometimes felt at our best while "under the
influence," we can see in retrospect that this wasn't true.
We're great at rationalizing. When our lives are consumed
by addictions, we're just not at our best. Many of us may even
have believed that our work was enhanced by our addictions.
Being sober, we can look back at our work with new perspective.
We probably realize that our job performance deteriorated and
our attitudes suffered. The fact is: we weren't giving our best.

The apostle Paul wrote, "Slaves, obey your earthly masters
in everything you do. Try to please them all the time, not just when
they are watching you. Serve them sincerely because of your rever-
ent fear of the Lord. Work willingly at whatever you do, as though
you were working for the Lord rather than for people. Remember
that the Lord will give you an inheritance as your reward. . . . But if
you do what is wrong, you will be paid back for the wrong you have
done. For God has no favorites" (Colossians 3:22-25).

We fill a needed role in society, however lowly we may esti-
mate that role to be. God knows that our contribution matters.
When we don't do our best, others are affected. When have people
been harmed because we didn't do our best at work? Who has been
hurt by the negative attitudes we may have displayed?

*Regardless of our role in life, when we are in
recovery we can be our best.*

Day 14

Internal Changes
Bible Reading: Luke 19:1-10

> We made a list of all persons we had harmed and became
> willing to make amends to them all.

There are many kinds of thieves. Some of us stole to support our habits, when our addictions demanded it. Others of us have never stolen anyone's property, but are thieves in another sense. We may have robbed ourselves of opportunities or dignity. Perhaps, we've stolen the heart of someone's spouse or robbed our children of their childhood. All these robberies have victims.

The apostle Paul said, "If you are a thief, quit stealing. Instead, use your hands for good hard work, and then give generously to others in need" (Ephesians 4:28). When Zacchaeus turned his life over to Christ he had to look at how many people he had cheated and stolen from in his unethical business deals. "Zacchaeus stood before the Lord and said, 'I will give half my wealth to the poor, Lord, and if I have cheated people on their taxes, I will give them back four times as much!'" (Luke 19:8).

Any time we take something that's not rightfully ours, or use something that doesn't belong to us without the permission of the rightful owner, that is stealing. People need to maintain clear boundaries of what belongs to them, whether in their material goods or in their committed relationships. If we have violated the boundaries and taken something belonging to others, we have spoiled their sense of security and brought them harm. We need to broaden our definition of stealing and ask God to show us everyone we've harmed in this way.

> Changes we see on the outside usually reflect changes
> that have already happened on the inside.

Amends with Children

Bible Reading: Ephesians 6:1-4

> We made a list of all persons we had harmed and became
> willing to make amends to them all.

All parents probably feel guilty at one time or another about how we have raised our kids. When there is addiction in the family, we are likely to be even harder on ourselves. We may just throw up our hands, giving up completely on parenting our children. If our needs weren't met during childhood, we may be totally at a loss; we may not know how to meet the needs of our little ones. We may be so overwhelmed by the responsibility of parenting that we stay in denial about how our lifestyles affect them.

The apostle Paul wrote, "Fathers, do not provoke your children to anger by the way you treat them. Rather, bring them up with the discipline and instruction that comes from the Lord" (Ephesians 6:4). "Fathers, do not aggravate your children, or they will become discouraged" (Colossians 3:21). Children also rely on their parents for their physical needs. Paul said, "Children don't provide for their parents. Rather, parents provide for their children" (2 Corinthians 12:14).

When we fail to provide for our children's needs, they are hurt. It may be hard to face because we feel so overwhelmed ourselves. We can make amends by letting them know that it's not their fault. We can reaffirm our love for them and let them know that we're taking steps to change.

❦

The fact of our recovery is best proven in our homes,
with those we love.

Day 16

Loving Submission
Bible Reading: Ephesians 5:21-33

> We made a list of all persons we had harmed and became willing to make amends to them all.

Those closest to us cannot escape being harmed by the consequences of our actions. If we are married, our addictions are harmful to our marriage partners, even if we hate to admit it.

The Bible tells us that marriage should be a relationship that satisfies the needs of both partners. The apostle Paul wrote, "Submit to one another out of reverence for Christ. . . . Husbands ought to love their wives as they love their own bodies. For a man who loves his wife actually shows love for himself. No one hates his own body but feeds and cares for it, just as Christ cares for the church. And we are members of his body. As the Scriptures say, 'A man leaves his father and mother and is joined to his wife, and the two are united into one.'. . . So again I say, each man must love his wife as he loves himself, and the wife must respect her husband" (Ephesians 5:21, 28-31, 33).

God says that our lives are literally intertwined with the lives of our mates. It may be a healthy union or a dysfunctional one. In either case, we're united. The behavior of one always affects the other. Any time we fail to break the bonds with our parents, fail to love sacrificially, or fail to show respect for our spouse, we are hurting them and ourselves. Surely, they have hurt us, too; but for now, we're dealing with our own issues.

❧

The most important amends we face are with those to whom we are closest.

Harming Ourselves

Bible Reading: Luke 6:36-38

We made a list of all persons we had harmed and became
willing to make amends to them all.

W e all know that we've been hurt. But some of us are so
focused on how we've been victimized and how others
have hurt us that we fail to see how we've been hurting ourselves. We may spend a lot of time and energy on trying to
change how others treat us, but to no avail. Perhaps we need to
begin by looking at ways we've been hurting ourselves. Then we
can work on changing them.

The Bible points out many danger areas where we are likely
to hurt ourselves. Here are some of them: "Stop telling lies. Let us
tell our neighbors the truth, for we are all parts of the same body"
(Ephesians 4:25). "Run from sexual sin! No other sin so clearly
affects the body as this one does. For sexual immorality is a sin
against your own body" (1 Corinthians 6:18). Jesus said, "Do not
condemn others, or it will all come back against you. Forgive others, and you will be forgiven. Give, and you will receive" (Luke
6:37-38).

God loves us every bit as much as he loves the people we've
harmed. He understands the actions that cause us pain and wants
to help us avoid them. We may be guaranteeing our continued
pain by continuing to do things that are guaranteed to hurt us.
Being willing to make amends to ourselves includes being willing
to renounce and give up the behaviors that destroy our lives. As we
are willing to give these things up, we'll begin to find good things
coming back our way.

When we've made bad choices, we first need to
make amends to ourselves.

235

Amends with God

Bible Reading: 1 Corinthians 6:15-17

> We made a list of all persons we had harmed and became
> willing to make amends to them all.

We're on intimate terms with God, whether we realize it
or not. We've probably thought a lot about how our sins
have hurt the people in our lives. But we may be surprised to find out how intimately acquainted God is with our sin,
and the emotional impact it has on him.

The apostle Paul warned, "Do not bring sorrow to God's
Holy Spirit by the way you live" (Ephesians 4:30). We can actually
cause God grief by our actions, because the Holy Spirit of God is
always with us. When we enter into sin, we take him with us. Paul
explained, "Don't you realize that your bodies are actually parts of
Christ? Should a man take his body, which is part of Christ, and
join it to a prostitute? Never! And don't you realize that if a man
joins himself to a prostitute, he becomes one body with her? For
the Scriptures say, 'The two are united into one.' But the person
who is joined to the Lord is one spirit with him" (1 Corinthians
6:15-17). When Potiphar's wife attempted to seduce Joseph, the
reason he gave for resisting was, "It would be a great sin against
God" (Genesis 39:9).

God is our loving Father! We may not realize it, but God
is intimately involved with our lives. He sees everything! He
knows the pain in store for us when we make bad decisions. And
he grieves deeply when we're doing things that will hurt us and
his other loved ones. We need to ask ourselves when we may have
caused God sorrow and grief.

Because God loves us so much, we hurt him
deeply when we sin.

236

Day 19

The Power of Words
Bible Reading: James 3:5-10

We made a list of all persons we had harmed and became
willing to make amends to them all.

Words can hurt terribly! We've all said things that we
regret. Stinging words leave their mark, and we can't
take away the sting or erase the emotional impact they
have. We may have made our tongues a tool of deception. Learning to tell lies expertly, we may have shattered someone's trust. We
may have used our words to attack and wound our children and
our spouses.

James recognized the terrible power of our words: "The
tongue is a small thing that makes grand speeches. But a tiny spark
can set a great forest on fire. And the tongue is a flame of fire. It is
a whole world of wickedness, corrupting your entire body. It can set
your whole life on fire, for it is set on fire by hell itself. People can
tame all kinds of animals, birds, reptiles, and fish, but no one can
tame the tongue. It is restless and evil, full of deadly poison. Sometimes it praises our Lord and Father, and sometimes it curses those
who have been made in the image of God. And so blessing and
cursing come pouring out of the same mouth" (James 3:5-10).

There seems to be no final cure for this unruly member of
our body. We need to respect what great damage it can do. Kids
may chant, "Sticks and stones can break my bones, but words will
never hurt me." But this is a weak defense against a verbal weapon
that can shatter our spirit. Whom have we hurt with our words?

❧

Our words are like fire: we cannot control them or
reverse the damage they cause.

Shared Addictions
Bible Reading: Proverbs 4:14-17

> We made a list of all persons we had harmed and became
> willing to make amends to them all.

Most of us didn't fall into sin alone. We may have softened our guilt about falling into addiction by bringing other people along with us. Whatever the addiction, it seems there's a tendency to lure others into the same pit. Whom have we harmed by bringing them down with us?

Solomon warned, "Don't do as the wicked do, and don't follow the path of evildoers. Don't even think about it; don't go that way. Turn away and keep moving. For evil people can't sleep until they've done their evil deed for the day. They can't rest until they've caused someone to stumble. They eat the food of wickedness and drink the wine of violence!" (Proverbs 4:14-17). Peter warned of false teachers who used their position to take advantage of those who were emotionally needy. He said of them, "They commit adultery with their eyes, and their desire for sin is never satisfied. They lure unstable people into sin" (2 Peter 2:14).

Solomon noted the power of seduction when he warned young men about the lure of a prostitute: "Don't let your hearts stray away toward her. Don't wander down her wayward path. For she has been the ruin of many; many men have been her victims. Her house is the road to the grave" (Proverbs 7:25-27).

We see the devastating effect we can have when we lure and seduce others to join us in sin. Whom have we harmed by breaking down their will to do good, and luring them back into trouble?

> No one stands alone; our addictions are usually tied
> to the addictions of others.

Day 21

Undoing the Damage
Bible Reading: Romans 8:28-30

We made a list of all persons we had harmed and became
willing to make amends to them all.

We may feel a bit discouraged after thinking of all the people we've hurt. We see that even though we are willing
to make amends, we won't be able to undo all the damage we've done. But there's still good reason to be encouraged.

The Bible has promised, "And we know that God causes
everything to work together for the good of those who love God
and are called according to his purpose for them. For God knew
his people in advance, and he chose them to become like his Son,
so that his Son would be the firstborn among many brothers and
sisters. And having chosen them, he called them to come to him.
And having called them, he gave them right standing with himself" (Romans 8:28-30).

Here's how one sin was turned around to be used by God for
good. Judah had sex with a woman he assumed to be a prostitute.
She was really his widowed daughter-in-law, who was upset that he
hadn't given her his other son for a husband. She had twin boys,
Perez and Zerah, who had their grandpa for a father! (Genesis 38).
Many were hurt by this unsavory situation.

Our hope lies in seeing how God can bring about good,
even through our worst sins. In Matthew 1:3 we see that Perez
and Zerah, the sons of Judah and Tamar, are in the direct lineage
that brought Jesus Christ into the world! We can be encouraged
that God has forgiven our sins and he has the power to bring good
things out of horrible circumstances.

God can turn our greatest tragedies into events that
bring honor to him.

Day 22

No Small Sins

Bible Reading: 1 Samuel 21:1-10; 22:21-23

> We made a list of all persons we had harmed and became willing to make amends to them all.

Sometimes we end up hurting innocent victims. When we started down the road seeking pleasure, or a path of safety or escape from our problems, we never imagined that our actions would lead to the destruction of innocent lives.

When young David was escaping from the wrath of King Saul, he ran to the priest, Ahimelech. "'The king has sent me on a private matter,' David said. 'He told me not to tell anybody why I am here. . . . The king's business was so urgent that I didn't even have time to grab a weapon!'" (1 Samuel 21:1-2, 8). The priest believed David's story and assisted him. But King Saul saw Ahimelech as a co-conspirator and had all eighty-five priests killed along with their entire families. Only one of Ahimelech's sons escaped to tell David what had happened. David responded, "Now I have caused the death of all your father's family. Stay here with me, and don't be afraid. I will protect you with my own life" (22:22-23).

David never intended to hurt anyone. He was just trying to cover his own tracks and get what he needed in his desperation. He recognized his responsibility and tried to do what he could after the tragedy. When people suffer innocently because of things we do, it will help them and their families if we acknowledge our responsibility and do whatever we can to help.

In recovery we must take responsibility for the consequences of our actions.

Healing with Parents

Bible Reading: Proverbs 17:25; 19:13, 26

We made a list of all persons we had harmed and became
willing to make amends to them all.

Our parents are deeply connected to our lives on some level.
And whether our families are intact or not, whether our
parents acknowledge their love for us or not, whether
they've made a mess of their lives or are a picture of perfection,
they are still our parents. They once held us in their arms and had
hopes and dreams that our lives could be better than their own.
Parents are deeply vulnerable to hurt from their children. When
our lives are damaged by the effects of addiction, our parents will
be vulnerable to the pain.

Solomon had plenty to say about how wayward children can
hurt their parents. Here are some of those comments from the book
of Proverbs: "Foolish children bring grief to their father and bitterness to the one who gave them birth" (Proverbs 17:25). "A foolish
child is a calamity to a father" (19:13). "Young people . . . with wild
friends bring shame to their parents" (28:7). "Anyone who steals
from his father and mother and says, 'What's wrong with that?' is
no better than a murderer" (28:24). "Children who mistreat their
father or chase away their mother are an embarrassment and a public disgrace" (19:26).

We have the capacity to cause grief, bitter sorrow, calamity,
shame, and disgrace to our parents. These are many of the things
we reap in our own lives when we are dominated by an addiction.
Even if our parents have contributed to our problems, we can still
take responsibility for our side of the relationship by doing what we
can to make things right with them.

Coming to terms with our parents is an essential
part of our recovery.

241

Day 24

Missing the Party
Bible Reading: Luke 15:28-32

We made a list of all persons we had harmed and became willing to make amends to them all.

W hen we think about making amends and reconciling relationships we may find that some places in our hearts are unwilling to take a step toward the other person. There may be unresolved anger, jealousy, and resentment; we may feel unable to forgive.

Jesus told a story about a man whose younger son took an early inheritance and left home. He wasted his money on riotous living and returned in desperate need. The older brother was angry and complained to his father. "'All these years I've slaved for you and never once refused to do a single thing you told me to. And in all that time you never gave me even one young goat for a feast with my friends. Yet when this son of yours comes back after squandering your money on prostitutes, you celebrate by killing the fattened calf!' His father said to him, 'Look, dear son, you have always stayed by me, and everything I have is yours. We had to celebrate this happy day. For your brother was dead and has come back to life! He was lost, but now he is found!'" (Luke 15:29-32).

Unresolved anger, resentment, and jealousy are very harmful, even if we've done all the "good deeds" expected of us. We harm ourselves and others by our self-pity and emotional manipulation. If we face this kind of roadblock, we need to stop rehearsing everyone else's wrongs. We need to deal with the things that are keeping us from attending the "party" of life.

❦

When we resist making amends we cut ourselves off
from the joys of life.

242

Loving Hearts
Bible Reading: James 4:11-12

> We made a list of all persons we had harmed and became
> willing to make amends to them all.

W e can harm others by our attitudes as well as our actions.
We may see ourselves as "righteous," assuming a superior
attitude, ready to criticize at any moment. We may feel
we have the right to criticize because others aren't measuring up
to what we think should be expected. But our judgmental nagging
doesn't seem to help others improve their performance.

James wrote, "Don't speak evil against each other, dear
brothers and sisters. . . . But your job is to obey the law, not
to judge whether it applies to you" (James 4:11-12). Here's an
example of someone who was critical when he didn't understand
the whole situation. Eli the priest saw Hannah in the temple.
"Seeing her lips moving but hearing no sound, he thought she
had been drinking" (1 Samuel 1:13). Hannah was actually begging God to give her a child; her silent prayer was driven by a
sad heart, not a drunken mind.

We are not God! We haven't been designated as the judge
of the people around us. So we really don't have the right to criticize and speak evil of others. Besides, we may not fully understand
the problems involved and may end up adding to them instead
of helping. We need to consider how our negative, critical, and
self-righteous attitudes have harmed others and become willing to
make amends. Perhaps our focus on the wrongs of others is a way
to avoid our own problems.

As God loves us, he wants to create loving hearts within us.

Day 26

Full of Mercy

Bible Reading: Matthew 9:10-13

> We made a list of all persons we had harmed and became
> willing to make amends to them all.

I n families where addictions are forceful, there's usually someone
who falls into the role of being superhuman and self-righteous.
In the family system, this person balances out the identified
"addict," who feels subhuman. If we are one of the self-righteous
ones, it is harder for us to identify ourselves because we don't look
sick. We seem to be stable and have it all together. However, it can
become very lonely as we separate ourselves from everyone whom
we perceive to be below us.

The Pharisees once asked why Jesus associated with sinners. "Healthy people don't need a doctor—sick people do. . . .
For I have come to call not those who think they are righteous,
but those who know they are sinners" (Matthew 9:12-13). Here's
God's view of the self-righteous: "They say to each other, 'Don't
come too close or you will defile me! I am holier than you!' These
people are a stench in my nostrils, an acrid smell that never goes
away" (Isaiah 65:5).

We may not realize how harmful self-righteousness can be.
We can be hurting others by our lack of mercy, even though we're
doing all the "right" things. Self-righteousness is hard to see in
ourselves. We may need to ask our loved ones if this type of attitude has harmed them. Then we need to be willing to really listen
to the answer they give.

> As we become willing to make amends, mercy begins
> to grow in our hearts.

STEP EIGHT

The Gift of Gratitude
Bible Reading: Luke 17:11-19

> We made a list of all persons we had harmed and became
> willing to make amends to them all.

We can become so focused on our own struggles and pain
that we forget to show gratitude to God or to the people
who are instrumental in our healing. We may come to
expect special treatment and forget that those who are showing
care for our lives really deserve our thanks.

Jesus healed ten lepers and told them to go to the priests and
show them that they were healed. "And as they went, they were
cleansed of their leprosy. One of them, when he saw that he was
healed, came back to Jesus, shouting, 'Praise God!' He fell to the
ground at Jesus' feet, thanking him for what he had done. This man
was a Samaritan. Jesus asked, 'Didn't I heal ten men? Where are
the other nine? Has no one returned to give glory to God except
this foreigner?'" (Luke 17:14-18). The apostle Paul said, "Be thankful in all circumstances, for this is God's will for you who belong to
Christ Jesus" (1 Thessalonians 5:18).

Jesus was both God and man. As God he deserved the glory
and the gratitude for the miracle of curing this incurable disease.
Perhaps, in his humanity, his feelings were hurt by being so taken
for granted. He didn't have to heal them. He extended himself out
of love and compassion. Are there people in our lives who have
reached out in loving compassion to help us, only to be taken for
granted? Have we become so self-centered because of our own pain
that we've failed to express gratitude to those who have helped us?

> We receive the gift of great joy when we are able
> to receive God's other gifts with gratitude.

Sensitive Hearts
Bible Reading: Luke 16:19-31

> We made a list of all persons we had harmed and became
> willing to make amends to them all.

O ne of the pitfalls of recovery is that we tend to become
extremely self-focused and fail to see the needs of others.
If we've been a rescuer, we can go overboard in our recovery and ignore valid needs. If we're medicating our pain through
work, or some other drug or distraction, we can numb ourselves to
the needs of others while we're numbing our own pain. Perhaps,
we need to consider those around us who were needy while we
were consumed with our own lives.

"Jesus said, 'There was a certain rich man who was splendidly clothed in purple and fine linen and who lived each day in
luxury. At his gate lay a poor man named Lazarus who was covered
with sores. As Lazarus lay there longing for scraps from the rich
man's table, the dogs would come and lick his open sores. Finally,
the poor man died and was carried by the angels to be with Abraham. The rich man also died and was buried, and his soul went to
the place of the dead [Hades]'" (Luke 16:19-23).

The point for us to consider is not that we may go to hell
for neglecting the needs of others. Our salvation is insured by the
blood of Jesus, which covers all of our sins. But we need to consider
whether we have neglected the needs of those around us while we
were consumed with addictions or with our recovery. Our children,
spouse, or others may feel like they were bleeding on our doorstep and we didn't even notice because we were so self-consumed.
Whom have we hurt by neglecting their valid needs?

> Our recovery is only successful to the extent that we
> grow more sensitive to those around us.

Day 29

Making Restitution
Bible Reading: Exodus 22:10-15

We made a list of all persons we had harmed and became
willing to make amends to them all.

I rresponsibility is often associated with those who are caught up
in addictive family systems. We may see ourselves as irresponsible and condemn ourselves. Or we may notice our irresponsible
behavior, but excuse ourselves because of all that we've been dealing with. Or we may not even notice our irresponsible behavior,
but have recurrent problems with others because we fail to respect
their property.

The Bible clearly states, "If someone borrows an animal
from a neighbor and it is injured or dies when the owner is absent,
the person who borrowed it must pay full compensation" (Exodus
22:14). David once wrote, "The wicked borrow and never repay,
but the godly are generous givers" (Psalm 37:21).

The Bible does tell us that it's important to take responsibility for the things we borrow. We may feel like we're being
condemned as chronically evil if we've had a problem with irresponsibility. The word translated "wicked" really means one who
is morally wrong or a person who acts badly. God sees irresponsible
behavior as a bad action which can be corrected. He doesn't see us
as hopelessly bad. Regardless of what we've been through, we are
still held responsible to respect the property of others. We need
to consider who we've harmed by being negligent or irresponsible
with the use of their property.

❧

Paying restitution builds bridges with others and
establishes peace within ourselves.

Day 30

Too Busy!
Bible Reading: Luke 10:38-42

We made a list of all persons we had harmed and became
willing to make amends to them all.

W e may be the one who tries to hold it all together in the
family. We figure that if we don't take care of things,
they just won't be taken care of. So we rush around trying to make sure that everything is as it should be. We may fume
that others don't pitch in and help. We may simmer in our own
self-pity, as we silently hope that someone will notice that we need
help. We may hurt others by lashing out unexpectedly or by blaming them.

Jesus dealt compassionately with a woman who behaved in a
similar way. Jesus and the disciples "came to a certain village where
a woman named Martha welcomed him into her home. Her sister,
Mary, sat at the Lord's feet, listening to what he taught. But Martha was distracted by the big dinner she was preparing. She came
to Jesus and said, 'Lord, doesn't it seem unfair to you that my sister
just sits here while I do all the work? Tell her to come and help
me.' But the Lord said to her, 'My dear Martha, you are worried and
upset over all these details! There is only one thing worth being
concerned about. Mary has discovered it, and it will not be taken
away from her'" (Luke 10:38-42).

Martha deprived herself by trying to be available to everyone. She deprived herself of what she really needed, while playing
the martyr. The result was resentment, self-pity, and indignation
that no one came to her rescue. Whom have we hurt, ourselves
included, by behaving as Martha did?

Keeping busy with the wrong things robs us of the even
better things God has for us.

STEP NINE

We made direct amends to such people wherever possible,
except when to do so would injure them or others.

*"If someone says, 'I love God,' but hates a Christian brother or sister,
that person is a liar. . . . He has given us this command:
Those who love God must also love their Christian brothers and sisters"
(1 John 4:20-21).*

Day 1

Keeping Promises
Bible Reading: 2 Samuel 9:1-9

> We made direct amends to such people wherever possible,
> except when to do so would injure them or others.

How many people are still living in the shadow of our unkept promises? Is it too late to go back now and try to make it up to them?

King David had made some promises to his friend Jonathan. "One day David asked, 'Is anyone in Saul's family still alive—anyone to whom I can show kindness for Jonathan's sake?'" (2 Samuel 9:1).

Jonathan's only living son, Mephibosheth, had lived a long time with the pain of David's unkept promise. It had shaped his lifestyle, his emotional condition, the way he thought about himself. His grandfather, King Saul, had mistreated David before David became king. Perhaps Mephibosheth was afraid that David would mistreat him on account of his grandfather. Perhaps he had begun to take the guilt of his grandfather's sins upon himself. Generations of fear and guilt had been laid upon him—until David remembered and fulfilled his promise.

There are probably people in our lives who have been affected by promises we've failed to keep. It is important that we try to fulfill whatever promises we are able to. When we can't, the least we can do is to ask what our neglect meant to those we disappointed.

❧

> As we make amends we restore to others what
> rightfully belongs to them.

Day 2

From Takers to Givers
Bible Reading: Luke 19:1-10

We made direct amends to such people wherever possible,
except when to do so would injure them or others.

W hen we are feeding our addictions, it is easy to become
consumed by our own needs. Nothing matters except
getting what we crave so desperately. We may have to
lie, cheat, kill, or steal; but that doesn't stop us. Within our families
and community we become known as "takers," trampling over the
unseen needs of others.

Zacchaeus had the same problem. His hunger for riches
drove him to betray his own people by collecting taxes for the
oppressive Roman government. He was hated by his own people as
a thief, an extortionist, and a traitor. But when Jesus reached out
to him, he changed dramatically. "Zacchaeus stood before the Lord
and said, 'I will give half my wealth to the poor, Lord, and if I have
cheated people on their taxes, I will give them back four times as
much!' Jesus responded, 'Salvation has come to this home today'"
(Luke 19:8-9).

Zacchaeus went beyond just paying back what he had taken.
For the first time in a long time, he saw the needs of others and
wanted to be a "giver."

Making amends includes paying back what we've taken,
whenever possible. Some of us may even seize the opportunity to
go even further, giving even more. As we begin to see the needs
of others and respond by choice, our self-esteem will rise. We will
begin to realize that we can give to others, instead of just being a
burden.

Making amends is the first step to becoming a giver.

Day 3

Rebuilding Relationships

Bible Reading: Acts 15:36-41

We made direct amends to such people wherever possible,
except when to do so would injure them or others.

How many times have we written people off because of some
dispute in the distant past? Years pass and people change;
yet we cling to our old ways of seeing them. Perhaps we
never saw them very clearly in the first place! For some of us, making amends will include reviewing our relationships. We may need
to change our estimation of some of those we've already judged.

Paul and Barnabas traveled together on a missionary journey, taking John Mark along as their assistant. When things got
tough, the young man deserted them and went home. Later, Barnabas wanted to give John Mark another chance, but Paul refused.
"Their disagreement was so sharp that they separated" (Acts
15:39). Much later in his life, Paul was put in prison. During that
time, he wrote to Timothy and asked for John Mark. He said, "He
is useful to me for ministry" (2 Timothy 4:11, NKJV).

The Bible doesn't tell us how Paul came to change his
opinion of John Mark. Perhaps he realized that he hadn't been
completely fair. Maybe John Mark had changed over the years.
At some point, though, they had reestablished their relationship
and repaired the emotional damage done.

Making amends includes going back and settling emotional
accounts. When we've judged someone harshly, we need to reexamine our relationship with that person. If we expect others to change
how they look at us, we will need to do the same for others.

✻

By making amends, we become open to God's life-changing power.

Day 4

Good Things from God

Bible Reading: Genesis 32:1-12

> We made direct amends to such people wherever possible, except when to do so would injure them or others.

There may be people whom we've hurt so badly that they hate us. There may be considerable risks involved in going back to face them. The pain may not be erased, even after many years. But as difficult as such a meeting might be, it may help in our healing process—if God is leading us to do it.

Jacob had so injured his brother Esau through his crafty schemes that Esau had vowed to kill him. Jacob ran away, fearing for his life. Twenty years later God told him to return home. So Jacob sent messengers ahead of him to see what kind of reception he could expect. "The messengers returned to Jacob and reported, 'We met your brother, Esau, and he is already on his way to meet you—with an army of 400 men!' Jacob was terrified at the news. . . . Then Jacob prayed, . . . 'O LORD, please rescue me from the hand of my brother, Esau. I am afraid that he is coming to attack me. . . . But you promised me, "I will surely treat you kindly"'" (Genesis 32:6-7, 9-12).

We can learn from Jacob's example in this situation. First, we must be certain that God is leading us. We can pray earnestly, remembering his previous provisions and trusting in his promises. Then, asking for protection, we must take steps toward reconciliation.

God's call to make amends will lead us down a path toward good things.

Day 5

Unfinished Business

Bible Reading: Philemon 1:13-16

> We made direct amends to such people wherever possible,
> except when to do so would injure them or others.

S ometimes we need to complete unfinished business before
we can move forward toward new opportunities in life. Some
of us may have left a trail of broken laws and relationships
behind us—things we need to address before moving on.

A new life doesn't excuse us from past obligations. While
the apostle Paul was in prison, he led a runaway slave named
Onesimus into a new life. Paul sent him back to his master, even
though Onesimus risked the death penalty for his offense. Since
his previous master was a friend of Paul's, and a Christian brother,
they hoped that Onesimus would be forgiven.

Onesimus carried a letter to his master from Paul, which
read, "I wanted to keep him [Onesimus] here with me. . . . But
I didn't want to do anything without your consent. . . . You lost
Onesimus for a little while so that you could have him back forever. He is no longer like a slave to you. He is more than a slave,
for he is a beloved brother. . . . If he has wronged you in any way
or owes you anything, charge it to me" (Philemon 1:13-16, 18).

Before we can move ahead we must face the unfinished
business of the past. This includes offering to pay back what we
owe, coming clean with the law, and going back to the people
from whom we ran away. We can't assume forgiveness from people,
although we can hope for it. In some cases we may be surprised to
find pardon and release from the bondage of our past.

❧

Making direct amends will release us from our
bondage to the past.

Something from Nothing

Bible Reading: Luke 15:11-24

> We made direct amends to such people wherever possible,
> except when to do so would injure them or others.

Some of us may have stolen things from others, but now have no means of paying them back. How can we face the people we've wronged when we have nothing to offer? Since working through Step Eight, we should be willing to humbly approach the people we've wronged. But if we can't repay our debts, what's the point?

Jesus told a story about a young son who demanded an early inheritance and left home. He wasted his fortune on riotous living. He hit bottom, so to speak, and decided to go back to his father. He had nothing left of what he had taken and no means with which to ever repay his father. We can imagine his feelings as he rehearsed what he would say.

"So he returned home to his father. And while he was still a long way off, his father saw him coming. Filled with love and compassion, he ran to his son, embraced him, and kissed him. . . . his father said to the servants, 'Quick! . . . We must celebrate with a feast, for this son of mine was dead and has now returned to life. He was lost, but now he is found.' So the party began" (Luke 15:20-24).

We may feel like we have nothing to offer. But to the people who love us, we are more important than anything else we could give them. The apostle Paul said, "Owe nothing to anyone—except for your obligation to love one another" (Romans 13:8). Though we may not be able to pay our debts right away, we can still offer our love.

Making amends can be the richest of gifts.

A Servant's Heart
Bible Reading: Philippians 2:1-8

> We made direct amends to such people wherever possible,
> except when to do so would injure them or others.

A t this point in recovery, most of us have experienced some major changes in our attitudes. At one time, we were so consumed by our addictions that we thought only of ourselves, failing to show any consideration for others. In this step, the focus is on the interests and needs of others.

The apostle Paul taught, "Don't be selfish; don't try to impress others. Be humble, thinking of others as better than yourselves. Don't look out only for your own interests, but take an interest in others too" (Philippians 2:3-4). Whether we make direct amends to others or choose not to because of the injury it would cause, we are concerned with protecting others from pain and suffering.

There may be situations where we will suffer if we go back to make amends. This is part of the work of recovery, and the potential pain should not deter us. The apostle Peter wrote, "If you suffer for doing good and endure it patiently, God is pleased with you. . . . Christ suffered for you. He is your example, and you must follow in his steps. He never sinned, nor ever deceived anyone. He did not retaliate when he was insulted, nor threaten revenge when he suffered. He left his case in the hands of God, who always judges fairly" (1 Peter 2:20-23).

This step can be very difficult as we face the painful consequences of past actions. During this time, we need to turn our lives over to the care of God. He will fairly and wisely decide what will happen to us.

❧

The best cure for selfishness is God's call to serve others.

Day 8

Making Peace
Bible Reading: Matthew 5:23-25

We made direct amends to such people wherever possible,
except when to do so would injure them or others.

We all suffer brokenness within ourselves, in our relationship with God, and in our relationships with others.
Brokenness tends to weigh us down and can easily lead
us back into our addictions. Recovery isn't complete until all areas
of brokenness are mended.

Jesus taught, "So if you are presenting a sacrifice at the altar
in the Temple and you suddenly remember that someone has something against you, leave your sacrifice there at the altar. Go and
be reconciled to that person. Then come and offer your sacrifice
to God" (Matthew 5:23-24). The apostle John wrote, "If someone says, 'I love God,' but hates a Christian brother or sister, that
person is a liar; for if we don't love people we can see, how can we
love God, whom we cannot see?" (1 John 4:20).

Much of recovery involves repairing the brokenness in our
lives. This requires that we make peace with God, within ourselves, and with others whom we've alienated. Unresolved issues
in relationships can disable us from being at peace with God and
ourselves. Once we go through the process of making amends, we
must keep our minds and hearts open to anyone we may have over-
looked. God will often remind us of relationships that need attention. When these come to mind, we should stop everything and go
to those we've offended, seeking to repair the damage.

Making direct amends brings peace—with ourselves,
others, and God.

Choosing to Love

Bible Reading: Luke 6:27-36

> We made direct amends to such people wherever possible,
> except when to do so would injure them or others.

As we set out to mend relationships, there are some things that are beyond our control. Some people may refuse to be reconciled, even when we do our best to make amends. This may leave us feeling like a victim. Once again we're stuck with the pain of unresolved issues. We may be left with negative feelings that continue to surface. What can we do to gain power in these situations?

Jesus said (emphasis added), "But to you who are willing to listen, I say, love your *enemies!* Do *good* to those who *hate* you. Bless those who *curse* you. Pray for those who *hurt* you. . . . Love your *enemies!* Do good to *them.* Lend to *them* without expecting to be repaid. Then your reward from heaven will be very great, and you will truly be acting as children of the Most High, for he is kind to those who are *unthankful* and *wicked*" (Luke 6:27-28, 35).

We no longer need to be controlled by other people's dispositions. Even when we've done our best to make amends for the wrongs we've done, the situations may not change. And even when we've come to terms with the wrongs that have been done against us, our feelings may not change. But we don't have to be held captive by our feelings or the feelings of others. We can choose to act in a loving way. This will free us from being controlled by anyone other than God. As we choose to do good, our feelings will follow with time.

❧

Our recovery is not decided by the responses of others;
it is in God's hands alone.

Imperfect Love

Bible Reading: John 21:14-19

> We made direct amends to such people wherever possible,
> except when to do so would injure them or others.

We may wonder how we can love others but still hurt them. This paradox causes shame, sometimes erecting a barrier between us and the ones we love. We may be afraid to say that we love them, thinking, *If I really loved them, I wouldn't let them down the way I have.*

Peter had once sworn his love for Jesus. But then, after Jesus was arrested, Peter protected himself by denying that he even knew him. Jesus wasn't surprised. But Peter had a hard time forgiving himself. After Jesus rose from the dead, he had this conversation with Peter. "Jesus asked Simon Peter, 'Simon son of John, do you love me more than these?' 'Yes, Lord,' Peter replied, 'you know I love you.' . . . A third time he asked him, 'Simon son of John, do you love me?' Peter was hurt that Jesus asked the question a third time. He said, 'Lord, you know everything. You know that I love you'" (John 21:15-17).

Jesus allowed Peter to affirm his love the best he could and accepted him as he was. In this way, Jesus reduced the shame and restored the relationship. Shame and isolation can lead us back to our addictions. For the sake of our recovery, we must not let our shame cause us to avoid the people we love. It's all right if we love others imperfectly—no one is perfect. But we must keep our love relationships together until they've had time to heal.

✿

Making amends for our imperfections will help us
understand the true nature of love.

Covering the Past
Bible Reading: Ezekiel 33:10-16

> We made direct amends to such people wherever possible,
> except when to do so would injure them or others.

W hen we walk down the wrong paths in life, we end up in bad places and experience devastating losses. If we go far enough down those paths, we endanger our very lives. We may wonder if we've already gone too far. Is a new way of life still possible, even if we turn from our old ways and make amends?

Even under the Old Testament laws, there was hope for those who chose to turn around and make amends. The Lord spoke through Ezekiel, saying, "Give the people of Israel this message: You are saying, 'Our sins are heavy upon us; we are wasting away! How can we survive?' As surely as I live, says the Sovereign LORD, I take no pleasure in the death of wicked people. I only want them to turn from their wicked ways so they can live. Turn! Turn from your wickedness, O people of Israel! Why should you die? Son of man, give your people this message: The righteous behavior of righteous people will not save them if they turn to sin, nor will the wicked behavior of wicked people destroy them if they repent and turn from their sins. . . . Suppose I tell some wicked people that they will surely die, but then they turn from their sins and do what is just and right. For instance, they might give back a debtor's security, return what they have stolen, and obey my life-giving laws, no longer doing what is evil. If they do this, then they will surely live and not die. None of their past sins will be brought up again, for they have done what is just and right, and they will surely live" (Ezekiel 33:10-12, 14-16).

There's hope for everyone who turns around and makes amends. Our past sins can be overshadowed by the new life ahead of us.

❧

Recovery leads to right actions, and then, to restitution.

Day 12

Desperate Hunger

Bible Reading: Proverbs 6:30-31

We made direct amends to such people wherever possible,
except when to do so would injure them or others.

There are conditions that drive us to our addictions. There's
some need inside that makes it worth the risk involved.
It deadens us to our own sense of what is right and wrong.
We'll do anything to satisfy the hunger our addiction feeds. We
wish people could understand that we don't risk everything good
in our lives on a whim. We feel like we're starving. By now, we're
coming to realize that although there are conditions that drive us
to our addictions, we still must take responsibility for the wrong
that we do.

King Solomon once wrote, "Excuses might be found for a
thief who steals because he is starving. But if he is caught, he must
pay back seven times what he stole, even if he has to sell everything in his house" (Proverbs 6:30-31).

God understands that there can be areas of starvation within
us that drive us to do wrong. Certainly, once we identify those
areas we will have more compassion for ourselves and from others
who understand. But we're still responsible to make amends, even
though this may be costly. The cost of making amends will help us
face the immediacy of our need to deal with the starvation. Perhaps
when we understand the hungers involved, we will be able to find
the help we need to satisfy them. Only when the starvation is satisfied will we be able to remain free from our addictions.

In recovery we learn not to destroy ourselves
through unwise actions.

Day 13

Regaining Control
Bible Reading: Exodus 22:5-6

> We made direct amends to such people wherever possible,
> except when to do so would injure them or others.

When we give in to our addictions, we feel isolated. We feel alone in our pain and need something to overcome it. We never expected our behaviors to affect the lives of others. We weren't thinking about the people around us; we were focused on our own pain. We just wanted to feel better. Our addictions seemed to promise us a way to destroy the pain without hurting anyone else.

The Old Testament says, "If you are burning thornbushes and the fire gets out of control and spreads into another person's field, destroying the sheaves or the uncut grain or the whole crop, the one who started the fire must pay for the lost crop" (Exodus 22:6).

This law was especially important in the farming community of early Israel. It stated a person's responsibility for damages caused when his attempt to burn up thornbushes in his own field got out of control and burned the valuable grain in adjoining fields. Here's an analogy: The thorns represent the pain we're trying to consume with the fire of our addictions. At first we don't realize how our lives are connected to others, or the damage that can result when our addictions get out of control. In retrospect, however, we can see how the fire of our addictions has destroyed much more than the thornbushes of our pain. Making amends means we need to account for all the losses that have resulted from the fire we started.

Making amends helps us take responsibility for the
pain we've caused.

Civic Duty
Bible Reading: Matthew 17:24-27

> We made direct amends to such people wherever possible,
> except when to do so would injure them or others.

We sometimes neglect our obligations because we disagree with the systems of which we are a part. This is a natural tendency. But it can become a greater problem when we're burdened with the pressures of addiction. Part of our recovery may involve realigning ourselves with some of society's expectations and demands, even when we may not be in full agreement with them.

Even Jesus had problems with the IRS of his day. Jesus asked Peter, "'What do you think, Peter? Do kings tax their own people or the people they have conquered?' 'They tax the people they have conquered,' Peter replied. 'Well, then,' Jesus said, 'the citizens are free! However, we don't want to offend them, so go down to the lake and throw in a line. Open the mouth of the first fish you catch, and you will find a large silver coin. Take it and pay the tax for both of us'" (Matthew 17:25-27).

The kings of Jesus' day drew their tax revenues from the nations they had conquered. Since Jesus was the Son of God, he should have been exempt from taxation by the Temple leaders—the representatives of God. Jesus still submitted himself to the demands of the society he lived in. We, too, need to be in good standing with our government. We need to pay our taxes and fulfill any other civic obligations demanded by the law.

We need to make things right even if we don't agree with all the stipulations.

Day 15

Authorities
Bible Reading: 1 Peter 2:13-17

> We made direct amends to such people wherever possible,
> except when to do so would injure them or others.

By turning our lives over to the care of God, we'll experience God's power for good. This will naturally lead us to make amends. We may be known for being at odds with society and the laws of the land. So when we begin to change, we may cause some heads to turn. People who have never experienced God's power will see the effect it's had on us. They will probably wonder what could have changed us so drastically.

The apostle Peter wrote, "For the Lord's sake, respect all human authority—whether the king as head of state, or the officials he has appointed. For the king has sent them to punish those who do wrong and to honor those who do right. It is God's will that your honorable lives should silence those ignorant people who make foolish accusations against you. For you are free, yet you are God's slaves, so don't use your freedom as an excuse to do evil. Respect everyone, and love your Christian brothers and sisters. Fear God, and respect the king" (1 Peter 2:13-17).

Obeying the law and meeting our obligations to society are important parts of making amends. We need to deal with our attitudes toward the laws of our land and the people in law enforcement. We may feel like we haven't hurt anyone, but if we've violated the law, we're responsible to face the consequences.

❧

As we make amends we must face how we feel
about authority figures.

Free from Fear

Bible Reading: Genesis 26:1-11

We made direct amends to such people wherever possible,
except when to do so would injure them or others.

Making amends is one of the most difficult steps in recovery. So for encouragement, perhaps we should consider some of the benefits we can gain. Before coming clean, we live with the gnawing fear of being found out. Most addictions require us to live a lie; we are haunted by the hidden fear that everything is about to unravel. Our families also are burdened by hidden fears and shame. Setting out to make amends can change all this.

Here's a story of how one family was affected by having to live a lie. "Isaac stayed in Gerar. When the men who lived there asked Isaac about his wife, Rebekah, he said, 'She is my sister' . . . He thought, 'They will kill me to get her, because she is so beautiful.' But some time later, Abimelech, king of the Philistines, looked out his window and saw Isaac caressing Rebekah. Immediately, Abimelech called for Isaac and exclaimed, 'She is obviously your wife! Why did you say, "She is my sister"?' 'Because I was afraid someone would kill me to get her from me,' Isaac replied" (Genesis 26:6-9).

Imagine the negative effect this lie had on Isaac and Rebekah's relationship. When they weren't pretending, they lived with constant fear. When we make amends and learn to live with the truth there is a great relief from fear. We are freed up from the pressures of always having to pretend to be something we're not. This relief can bring new life to all our intimate relationships.

❦

In making amends we discover the freedom that
comes by way of the truth.

Day 17

Free from Shame
Bible Reading: Genesis 3:6-10

> We made direct amends to such people wherever possible,
> except when to do so would injure them or others.

B efore we make amends, constant guilt plagues our relationships with the people we've hurt. We actually give them
power over us. We avoid them, feeling uncomfortable in
social situations where they're present. We exclude them from
our circle of friends. We become evasive and always hope that we
won't have to deal with the shame of facing them. Living in hiding
is not a good feeling.

Look at these two examples of people in hiding: "At that
moment their eyes were opened, and they [Adam and Eve] suddenly felt shame at their nakedness. So they sewed fig leaves together
to cover themselves. When the cool evening breezes were blowing,
the man and his wife heard the LORD God walking about in the
garden. So they hid from the LORD God among the trees. Then the
LORD God called to the man, 'Where are you?' He replied, 'I heard
you walking in the garden, so I hid'" (Genesis 3:7-10). "One day
Cain suggested to his brother, 'Let's go out into the fields.' And
while they were in the field, Cain attacked his brother, Abel,
and killed him. Afterward the LORD asked Cain, 'Where is your
brother? Where is Abel?' 'I don't know,' Cain responded. 'Am I my
brother's guardian?'" (4:8-9).

These are not stories of happy people! Living a lie necessarily forces us to live in shame and isolation. We begin to live
constantly on the defensive. When we make amends, we're free
to resume our relationships with God and others, and without the
fear or shame.

Making things right with others will bring freedom from shame.

Surprised by Love
Bible Reading: Luke 15:18-21

We made direct amends to such people wherever possible,
except when to do so would injure them or others.

Often our behaviors result not only in harming others, but also in alienating us from the people who love us. We begin to feel embarrassed around others. We wonder how we'll be received when we meet the people we've hurt. Step Nine says that we are to make *direct* amends wherever possible. This can be an intimidating task.

When the Prodigal Son was preparing to make direct amends to his father, he felt the need to rehearse a little speech. "I will go home to my father and say, 'Father, I have sinned against both heaven and you, and I am no longer worthy of being called your son. Please take me on as a hired servant.' So he returned home to his father. And while he was still a long way off, his father saw him coming. Filled with love and compassion, he ran to his son, embraced him, and kissed him. His son said to him, 'Father, I have sinned against both heaven and you, and I am no longer worthy of being called your son'" (Luke 15:18-21).

He didn't even get to finish his speech! His father embraced him, welcomed him home with love and compassion, and threw the biggest party they'd ever had! One of the surprise benefits we may experience from making amends is that it may not be as hard as we expect. In some cases, those we love will have compassion for us and be thrilled to see us at their door. They will embrace us, forgiving all the harm we've done in the past. These positive experiences should then help us face the more painful and difficult ones.

The hardest part of making amends is in making the
decision to do so.

Day 19

In the Light

Bible Reading: Psalm 19:7-11

> We made direct amends to such people wherever possible,
> except when to do so would injure them or others.

When we're living under the influence of an addiction, we're likely to see the world in a distorted fashion. What we perceive to be right and wrong becomes confused. Our perceptions of reality become blurred. We get out of sync with society's norms and ignore the proper boundaries for governing our behavior.

The books of Exodus, Leviticus, Numbers, and Deuteronomy are filled with laws and rules of conduct that were to govern every facet of Jewish life. They form the basis for our laws in the Judeo/Christian tradition. There were laws regarding diet, proper hygiene, relationships, business dealings, livestock, worship, marriage, sexuality, crime, and punishment. These clearly defined boundaries were set up by God to protect everyone and to help them maintain good relationships with him and with each other. King David once wrote, "The instructions of the LORD are perfect, reviving the soul. The decrees of the LORD are trustworthy, making wise the simple. The commandments of the LORD are right, bringing joy to the heart. The commands of the LORD are clear, giving insight for living. Reverence for the LORD is pure, lasting forever. The laws of the LORD are true; each one is fair" (Psalm 19:7-9).

Making amends will bring us back into line with the protective norms our society has set up. We need to recognize where we've overstepped boundaries. Making amends while using God's laws as the standard for wise behavior should help us learn to respect the dignity of others. It should also give us a clear vision of reality and, ultimately, will allow us to have joy and success.

*Aligning ourselves with God's laws for recovery will
bring light to our paths.*

Day 20

Free from Sin's Penalty

Bible Reading: Colossians 2:13-15

> We made direct amends to such people wherever possible,
> except when to do so would injure them or others.

S ometime during the recovery process we will probably notice that we've begun to grow spiritually. And with this growth, we may realize that we've hurt God through the things we've done to ourselves and others. We may feel an obligation to try to do something to make it up to him. But what can we do? How can we ever make up for the long list of sins we've committed?

In Jesus' day, a criminal's charges were set out on a list to be brought before the court. If the criminal was sentenced to crucifixion for his crimes, the list would be nailed to the cross where he was to be executed. The crimes on the list were then fully paid for by his death. The apostle Paul wrote, "You were dead because of your sins and because your sinful nature was not yet cut away. Then God made you alive with Christ, for he forgave all our sins. He canceled the record of the charges against us and took it away by nailing it to the cross. In this way, he disarmed the spiritual rulers and authorities. He shamed them publicly by his victory over them on the cross" (Colossians 2:13-15).

All the sins we would ever commit were listed and nailed to the cross of Christ. His blood covered them all; they were paid for in full. When it comes to making amends to God, there's nothing left to do!

Since we're already forgiven by God, we are free
to seek forgiveness from others.

Day 21

Good and Bad
Bible Reading: Galatians 3:10-13

> We made direct amends to such people wherever possible,
> except when to do so would injure them or others.

W e may still feel like we're basically good people. Yes, our lives may have gotten a bit out of control, but the good we've done surely outweighs the bad. Maybe we don't need to turn our lives over to Jesus Christ and accept him as our Savior. Perhaps we can just make amends for the wrongs we've done and do our best to be good in the future. Then everything will be fine.

Maybe not! The Bible doesn't say that God weighs our good deeds out against our bad. Here's what God says: "For the person who keeps all of the laws except one is as guilty as a person who has broken all of God's laws" (James 2:10). "'Cursed is everyone who does not observe and obey all the commands that are written in God's Book of the Law.' So it is clear that no one can be made right with God by trying to keep the law. For the Scriptures say, 'It is through faith that a righteous person has life'" (Galatians 3:10-11). "For the wages of sin is death, but the free gift of God is eternal life through Christ Jesus our Lord" (Romans 6:23).

The Bible makes it clear that if we reject Jesus Christ's payment for our sins, we will have to pay the debt ourselves. The only acceptable payment is death. Not even a lifetime of our good deeds is enough to make amends for the bad deeds we've done, no matter how few they may be.

> The Cross frees us from having to be "good," so we can
> freely admit we are bad.

Nothing Added

Bible Reading: Galatians 2:17-19

> We made direct amends to such people wherever possible,
> except when to do so would injure them or others.

As we think about making amends to God, it seems there must be something we can do beyond placing our faith in Christ. What if God does expect us to do good works to make up for our sins? All right, maybe the sins we committed before we became Christians have been covered. But what about all the sins we've committed since then? Wouldn't it be wise to be on the safe side? Why not figure out some sort of payment system—adding to what Christ did—just to be safe?

The Christians of Paul's day asked similar questions. They thought, "But suppose we seek to be made right with God through faith in Christ and then we are found guilty because we have abandoned the law. Would that mean Christ has led us into sin?" Paul replied to this question, "Absolutely not! Rather, I am a sinner if I rebuild the old system of law I already tore down. For when I tried to keep the law, it condemned me. So I died to the law—I stopped trying to meet all its requirements—so that I might live for God" (Galatians 2:17-19).

Christ paid in full for all our sins. We can trust him fully to make amends for us with God. We don't have to rely partly on our own ability to make amends to God. It's already done!

Jesus Christ has made direct and complete amends on our behalf.

271

A Clean Slate

Bible Reading: Ephesians 2:8-10

> We made direct amends to such people wherever possible,
> except when to do so would injure them or others.

Recovery is hard work. Step Nine is one of the hardest. Notice, however, that this step focuses our attention on making amends to people, not God. Once we realize that our amends to God have already been settled, we are free to focus our attention on making amends to the people in our lives.

The apostle Paul wrote, "Everyone has sinned; we all fall short of God's glorious standard. Yet God, with undeserved kindness, declares that we are righteous. He did this through Christ Jesus when he freed us from the penalty for our sins" (Romans 3:23-24). "God saved you by his grace when you believed. And you can't take credit for this; it is a gift from God. Salvation is not a reward for the good things we have done, so none of us can boast about it. For we are God's masterpiece. He has created us anew in Christ Jesus, so we can do the good things he planned for us long ago" (Ephesians 2:8-10).

We don't need to give God anything to make amends for our sins. What we can do is turn our attention toward healing our relationships with the people close to us. God loves us all. Now that we have been freed up from having to worry about our forgiveness from God, we can spend our lives helping others. When we make amends for the harm we've caused, we are helping others. We are acknowledging the value of their lives, their feelings, and their property.

❧

> Since our slate is clean with God, we are free to
> make things right with others.

Day 24

Proper Sensitivity
Bible Reading: 1 Corinthians 10:23-33

> We made direct amends to such people wherever possible,
> except when to do so would injure them or others.

When we're making amends, we need to be wise in the way we go about it. We may be so anxious to get things off our chest that we may blurt things out without fully considering the people involved. We need to consider how our actions may injure them. We may feel so pressured by guilt and fear of exposure that we rush ahead and make mistakes we can't erase.

Many of the people in the apostle Paul's world worshiped idols. Part of their pagan worship included sacrificing an animal, and then cooking and eating the meat. The Christians of that day struggled with the rightness of eating this sacrificed meat. Paul explained that there was nothing wrong with eating the meat, but he advised them not to eat it if it would offend another Christian's conscience. Paul said, "Don't be concerned for your own good but for the good of others. . . . It might not be a matter of conscience for you, but it is for the other person. . . . I, too, try to please everyone in everything I do. I don't just do what is best for me; I do what is best for others" (1 Corinthians 10:24, 29, 33).

When making amends we need to weigh the feelings and needs of the people who will be exposed to what we say and do. Since we are not always the best judge of what needs to be disclosed and when, we can rely on our support group for help in these decisions. We need to make sure that no one will be hurt by our disclosures.

Recovery will bring with it renewed sensitivity in our relationships.

Sexual Boundaries
Bible Reading: Leviticus 18:6-26

> We made direct amends to such people wherever possible,
> except when to do so would injure them or others.

W hile under the influence we may have violated someone's
sexual boundaries. This may have involved some form of
incest, molestation, rape, or other behavior that violated
another person's privacy. Or we may have been taken advantage
of in this way. In dealing with something so shameful and damag-
ing, it's common to be in denial. Our denial continues the cycle of
shame and devastation in the lives of everyone involved.

God made a long list of forbidden sexual practices including
rape, incest, and molestation. Offenders of these laws were sentenced to death. God listed almost every conceivable sexual violation and set up definite boundaries to protect our sexuality. Here
are a few: "None of you shall approach anyone who is near of kin
to him, to uncover his nakedness: I am the LORD" (Leviticus 18:6,
NKJV). "The nakedness of your son's daughter or your daughter's
daughter, their nakedness you shall not uncover" (18:10, NKJV). "If
a man takes his sister, his father's daughter or his mother's daughter,
and sees her nakedness and she sees his nakedness, it is a wicked
thing. . . . He shall bear his guilt" (20:17, NKJV).

Our nakedness—our sexual identity—is precious. It's meant
to be ours alone until it's given to a husband or wife. If we have
violated another's sexual boundaries, we need to admit the devastation we've caused and get help. If we've been the victim, we need
to acknowledge the violation and get help for ourselves.

❧

> By admitting our faults, we begin the process toward
> healing even the deepest of devastations.

Day 26

Giving Something Back
Bible Reading: Romans 13:7-10

> We made direct amends to such people wherever possible,
> except when to do so would injure them or others.

I t's relatively easy to know how to make amends for the property we've damaged. It's much harder to know how to make
amends when it comes to the intangible losses in our human
relationships.

The apostle Paul wrote, "Give to everyone what you owe
them: . . . give respect and honor to those who are in authority.
Owe nothing to anyone—except for your obligation to love one
another. If you love your neighbor, you will fulfill the requirements
of God's law" (Romans 13:7-8). Regarding marriage he said, "The
husband should fulfill his wife's sexual needs, and the wife should
fulfill her husband's needs. The wife gives authority over her body
to her husband, and the husband gives authority over his body to
his wife. Do not deprive each other of sexual relations" (1 Corinthians 7:3-5).

When we were under the influence, we may have failed to
show respect and honor to others. We can go back now and express
our feelings of love and respect. Whenever we're not sure what to
do, we can never go wrong by expressing love. This entails treating
others as we would like to be treated. In marriage, it's not enough
to stop giving ourselves to our addiction or to others. We need
to give ourselves back to our spouses, devoting ourselves to them
sexually and in every other appropriate way.

As Christ has loved us, so we ought to love others.

Day 27

Trusting Again
Bible Reading: Acts 5:1-11

> We made direct amends to such people wherever possible,
> except when to do so would injure them or others.

Deception and addictions go hand in hand. We've probably lost the trust of others, if we've told lies and hidden the truth. Making amends includes reestablishing a healthy trust.

In the early church many people sold their possessions and donated the money to the poor. "There was a certain man named Ananias who, with his wife, Sapphira, sold some property. He brought part of the money to the apostles, claiming it was the full amount. With his wife's consent, he kept the rest. Then Peter said, '. . . You lied to the Holy Spirit, and you kept some of the money for yourself. The property was yours to sell or not sell, as you wished. And after selling it, the money was also yours to give away. How could you do a thing like this? You weren't lying to us but to God!' As soon as Ananias heard these words, he fell to the floor and died. Everyone who heard about it was terrified. . . . About three hours later his wife came in, not knowing what had happened. Peter asked her, 'Was this the price you and your husband received for your land?' 'Yes,' she replied, 'that was the price.' . . . Instantly, she fell to the floor and died" (Acts 5:1-5, 7-8, 10).

Ananias and Sapphira had a chance to make things right by being honest with Peter. Instead they chose to continue with the deception. Our recovery program will include making amends for the lies we've told and the truth we've hidden. We are making amends every time we choose to tell the truth. We're also allowing trust to be reestablished after a history of deception.

Trust can be recovered over time by means of truth and grace.

Day 28

Testing the Water
Bible Reading: Genesis 32:13-21

We made direct amends to such people wherever possible,
except when to do so would injure them or others.

W hen we've deeply hurt someone and are preparing
to make amends, we may be hesitant. We may want
to spend some time considering the best strategy for
approaching them.

Jacob had deeply offended Esau. He was afraid as he
approached Esau after a twenty-year separation. Before they were
to meet, "Jacob stayed where he was for the night. Then he selected . . . gifts from his possessions to present to his brother, Esau."
The gift he prepared was a large herd of livestock. "He told his servants, 'Go ahead of me with the animals, but keep some distance
between the herds.' He gave these instructions to the men leading
the first group: 'When my brother, Esau, meets you, he will ask,
"Whose servants are you? Where are you going? Who owns these
animals?" You must reply, "They belong to your servant Jacob, but
they are a gift for his master Esau. Look, he is coming right behind
us."' Jacob gave the same instructions to the second and third
herdsmen and to all who followed behind the herds: 'You must say
the same thing to Esau when you meet him. And be sure to say,
"Look, your servant Jacob is right behind us."' Jacob thought, 'I will
try to appease him by sending gifts ahead of me. When I see him in
person, perhaps he will be friendly to me'" (Genesis 32:13-20).

Notice that Jacob told the servants to call Esau "master."
When Jacob left home he had stolen Esau's birthright to be master
over him. The words and gift were designed to bring peace. There
are times when it may be wise to send a gift and a pacifying message to test the waters before a face-to-face meeting.

We need to take precautions as we seek to make amends—
it's OK to test the waters.

Day 29

Long-Awaited Healing
Bible Reading: Genesis 33:1-11

We made direct amends to such people wherever possible, except when to do so would injure them or others.

R eturning to someone we've hurt is a scary thing. The passing years, lack of communication, and memories of the anger and hateful exchanges of emotion can all create a tremendous weight of fear. Even though we may make some contact through a third party, there will still be tension until we see that person face-to-face.

This was the case for Jacob upon returning to see Esau. "Then Jacob looked up and saw Esau coming with his 400 men. . . . Then Jacob went on ahead. . . . Then Esau ran to meet him and embraced him, threw his arms around his neck, and kissed him. And they both wept." After being introduced to Jacob's family, Esau asked, "'And what were all the flocks and herds I met as I came?' . . . Jacob replied, 'They are a gift, my lord, to ensure your friendship.' 'My brother, I have plenty,' Esau answered. 'Keep what you have for yourself.' But Jacob insisted, 'No, if I have found favor with you, please accept this gift from me. And what a relief to see your friendly smile. It is like seeing the face of God! Please take this gift I have brought you, for God has been very gracious to me. I have more than enough.' And because Jacob insisted, Esau finally accepted the gift" (Genesis 33:1, 3-4, 8-11).

Jacob's tremendous fear gave way to relief. The last time Jacob had seen Esau, he was being restrained to keep him from killing Jacob. With the passing of time, both of them had changed. When Jacob faced his brother, he found that there was still affection, even though they both remembered the pain.

🌿

Time can heal only those hurts we've brought out into the open.

A Time for Mending
Bible Reading: Hosea 3:1-3

We made direct amends to such people wherever possible,
except when to do so would injure them or others.

I f we have broken trust with a spouse, especially if we've violated our marriage vows, making amends will take time. Perhaps
we've made so many false promises in the past that our spouse
will need time before fully resuming the relationship.

The prophet Hosea was told by God to marry a prostitute.
His marriage was to be a living example to the nation of Israel of
her infidelity toward God. It had to hurt Hosea deeply when she
returned to her life of prostitution. Hosea said, "Then the LORD
said to me, 'Go and love your wife again, even though she commits adultery with another lover. This will illustrate that the LORD
still loves Israel, even though the people have turned to other gods
and love to worship them.' So I bought her back [from her slavery]
for fifteen pieces of silver and five bushels of barley and a measure
of wine. Then I said to her, 'You must live in my house for many
days and stop your prostitution. During this time, you will not have
sexual relations with anyone, not even with me'" (Hosea 3:1-3).

Hosea needed some time before he could be close to her
again. Sometimes the best way we can make amends with our mate
is to allow time to go by. During that time, we need to prove to our
spouse that there is no reason to fear that our wrong behavior has
continued. If a time of separation is needed to see that our commitment is real, we need to give our spouse that time and focus on our
own recovery.

As God has bought us back, we need to restore our
most important relationships.

STEP TEN

We continued to take personal inventory, and when we were
wrong, promptly admitted it.

"Keep putting into practice all you learned and received from me—
everything you heard from me and saw me doing. Then the God of peace
will be with you" (Philippians 4:9).

Looking in the Mirror
Bible Reading: James 1:21-25

> We continued to take personal inventory, and when we
> were wrong, promptly admitted it.

How many times do we look in the mirror each day? Suppose we saw someone looking in the mirror who found that he had mustard smeared around his mouth. We would find it very strange if he didn't immediately wash his face and clear up the problem. In the same way, we need to routinely look at ourselves in a spiritual mirror. Then if anything is wrong, we can make the proper adjustments.

James used a similar illustration to show how God's Word should be like a spiritual mirror in our lives. He said, "Don't just listen to God's word. You must do what it says. Otherwise, you are only fooling yourselves. For if you listen to the word and don't obey, it is like glancing at your face in a mirror. You see yourself, walk away, and forget what you look like. But if you look carefully into the perfect law that sets you free, and if you do what it says and don't forget what you heard, then God will bless you for doing it" (James 1:22-25).

We can use this illustration to support the sensibility of doing routine personal inventories. As we examine ourselves, we need to respond with immediate action if something has changed since we last looked. If we put off taking care of a problem that we see, it may soon slip our minds. Just as we would think it foolish to go all day with mustard on our face, it's absurd to notice a problem that could lead to a fall and not correct it promptly.

The mirror of God's Word helps us to see what we
should become.

Day 2

Dealing with Anger
Bible Reading: Ephesians 4:26-27

We continued to take personal inventory, and when we
were wrong, promptly admitted it.

Many of us have a hard time dealing with anger. Some of
us have a history of rage, so we try to stifle our feelings.
Others of us stuff down the feelings of anger; we pretend
they don't exist because we were never allowed to express them
in the past. If some of our problems stem from not knowing how
to express anger properly, we may try to avoid dealing with it altogether. We may try to just "put it off" and hope it goes away. Evaluating how to deal with anger appropriately is an important part of
our daily inventory.

The apostle Paul once said, "'Don't sin by letting anger control you.' Don't let the sun go down while you are still angry, for
anger gives a foothold to the devil" (Ephesians 4:26-27). One key
is to have a daily time limit for handling our feelings of anger—a
time to find a way to express the feelings and then let them go.

Dealing with anger promptly is important because when it
is left to fester, it becomes bitterness. Bitterness is anger that has
been buried and given time to grow. The Bible warns us, "Watch
out that no poisonous root of bitterness grows up to trouble you,
corrupting many" (Hebrews 12:15).

AA teaches that we should never allow ourselves to become
too hungry, angry, lonely, or tired. We can accomplish this by
promptly dealing with our anger as it occurs.

We need to deal with short-term anger before it
causes long-term destruction.

Preventing Relapse
Bible Reading: Hebrews 4:12-13

> We continued to take personal inventory, and when we
> were wrong, promptly admitted it.

Who among us takes a fall without a preceding thought,
a flirtation with desire, or a season of being enticed?
Who among us falls into a pit without walking near
the edge? Relapse doesn't appear from nowhere to grab us by the
throat. There are warning signs of complacency, confusion, and
compromise that we can watch for as a precaution.

In order to safeguard against relapse, we must ask God to
help us keep a close watch on our motives, desires, and thoughts.
He has the power to do this. "For the word of God is alive and
powerful. It is sharper than the sharpest two-edged sword, cutting
between soul and spirit, between joint and marrow. It exposes our
innermost thoughts and desires" (Hebrews 4:12). As God shines
his light into the darkness of our souls, we are enabled to see the
problems lurking there. Then we can ask for God's help in dealing
with them.

Temptation is progressive. James wrote, "Each one is tempted when he is drawn away by his own desires and enticed. Then,
when desire has conceived, it gives birth to sin; and sin, when it is
full-grown, brings forth death" (James 1:14-15, NKJV).

As we continue to take personal inventory, we can't afford
to wait for harmful behaviors to surface before dealing with them.
We need to look at the attitudes in our hearts that cause those
behaviors. In this way, we can be alerted to problem areas and
deal with our temptations before they become full-grown and
overpowering.

God's Word will help us to continue in recovery and
avoid the devastation of a relapse.

Day 4

Dangerous Pride

Bible Reading: 1 Corinthians 10:12-13

> We continued to take personal inventory, and when we
> were wrong, promptly admitted it.

W hen we begin to experience the benefits of recovery, it's easy to forget the power of our addictions. When we grow comfortable in our sobriety, we may begin to trust ourselves more than we should. We need to stay on the lookout for pride; it is a danger each of us must seek to crush.

King Solomon wisely noted, "Pride goes before destruction, and haughtiness before a fall" (Proverbs 16:18). The apostle Paul also cautioned us, "If you think you are standing strong, be careful not to fall. The temptations in your life are no different from what others experience. And God is faithful. He will not allow the temptation to be more than you can stand. When you are tempted, he will show you a way out so that you can endure" (1 Corinthians 10:12-13).

Pride whispers to us, "Don't worry, you can handle this one; you're not like those addicts anymore." It is pride that pushes us to take foolish chances by walking into situations that support our addictions. We will never be able to "handle" making provisions for our compulsive inclinations. When we start to tell ourselves that we can, we're entertaining pride, which will only lead to our downfall. Pride often masquerades behind progress. We must be vigilant to reveal and abandon it whenever it tiptoes into our lives.

> Even the pride we feel in our recovery can set us up for
> temptation and relapse.

Day 5

Spiritual Exercises
Bible Reading: 1 Timothy 4:7-8

> We continued to take personal inventory, and when we were wrong, promptly admitted it.

I t is amazing to behold what a human being can achieve through a consistent, disciplined effort. How many times have we watched seasoned gymnasts or other athletes and marveled at the ease with which they performed their sport? We realize that they developed that ability through rigorous training, which is what sets the true athlete apart from the spectator. There are parallels to the discipline of continuing our inventories.

Paul wrote to Timothy, "Train yourself to be godly. 'Physical training is good, but training for godliness is much better'" (1 Timothy 4:7-8). The word translated *training* specifically referred to the disciplined training done by gymnasts in Paul's day.

Spiritual strength and agility only come through practice. We need to develop our spiritual muscles through consistent effort and daily discipline. Continuing to take personal inventory is one of the disciplines we can develop. The Bible describes it as having our "senses exercised to discern both good and evil" (Hebrews 5:14, NKJV). Like the athlete, we can motivate ourselves to continue in a disciplined routine by looking to our reward. This kind of discipline "is much better, promising benefits in this life and in the life to come" (1 Timothy 4:8). We must not expect overnight results. As we continue practicing these disciplines each day, we'll eventually grow to enjoy the benefits.

Our continued inventory will keep us spiritually fit and strong in the face of temptation.

Personal Boundaries
Bible Reading: Genesis 31:45-55

> We continued to take personal inventory, and when we
> were wrong, promptly admitted it.

We all have particular weaknesses and it is often helpful to establish personal boundary lines to support these weaker areas. We may need to clearly define our commitments to others; we may need to agree on certain limitations in order to maintain peace. Once the boundaries have been established, honesty is needed to maintain them. An assessment of our honesty in keeping our commitments needs to be part of our regular inventory.

Jacob and his father-in-law, Laban, had some conflicts. As they were working them out, they entered into an agreement by drawing a clearly defined boundary line and setting up a monument to remind them of that commitment. "'May the LORD keep watch between us to make sure that we keep this covenant when we are out of each other's sight. . . . See this pile of stones,' Laban continued, 'and see this monument I have set between us. They stand between us as witnesses of our vows. . . .' So Jacob took an oath before the fearsome God of his father, Isaac, to respect the boundary line" (Genesis 31:49, 51-53).

Restoring trust in our relationships is part of recovery. To do this we should define our expectations and cautiously enter into commitments. We are not merely responsible for what the other person knows about. We are personally responsible for our own honesty before the watchful eyes of God. These relational commitments are not to be entered into lightly. But when we make them, they must be vigilantly maintained.

❧

Honest inventories help us maintain boundaries
important to our recovery.

Positive Thoughts
Bible Reading: Philippians 4:8-9

> We continued to take personal inventory, and when we
> were wrong, promptly admitted it.

A s we take personal inventory, we will probably be inclined to focus on the bad things in our lives. Early on in recovery it's hard to see much that's very good. It's easy to get our perspective out of focus, allowing pessimism to grow. We may even feel awkward about taking inventory of the good things in our lives.

The apostle Paul advised, "Fix your thoughts on what is true, and honorable, and right, and pure, and lovely, and admirable. Think about things that are excellent and worthy of praise. Keep putting into practice all you learned and received from me—everything you heard from me and saw me doing. Then the God of peace will be with you" (Philippians 4:8-9).

Balance is an important part of our recovery. Our daily balance sheet needs to have two sides, since there is both good and bad in all of us. We'll make choices that are right and choices that are wrong. We may take a step back now and again, but we should also take into account the two steps we took forward. Let's not get overwhelmed by focusing on the failure in ourselves and others. It is good to confess our wrongs and receive God's forgiveness on a daily basis. But once we've done this, it's time to stop and consider what remains in our lives. We should look for everything that is right and pure, the things that are lovely and admirable. Let's take some time during our continuing inventory to count our blessings. Let's take note of everything we can praise God for in our lives!

❦

What we keep in our minds and hearts often
determines what we do and say.

Perseverance
Bible Reading: 2 Timothy 2:3-7

> We continued to take personal inventory, and when we
> were wrong, promptly admitted it.

Recovery is a lifelong process. There will be times when we grow tired and weary, times when we want to throw in the towel. We'll experience pain, fear, and a host of other emotions. We'll win some battles but lose others in our war to gain wholeness. We may get discouraged at times when we can't see any progress, even though we've been working hard. But through it all, we must persevere or lose the ground we've gained.

The apostle Paul used three illustrations to teach about perseverance. He wrote to Timothy, "Endure suffering along with me, as a good soldier of Christ Jesus. Soldiers don't get tied up in the affairs of civilian life, for then they cannot please the officer who enlisted them. And athletes cannot win the prize unless they follow the rules. And hardworking farmers should be the first to enjoy the fruit of their labor. Think about what I am saying. The Lord will help you understand all these things" (2 Timothy 2:3-7).

Like the soldier, we're in a war that we can only win if we fight to the end. Like the athlete, we must train for a new way of life and follow the steps of recovery to the finish line. Like the farmer, we must do our work in every season and then wait patiently until we see the growth. If we stop working our program before reaching our aim, we may lose everything we've fought for, trained ourselves for, and worked hard for.

> You cannot win the race for recovery by going just
> part of the way.

Our Defender
Bible Reading: 1 John 2:1-2

We continued to take personal inventory, and when we were wrong, promptly admitted it.

A t times we may feel like we're the worst sinner in the whole world. We just seem to keep doing the same things over and over again. We feel guilty! Can God just wink at our sin and pretend that it's all right? How can he repeatedly forgive us for committing the same wrongs?

The apostle John said, "My dear children, I am writing this to you so that you will not sin. But if anyone does sin, we have an advocate who pleads our case before the Father. He is Jesus Christ, the one who is truly righteous. He himself is the sacrifice that atones for our sins—and not only our sins but the sins of all the world" (1 John 2:1-2).

God takes sin very seriously. As a righteous Judge, he can't just ignore sin and act like it doesn't matter. But we can be forgiven completely and repeatedly. The words used here are legal terms. Jesus is our advocate, a defense attorney in a court of law, who intercedes for us, the lawbreakers. But he is not only the defense attorney; he's also "the sacrifice that atones for our sins." This means that his death has been accepted by the court as admissible payment for all of our sins. We're all guilty. The sentence is death! But our sentence has already been paid by Jesus, if we've trusted in him. When we bring our sin to Jesus, he goes back to the Judge on our behalf, reminding him that the sentence has already been served.

There is nothing in our lives that Jesus can't handle.

Day 10

No Shortcuts
Bible Reading: Matthew 4:1-11

> We continued to take personal inventory and when we were
> wrong promptly admitted it.

W e may be searching for a shortcut to happiness. The road
of life often takes us through painful places we'd rather
avoid. Some of us have gotten off the right track, lured
away by hopes of a faster and easier way to "the good life."

Jesus faced this same temptation. He was destined to
become the King of all the earth. The plan was that he would
come to earth as a man, live a sinless life, die to pay for our sins,
rise from the dead, and go back to heaven to wait for those who
would be his. Then he would return to earth to claim his people
and his rightful place as King of kings. Satan offered him a shortcut. "The devil . . . showed him [Jesus] all the kingdoms of the
world and their glory. 'I will give it all to you,' he said, 'if you will
kneel down and worship me.' 'Get out of here, Satan,' Jesus told
him. 'For the Scriptures say, "You must worship the LORD your
God and serve only him"' (Matthew 4:8-10). If Jesus had fallen
for this trick, he would have sinned and lost everything.

We need to beware of "shortcuts" that take us even one step
outside of God's will. We're warned, "Resist the devil, and he will
flee from you" (James 4:7). This resistance is sometimes shown by
ignoring offers that are "too good to be true." There are really no
quick fixes in life. The path of recovery can be long and hard, but
many have gone before us and made it. As we stay on the path,
taking one step at a time, we'll find the good things in life.

> On our journey toward recovery, shortcuts are only
> stepping-stones to a relapse.

Day 11

Daily Recovery
Bible Reading: Romans 7:18-25

We continued to take personal inventory, and when we
were wrong, promptly admitted it.

We may feel like we're just no good. Deep down inside
there is a sense of brokenness that is a constant
reminder of our humanity. Hopefully, we'll get to a
place where our behavior is under control and we'll be able to
maintain sobriety. But we should always be aware that as long
as we're in this human body, we'll have to contend with our
lower nature.

Paul said of himself, "I know that nothing good lives in me,
that is, in my sinful nature. I want to do what is right, but I can't.
. . . There is another power within me that is at war with my mind.
This power makes me a slave to the sin that is still within me"
(Romans 7:18, 23). King David described God's tenderness toward
us because of our human condition: "The LORD is like a father to
his children, tender and compassionate to those who fear him. For
he knows how weak we are; he remembers we are only dust. Our
days on earth are like grass" (Psalm 103:13-15).

No matter how far we progress, our lower nature will always
be inclined toward and susceptible to the lure of our addictions.
We can't afford to forget this or let down our guard. Paul wrote,
"Make no provision for the flesh, to fulfill its lusts" (Romans 13:14,
NKJV). It is this realization that should convince us that maintaining sobriety is something we will need to nurture for the rest of our
lives, one day at a time.

We will always be tempted by our old lives; but we need
not always fall prey to them.

Day 12

Self-Nourishment
Bible Reading: 1 Samuel 14:20-45

We continued to take personal inventory, and when we
were wrong, promptly admitted it.

W e once used our addictions to find comfort and to help
us cope with life's daily battles. In recovery, we may
have become so focused on the battle at hand that
we've neglected our basic physical needs. We may have forgotten
our need to enjoy some of the sweet things of life. Failure to take
care of ourselves can leave us weak and vulnerable.

During a difficult battle, King Saul had declared, "'Let a
curse fall on anyone who eats before evening—before I have full
revenge on my enemies.' . . . But Jonathan had not heard his
father's command, and he dipped the end of his stick into a piece
of honeycomb and ate the honey. After he had eaten it, he felt
refreshed. But one of the men saw him and said, 'Your father made
the army take a strict oath that anyone who eats food today will
be cursed. That is why everyone is weary and faint.' 'My father has
made trouble for us all!' Jonathan exclaimed. 'A command like
that only hurts us. See how refreshed I am now that I have eaten
this little bit of honey'" (1 Samuel 14:24, 27-29).

When we're in recovery, we already feel deprived. We need
to make sure that we're being good to ourselves in healthy ways,
eating good food and tasting some of the sweet things that life naturally provides. Recovery isn't a time for unnecessary deprivation.
If we allow ourselves to become too hungry, physically or emotionally, we'll find ourselves weary and less able to fight the battles we
face each day.

❧

We should be more interested in what is right than
in looking good.

STEP TEN

Day 13

True Wisdom
Bible Reading: James 3:17-18

> We continued to take personal inventory, and when we
> were wrong, promptly admitted it.

Many of us in recovery are learning to think and act in new ways. So we may find it hard to recognize true wisdom, even when it's staring us in the face. We may need some guidelines to help us identify wisdom in our thoughts and choices of action.

According to the Bible, there are two aspects of wisdom: the spiritual and the practical. Spiritual wisdom gives insight into the true nature of things. It includes things like, "ask God to give you complete knowledge of his will and to give you spiritual wisdom and understanding. . . . Learn to know God better and better" (Colossians 1:9-10). Special wisdom is also sometimes given "that your hearts will be flooded with light so that you can understand the confident hope he has given to those he called" (Ephesians 1:18).

Wisdom can be evaluated by its qualities. The Bible tells us that God's wisdom is "first of all pure. It is also peace loving, gentle at all times, and willing to yield to others. It is full of mercy and good deeds. It shows no favoritism and is always sincere" (James 3:17).

On the practical level, our wisdom can be judged by whether our actions conform to God's instructions or not. God's instructions were given to us because they naturally lead to healthy living. Using them, we can find the wisdom we need to walk progressively toward wholeness. This can be one of the standards we use in our continuing daily inventory.

❧

> True wisdom will always lead those who follow it toward
> peace and wholeness.

293

Day 14

Moderation in Everything
Bible Reading: Hebrews 12:16-17

> We continued to take personal inventory, and when we
> were wrong, promptly admitted it.

Our appetites can overtake us and make us their slaves.
Perfectly good activities can get us into trouble when
we fail to practice them in moderation. Or there may be
times when we don't feed our appetites in a balanced way. Then
we find ourselves so starved that we fall to our addictions at the
first opportunity.

This happened to Esau. One day he came home so hungry
that he promised his birthright to his younger brother in exchange
for a bowl of porridge. We're warned, "Make sure that no one
is immoral or godless like Esau, who traded his birthright as the
firstborn son for a single meal. You know that afterward, when he
wanted his father's blessing, he was rejected. It was too late for
repentance, even though he begged with bitter tears" (Hebrews
12:16-17). The apostle Paul wrote, "You say, 'I am allowed to do
anything'—but not everything is good for you. And even though
'I am allowed to do anything,' I must not become a slave to anything" (1 Corinthians 6:12).

We need to satisfy our appetites in appropriate ways, so we
don't become starved and become more susceptible to temptation.
There may be some good things that have such control over us that
it's best to avoid them altogether. If we allow the demands of our
appetites to become overpowering, we risk losing things (or people)
that we might never get back.

❧

> We must learn to evaluate the long-range effects of our
> choices and actions.

Softened Hearts

Bible Reading: Matthew 13:1-9, 18-23

> We continued to take personal inventory, and when we
> were wrong, promptly admitted it.

As we move through our recovery, our attitudes can change. We long to live a productive life. We may be exposing ourselves to new ideas, even to the Bible, much more than we ever did before. Yet as we examine ourselves in our personal inventory, we may not see the kind of growth we had hoped for. If this is true, we may need to ask whether our minds and emotions are really receptive to the new thoughts and truths we're hearing.

Jesus told a story to illustrate four ways that the human heart responds to God's Word. Describing the first way, he said, "A farmer went out to plant some seeds. As he scattered them across his field, some seeds fell on a footpath, and the birds came and ate them. . . . The seed that fell on the footpath represents those who hear the message about the Kingdom and don't understand it. Then the evil one comes and snatches away the seed that was planted in their hearts" (Matthew 13:3-4, 19).

We may find the Bible to be confusing. Maybe we're not able to understand because we are defensive toward God, still feeling that he's rejected us. Perhaps we're angry because of the pain he's allowed in our lives. It won't do us any good, however, if God's Word is getting into our minds, but not our hearts. We can ask God to help us understand and overcome whatever is causing our resistance toward him. As our hearts grow softer, we will begin to see positive spiritual growth.

❧

> We don't need to understand everything; God will open
> our minds and soften our hearts.

Day 16

Dealing with Disappointment
Bible Reading: Matthew 13:1-9, 18-23

> We continued to take personal inventory, and when we
> were wrong, promptly admitted it.

W hen we first began our recovery, we may have been surprised to find that God wasn't the enemy we'd thought
him to be. Perhaps we were enthusiastic about our
new relationship with God. We may have expected that when
we turned our will and our life over to God, the struggle with our
addictions would miraculously disappear. That sounded great!
Finally there was an escape from the pain! But as we progressed in
our recovery, we discovered that we still had to live life in the real
world. We had access to God and his power, but we still had to
fight the battles. This may have caused us to get discouraged about
our relationship with God, causing our spiritual life to wilt.

Jesus described a similar condition using a farming illustration: "Other seeds fell on shallow soil with underlying rock. The
seeds sprouted quickly because the soil was shallow. But the plants
soon wilted under the hot sun, and since they didn't have deep
roots, they died" (Matthew 13:5-6). Jesus explained, "The seed on
the rocky soil represents those who hear the message and immediately receive it with joy. But since they don't have deep roots, they
don't last long. They fall away as soon as they have problems or are
persecuted for believing God's word" (Matthew 13:20-21).

God never promised an easy life. If we're disappointed, it's
because our expectations were unrealistic. Have we allowed life's
troubles to destroy our budding faith?

※

> By continuing with our personal inventories, we
> allow the seeds of recovery to take root.

Day 17

Weeding the Garden
Bible Reading: Matthew 13:1-9, 18-23

> We continued to take personal inventory, and when we were wrong, promptly admitted it.

W hile growing in our recovery we may find that weeds crop up in our lives, threatening to choke out the good. We may find ourselves cynical and mistrusting; we become so self-centered that our relationships with others suffer. We may learn to take care of our own needs, which is healthy, but we may go beyond that to where we become greedy and demanding. We may be caught up with worries and fears of various kinds or lapse back into bouts of self-pity. These types of weeds can choke out the good that's growing out of our recovery.

Jesus described this danger in his illustration about the four types of soil. He said, "Other seeds fell among thorns that grew up and choked out the tender plants" (Matthew 13:7). Then he explained, "The seed that fell among the thorns represents those who hear God's word, but all too quickly the message is crowded out by the worries of this life and the lure of wealth, so no fruit is produced" (Matthew 13:22).

As we continue to take personal inventory, we need to watch for the weeds that spring up in our lives. We may have had the chance to taste a better way of life. But once the crisis of confronting our addiction is past, there are new types of distractions that can choke out our spiritual life. We need to take a few moments each day to weed out all the greed, worry, fear, selfishness, cynicism, self-pity, and other negative tendencies that may take root in our hearts. Our support group can help us see when these "weeds" start inhibiting our growth.

> Continuing our personal inventory is like weeding a garden; it allows the good things to grow.

297

Day 18

Open to Growth
Bible Reading: Matthew 13:1-9, 18-23

We continued to take personal inventory, and when we
were wrong, promptly admitted it.

Our initial goal was to stop the addictions that made our
lives unmanageable. Once that was done, we may have
experienced some confusion about what should come next.
We may now wonder what life should be like with our addictions
out of the way. Being free from our addictions may produce opportunities for us to put our talents and abilities to work. If we don't
find worthwhile outlets for the new life growing in us, we may
become frustrated.

One of Jesus' parables relates to this. He said, "Other seeds
fell on fertile soil, and they produced a crop that was thirty, sixty,
and even a hundred times as much as had been planted!" (Matthew 13:8). He explained, "The seed that fell on good soil represents those who truly hear and understand God's word and produce
a harvest of thirty, sixty, or even a hundred times as much as had
been planted!" (Matthew 13:23).

Jesus described how God's Word, received and understood,
can take root in people's lives. Its growth there will cause them
to develop into the productive people God created them to be.
There's great potential within each of us! As we accept God's
perspective on our lives and respond openly to him, new life will
sprout in us. This new life will then find expression in our talents
and abilities. There's a world of opportunities for growth. As we
take our inventory, we need to check for signs of frustration about
not using our talents and look for ways to develop them.

As we admit our wrongs, the seeds of God's goodness
and love blossom in our lives.

Day 19

New Life
Bible Reading: 1 Peter 2:1-3

We continued to take personal inventory, and when we
were wrong, promptly admitted it.

Recovery often brings us into a new life. Everything may
seem so new to us! We may feel like a little child, somewhat
helpless and not yet able to take care of ourselves the way
other people do. A new life is great, but we still need to grow up.
As we continue to take personal inventory we can monitor how
regularly we are feeding ourselves on God's Word, which will help
us grow. We can also keep our eyes open for the feelings and behavior patterns that characterized our old life. It's not unusual for some
of them to crop up again.

The apostle Peter wrote, "So get rid of all evil behavior. Be
done with all deceit, hypocrisy, jealousy, and all unkind speech.
Like newborn babies, you must crave pure spiritual milk so that
you will grow into a full experience of salvation. Cry out for this
nourishment, now that you have had a taste of the Lord's kindness"
(1 Peter 2:1-3). Here is another rendering of Peter's words: "If you
have tasted the Lord's goodness and kindness, cry for more, as a
baby cries for milk. Eat God's Word—read it, think about it—and
grow strong in the Lord and be saved."

Our old patterns of hatred, pretending, dishonesty, jealousy,
gossip, and the like have to be dealt with as they arise. They will
show up! But as they do, we need to get rid of them, one by one.
We also need to feed on God's Word every day so that we can continue in to grow in our new life.

🌱

The longer we continue in recovery, the more we want to recover.

Day 20

A Sensitive Conscience
Bible Reading: 1 Timothy 1:18-20

> We continued to take personal inventory, and when we
> were wrong, promptly admitted it.

W e've probably experienced the feelings that result when we do something our conscience has warned us against. We've felt the shame, and we may have distanced ourselves from God as a result. We may find that our conscience has been revived as we've worked through recovery. A healthy conscience is a necessary tool for recognizing wrong and taking a personal inventory. There are things we can do to help reactivate a conscience that has been damaged or put to sleep.

Paul told Timothy, "Cling to your faith in Christ, and keep your conscience clear" (1 Timothy 1:19). The word *conscience* literally means "having a co-perception." It describes the act of perceiving our will and the will of God simultaneously. As we learn what the will of God is, we can set that perception alongside our own, thus strengthening our conscience. As we exercise our choice to do what is right (i.e., God's will), our conscience will be clear.

One way to strengthen our conscience is to apply ourselves to study the Bible. Paul said, "Work hard so you can present yourself to God and receive his approval. Be a good worker, one who does not need to be ashamed and who correctly explains the word of truth" (2 Timothy 2:15). Doing these things will help us become better able to recognize the sin in our lives, so we can promptly deal with it.

❧

> When we've discovered what God wants of us, we've also
> discovered the shortest road to inner peace.

Day 21

Filling the Empty Places
Bible Reading: Luke 11:24-26

We continued to take personal inventory, and when we were wrong, promptly admitted it.

Our addictions once played an important role in our lives. We used them to help us cope with an emptiness, a nameless pain, or some other lack, deep inside. We may have stopped using or acting out our addictions, but have we filled the needs that prompted them? Have we dealt with the empty places that the addictions once filled?

Jesus said, "When an evil spirit leaves a person, it goes into the desert, searching for rest. But when it finds none, it says, 'I will return to the person I came from.' So it returns and finds that its former home is all swept and in order. Then the spirit finds seven other spirits more evil than itself, and they all enter the person and live there. And so that person is worse off than before" (Luke 11:24-26).

Jesus saw into the spiritual realm as clearly as he saw into the natural realm. He knew demonic oppression when he saw it. For us the picture isn't as clear. It's hard for us to know how much the spiritual forces of darkness are involved in our addictions. We can use this as a good analogy, at the least, and perhaps as a glimpse into a spiritual reality behind our addictions. Either way, we have a problem if we get rid of something bad and fail to fill the vacancy with something strong and good.

The failure to fill the vacancy can lead to a relapse. We need to consider whether our lives are being filled with God's power. We also need to make sure that the areas of vulnerability in our lives are being filled in healthy ways.

The empty places in our lives can be filled only by God.

Day 22

Admitting Our Flaws
Bible Reading: James 4:7-10

> We continued to take personal inventory, and when we
> were wrong, promptly admitted it.

For those of us who tend toward perfectionism, admitting we are wrong can be very difficult. Great fear may be generated at the thought of admitting our flaws, faults, and weaknesses. Sometimes the fear can be so intense that we feel like we would be utterly destroyed if we admitted all of our wrongs. This fragile sense of self is often hidden by a false front of confidence. We may even be perceived as a know-it-all. But in reality, it's our lack of confidence that keeps us from being able to admit it when we're wrong.

James wrote, "Humble yourselves before the Lord, and he will lift you up in honor" (James 4:10). The apostle Peter said, "Humble yourselves under the mighty power of God, and at the right time he will lift you up in honor" (1 Peter 5:6).

Our feelings of weakness and worthlessness are not a surprise to God. King David once wrote, "The LORD is like a father to his children, tender and compassionate to those who fear him. For he knows how weak we are; he remembers we are only dust" (Psalm 103:13-14).

When we take our personal inventory we are not told to admit our faults to everyone. If we find it hard to admit them openly, we can start by admitting them to God. By humbling ourselves before him in this way, we'll receive his help and he will lift us up. As our trust in God grows, we'll be freed from the fear of being destroyed when we admit our faults.

> Admitting our flaws to God is the first step toward
> admitting them to others.

Helping Hands
Bible Reading: Matthew 18:19-20

We continued to take personal inventory, and when we were wrong, promptly admitted it.

We've probably already been convinced that we need the support of others in our recovery. We know whom we can trust to be supportive and who will be destructive. We know who will help us walk along the path of God's will, and who will just preach at us and condemn us. We know those who struggle as we do, who can be depended on for encouragement when we slip up. We're also learning that we can be a support to others.

James advised, "Confess your sins to each other and pray for each other so that you may be healed. The earnest prayer of a righteous person has great power and produces wonderful results" (James 5:16). Jesus told us, "If two of you agree here on earth concerning anything you ask, my Father in heaven will do it for you. For where two or three gather together as my followers, I am there among them" (Matthew 18:19-20).

There is great power in coming together and being concerned for one another's needs. We all need encouragement and support as we go through the steps of recovery, especially when we have to deal with weaknesses and wrongs. We need to nurture relationships with real, flesh-and-blood people who are willing to accept us in our imperfect condition. We need to be praying with them when we stumble, and praying for them when they do. We can help each other see areas that need attention; areas we might miss all alone. We should devote some of our time and energy to maintaining the positive relationships that encourage our recovery.

❦

A cord with three strands is not easily broken.

Day 24

An Honest Assessment
Bible Reading: Philippians 3:11-14

We continued to take personal inventory, and when we
were wrong, promptly admitted it.

L ife is a journey that takes us beyond recovery from our past
and into a hopeful future. By realizing we haven't "arrived,"
we can experience the excitement of pursuit. We can know
the thrill of seeking after and achieving our goals. We don't have to
pretend to be perfect or to know everything. We don't need to fear
that one wrong move will destroy everything.

Part The apostle Paul said, "One way or another I will experience
the resurrection from the dead! I don't mean to say that I have
already achieved these things or that I have already reached perfection. But I press on to possess that perfection for which Christ
Jesus first possessed me. No, dear brothers and sisters, I have not
achieved it, but I focus on this one thing: Forgetting the past, . . .
I press on to reach the end of the race and receive the heavenly
prize for which God, through Christ Jesus, is calling us" (Philippians 3:11-14).

Part Paul could commit himself to know the "mighty power that
raised him [Christ] from the dead" (Philippians 3:10) and admit his
imperfections in the same breath. So can we! We haven't learned
everything we need to know. So we, too, can pursue the future
and leave the past behind us. As we take our inventory we need to
check to see that we don't get stuck in the past. We need to make
sure that recovery becomes a bridge to a bright new future instead
of a circle of revolving past hurts.

The bridge to a hopeful future cannot be crossed
with burdens from the past.

Healing Hunger
Bible Reading: John 6:32-35

> We continued to take personal inventory, and when we were wrong, promptly admitted it.

There is a hunger in every human soul—a hunger for true love, a hunger to be understood, a hunger to be valued. There's a hunger for God. He created that hunger to drive us to himself. We may have fed our hunger with the stuff that tasted good emotionally, but it was never satisfied.

The Lord spoke through the prophet Isaiah asking, "Is anyone thirsty? Come and drink—even if you have no money! Come, take your choice of wine or milk—it's all free! Why spend your money on food that does not give you strength? Why pay for food that does you no good? Listen to me, and you will eat what is good. You will enjoy the finest food" (Isaiah 55:1-2).

Jesus said, "And now he [my Father] offers you the true bread from heaven. The true bread of God is the one who comes down from heaven and gives life to the world. . . . I am the bread of life. Whoever comes to me will never be hungry again. Whoever believes in me will never be thirsty" (John 6:32-33, 35).

Jesus Christ claimed to be the Person we're all really hungry for. We could be just filling ourselves up on meetings and even religious rituals without nourishing ourselves on a relationship with him. We may not be using our previous addictions to deal with our hunger, but are we really finding satisfaction? What are we doing to make sure that we're taking in the "true bread," which can satisfy the deepest of needs?

> Our dependencies cannot fill the void that only God was meant to fill.

Day 26

Opening Up
Bible Reading: Acts 13:21-23

We continued to take personal inventory, and when we
were wrong, promptly admitted it.

W e may be inclined to cover up our wrongs or insist that
our way is right, even though it's contrary to what God
says in the Bible. This attitude may have played a significant role in our past problems. We may not yet believe that it's better to honestly and repeatedly admit our wrongs than to work hard
at covering them up.

In recounting the history of Israel, the apostle Paul said,
"The people begged for a king, and God gave them Saul . . . who
reigned for forty years. But God removed Saul and replaced him
with David, a man about whom God said, 'I have found David . . .
, a man after my own heart. He will do everything I want him to
do'" (Acts 13:21-22).

King Saul looked great on the outside. He was tall and
handsome. He seemed to always have an answer to cover up his
wrongdoing. But God finally removed him from the kingship
because whenever he was wrong, he refused to admit it! (See
1 Samuel 15.) God replaced him with David. We might assume
that David was an exemplary man. But actually, David was a man
who committed many terrible sins, including adultery and murder. The one quality that distinguished him from Saul was that he
always agreed with God's view of morality. He immediately admitted his sins when he knew he had violated God's commands.

God isn't looking for someone who looks good on the surface. God has unfailing mercies and love for us when we agree with
his commands and admit our faults when we don't measure up.

❧

A spring cleaning is only possible after the dirty
rooms have been opened.

Repeated Forgiveness
Bible Reading: Romans 5:3-5

> We continued to take personal inventory, and when we
> were wrong, promptly admitted it.

We may grow impatient with ourselves when we continue to run into the same sins over and over again. This may cause us to get discouraged, or we may be afraid that we are doomed to relapse.

Peter asked Jesus, "Lord, how often should I forgive someone who sins against me? Seven times? 'No, not seven times,' Jesus replied, 'but seventy times seven!'" (Matthew 18:21-22). If this is to be our attitude toward others, doesn't it make sense that we should extend the same grace to ourselves? We need to be patient with ourselves.

Paul wrote, "We can rejoice, too, when we run into problems and trials, for we know that they help us develop endurance. And endurance develops strength of character, and character strengthens our confident hope of salvation. And this hope will not lead to disappointment. For we know how dearly God loves us, because he has given us the Holy Spirit to fill our hearts with his love" (Romans 5:3-5).

Learning to wait patiently is an important characteristic for us to develop. Each time we admit wrong and accept God's forgiveness, our hope of salvation has a chance to be exercised and to grow stronger. We no longer have to hide in shame every time we slip. We can admit our wrongs and move on. God's love is reaffirmed every time we rely on it. In this way, God helps us to hold our heads high no matter what happens.

❧

Our repeated failures afford us repeated opportunities
for healing and growth.

Recurrent Sins
Bible Reading: 1 John 1:8-10

> We continued to take personal inventory, and when we
> were wrong, promptly admitted it.

W e may feel awkward about bringing our recurrent sins before God. We may be embarrassed by the number of times we've had to deal with the same issues—issues that stubbornly refuse to be washed away. We may imagine that God is collecting a long list to be used against us.

The apostle John wrote, "If we claim we have no sin, we are only fooling ourselves and not living in the truth. But if we confess our sins to him, he is faithful and just to forgive us our sins and to cleanse us from all wickedness. [And it is perfectly proper for God to do this for us because Christ died to wash away our sins.] If we claim we have not sinned, we are calling God a liar" (1 John 1:8-10).

To confess means to agree with God that what he declares to be wrong really is. To do this, we need to recognize our wrongs when they occur. Notice that he says he will forgive us and cleanse of from *all* wickedness. Each time we confess a sin it is washed away. Our lives are like slates that have been wiped clean. Our sins are not recorded on some celestial list. They're gone forever! And each time we confess a sin we've dealt with before, it's forgiven all over again. Some areas of our lives need more cleaning than others! God doesn't get angry when we come back to him again and again. This is the process he set up to cleanse the areas in our lives that cause the most trouble. There's no need to feel awkward. God wants us to come every time we sin.

❧

Confession opens up our hearts to God's cleansing power.

Day 29

Healing Fellowship
Bible Reading: 1 Thessalonians 5:12-13

We continued to take personal inventory, and when we
were wrong, promptly admitted it.

W e've all had different experiences at the churches we've
attended. Some of us may have felt condemned and
shamed at a church when we desperately needed its
help. We may fear rejection. We may wish we were part of a church
but don't know how to find a good one. Or we may feel out of place
in the church we presently attend. Some of us may think that we
don't need a church, that we can do fine on our own.

The Bible makes it clear that no church is perfect, but
we're still told to join with a group of Christians. It is through our
relationships in the church that God molds us. The apostle Paul
once wrote, "Honor those who are your leaders in the Lord's work.
They work hard among you and give you spiritual guidance. Show
them great respect and wholehearted love because of their work"
(1 Thessalonians 5:12-13).

The Bible also says, "Let us not neglect our meeting
together, as some people do, but encourage one another" (Hebrews
10:25). The church should be a place where believers can encourage and give each other guidance. They should urge each other to
pursue a godly course of conduct. Notice that Paul's advice looks
to the future rather than looking back. In the church context, God
can raise up people to encourage us to keep moving ahead in our
spiritual development. Their perspective can help us to continue
taking stock of our lives as we recover.

The church community should provide help,
encouragement, and direction.

Human Weakness
Bible Reading: Zechariah 4:6-7

> We continued to take personal inventory, and when we
> were wrong, promptly admitted it.

As we continue to take personal inventory, we will be reminded that we are human. We are powerless in ourselves, weak and constantly in need of God's mighty power. Just before Jesus ascended into heaven, he told his disciples, "And now I will send the Holy Spirit, just as my Father promised. But stay here in the city until the Holy Spirit comes and fills you with power from heaven" (Luke 24:49). When Zerubbabel was given the responsibility for rebuilding the Jewish Temple, God sent him this message: "It is not by force nor by strength, but by my Spirit, says the LORD of Heaven's Armies. Nothing, not even a mighty mountain, will stand in Zerubbabel's way; it will become a level plain before him! And when Zerubbabel sets the final stone of the Temple in place, the people will shout: 'May God bless it! May God bless it!'" (Zechariah 4:6-7).

Every day we need to rely on God's Spirit to fill us with the power we need to live our new life. Just as Zerubbabel could not rely on his own might and power, we cannot trust in our own strength. But we can see our admitted weaknesses swallowed up in the power of God. We can succeed and scale whatever mountains we face by the power of God's Spirit. When we learn to live this way, we will be full of thanksgiving for God's mercy. We'll be able to tell everyone that it is the grace of God that keeps us.

Our weaknesses provide endless opportunities
for God to prove his power.

STEP ELEVEN

We sought through prayer and meditation to improve
our conscious contact with God, praying only for knowledge
of his will for us and the power to carry it out.

*"Those who trust in the LORD will find new strength. They
will soar high on wings like eagles. They will run and not
grow weary. They will walk and not faint"*
(Isaiah 40:31).

Day 1

Joy in God's Presence
Bible Reading: Psalm 65:1-4

> We sought through prayer and meditation to improve our
> conscious contact with God, praying only for knowledge of
> his will for us and the power to carry it out.

M ost of us need to desire something before we will whole-heartedly seek after it. Until we realize how much God loves us and cares about the details of our lives, we won't want to pray to him. Until we sincerely believe that he has completely forgiven us, we will be ashamed to face him. If we hold to our misconceptions about God, this step will be a formidable chore rather than a joy.

The life of King David gives us hope. Long after he had come face-to-face with his own sinfulness, he was able to sing, "What mighty praise, O God, belongs to you in Zion. We will fulfill our vows to you, for you answer our prayers. All of us must come to you. Though we are overwhelmed by our sins, you forgive them all. What joy for those you choose to bring near, those who live in your holy courts. What festivities await us inside your holy Temple" (Psalm 65:1-4). God wants us to be like those who live and serve in his temple, walking freely into his presence. He wants us to know that we are welcome and valued before him. (See also Matthew 10:29-31.)

The place where God lives can be a place of joy and happiness for us now. We can look forward to spending time with him and living in his presence every day.

❦

It is essential for our recovery that we draw close to God.

Pools of Blessing
Bible Reading: Psalm 84:5-11

> We sought through prayer and meditation to improve our
> conscious contact with God, praying only for knowledge of
> his will for us and the power to carry it out.

Where do we find the desire to seek after the knowledge of his will for us and the power to carry it out? We probably realize that seeking after our own will only brought us misery. Instead of happiness we found sorrow; instead of power we found that we became powerless. In following our own will we ended up depressed and exhausted, on a road leading nowhere.

The desire to seek after the knowledge of God's will comes from realizing that God's plan for us is good. The psalmist wrote, "What joy for those whose strength comes from the LORD, who have set their minds on a pilgrimage to Jerusalem. When they walk through the Valley of Weeping, it will become a place of refreshing springs. The autumn rains will clothe it with blessings. They will continue to grow stronger, and each of them will appear before God in Jerusalem" (Psalm 84:5-7).

Those who long and pray for God's will are on a road that leads to happiness. We may still walk through the "Valley of Weeping," but out of the sorrow will spring new life. Instead of depression, exhaustion, and a road to nowhere, we will find joy, strength, and a road that leads to heaven and the presence of a loving God.

> We are not alone in the Valley of Weeping; God
> walks there with us.

Day 3

Meditation

Bible Reading: Psalm 1:1-3

> We sought through prayer and meditation to improve our conscious contact with God, praying only for knowledge of his will for us and the power to carry it out.

I magination exerts amazing power! Many of us struggle with obsessive thoughts. Our imaginations are haunted by images of doing the things we crave. No matter how hard we try to exert willpower over our imaginations, our willpower loses the battle sooner or later. Instead of trying to summon up more willpower, perhaps we should try a different tactic.

The Lord told Joshua, "Study this Book of Instruction continually. Meditate on it day and night so you will be sure to obey everything written in it. Only then will you prosper" (Joshua 1:8). When the psalmist described people not caught up in evil, he said, "They delight in the law of the LORD, meditating on it day and night" (Psalm 1:2). Each of these passages describes meditating as a key to success in following God's will for our lives.

The word *meditate* in the Bible means "to imagine" and "to ponder repeatedly." The key to winning the battle over obsessive thoughts is to fill our imaginations with images of a life lived according to God's plan. There's a better way of life for us. When we begin to "delight in" imagining what that would be like, we will find that we begin to win more of our inner battles.

> The more we bask in the joy of God's presence, the more we will discover joy within.

Day 4

Powerful Secrets

Bible Reading: Psalm 119:9-11

> We sought through prayer and meditation to improve our
> conscious contact with God, praying only for knowledge of
> his will for us and the power to carry it out.

The secrets we hide away have enormous power over our lives. How many of our addictive/compulsive behaviors were hidden or covered up? When we took the step to admit the exact nature of our wrongs to another human being, we were amazed at the way the addiction lost power as it was exposed. The power of hidden behaviors and secrets can work for us as well as against us.

David said, "I have hidden your [God's] word in my heart, that I might not sin against you" (Psalm 119: 11). The word rendered *hidden* can be translated "to hide by covering over" or "to hoard secretly." If we "hide" God's Word in our hearts by memorizing and imagining it, we will find new power to keep our minds and hearts clean.

The power of secrets also will work to our advantage in our prayer lives. Jesus taught us, "But when you pray, go away by yourself, shut the door behind you, and pray to your Father in private. Then your Father, who sees everything, will reward you" (Matthew 6:6). Secrets have a way of being exposed. When we begin to use our ability to keep secrets for prayer and meditation, we'll find that power working for us. And if these secrets are "exposed," it will be God's rewards that people see.

> Special secrets with God can overpower the destructive
> secrets that hide within us.

Finding God
Bible Reading: Psalm 105:1-9

> We sought through prayer and meditation to improve our conscious contact with God, praying only for knowledge of his will for us and the power to carry it out.

As we work the Twelve Steps, we spend a lot of time looking back. We often think about the wrong things we've done in the past. As we proceed in our recovery, we will need strength to move along the path God wants us to follow. Part of this strength will come as we visualize God's constant presence with us.

The psalmist wrote, "Give thanks to the LORD and proclaim his greatness. Let the whole world know what he has done. . . . Remember the wonders he has performed. . . . He is the LORD our God. His justice is seen throughout the land. He always stands by his covenant—the commitment he made to a thousand generations" (Psalm 105:1, 5-8).

From now on when we look back we will see the "the wonders he has performed." We will look around to find his goodness "throughout the land" and look forward to the fulfillment of his promises. In prayer we thank him for what he's done; we seek him for the strength we need today; and we ask him to fulfill his promises for tomorrow. In meditation we remember our victories, ponder his presence with us today, and consider his faithfulness and the hope that gives us for tomorrow.

When we look, we will find God in the past,
the future, and the present.

Seeking and Finding
Bible Reading: John 14:15-24

> We sought through prayer and meditation to improve our
> conscious contact with God, praying only for knowledge of
> his will for us and the power to carry it out.

W e can only get to know people to the degree they allow
us to do so. We cannot get close to people who choose
not to reveal themselves. In most of our human relationships we find that love can open up the door to the heart of the
one we seek to know. It is the same way with God.

God reached out to us through the person of Jesus Christ.
When we genuinely seek after a love relationship with God, he will
then reveal himself to us. Jesus said, "If you love me, obey my commandments. And I will ask the Father, and he will give you another Advocate, who will never leave you. He is the Holy Spirit, who
leads into all truth. . . . No, I will not abandon you as orphans—I
will come to you. . . . All who love me will do what I say. My
Father will love them, and we will come and make our home with
each of them" (John 14:15-18, 23).

The way to find the knowledge of God's will is through the
person of the Holy Spirit who leads us into all truth. We find the
power through our relationship with the person of Jesus Christ. As
we seek God with a desire to know him and a willingness to obey,
he will reveal himself: Father, Son, and Holy Spirit.

As we reach out toward God, we will find his hand
already waiting.

Day 7

Patient Waiting
Bible Reading: Isaiah 40:28-31

> We sought through prayer and meditation to improve our
> conscious contact with God, praying only for knowledge of
> his will for us and the power to carry it out.

We all want to recover as quickly as possible. It's hard to be patient as we wait for the process to work. Sure, we realize that we didn't get to the difficult spot we're in overnight. We understand that we can't undo a lifetime of damage in a moment. But still, it is a challenge to wait patiently. Every part of recovery requires time and patience with ourselves. This step also requires that we learn to wait for God.

The prophet Isaiah gave us this promise: "Those who trust in the LORD will find new strength. They will soar high on wings like eagles. They will run and not grow weary. They will walk and not faint" (Isaiah 40:31). Jeremiah said, "The LORD is good to those who depend on him, to those who search for him. So it is good to wait quietly for salvation from the LORD" (Lamentations 3:25-26).

Waiting for salvation from the Lord has its rewards. We can remain calm when it appears that nothing is happening in our recovery. As we learn to respond to life in new ways, the winds of adversity will lift us up, like wind beneath the wings of an eagle, instead of immediately knocking us down. As we develop a patient faith in God we will be able to endure to the end of the race—and win.

Even the strongest of people tire, but God's power
never diminishes.

Paralyzed by Perfectionism
Bible Reading: Matthew 25:14-30

> We sought through prayer and meditation to improve our conscious contact with God, praying only for knowledge of his will for us and the power to carry it out.

Perfectionism can paralyze us. Perhaps we've been shamed for not being exactly what others wanted us to be. Now the shadow of their unrealistic expectations is cast over how we see ourselves, creating unrealistic expectations for our progress.

Jesus told a story of a man who loaned three servants money to invest for him while he was away. The first two men invested and doubled the money; the third hid his money in a hole. The third servant saw the master through the eyes of fear. He "came and said, 'Master, I knew you were a harsh man, harvesting crops you didn't plant and gathering crops you didn't cultivate. I was afraid I would lose your money, so I hid it in the earth. Look, here is your money back.' But the master replied, '. . . If you knew I harvested crops I didn't plant and gathered crops I didn't cultivate, why didn't you deposit my money in the bank? At least I could have gotten some interest'" (Matthew 25:24-27).

When we measure ourselves by others' expectations or by our own need to be perfect, we may not even try. All God asks is that we try to do something with our abilities and resources. When we allow ourselves the option of just making modest progress, we'll find courage to try. Even the least improvement is better than being doomed to complete failure by our perfectionism.

Being willing to try will open the door to new aspects of our recovery.

Antidote to Depression

Bible Reading: Psalm 42:4-11

We sought through prayer and meditation to improve our conscious contact with God, praying only for knowledge of his will for us and the power to carry it out.

I n bad times we may get lost in our memories of the "good old days." We may find ourselves struggling with conflicting emotions, teetering between the extremes of depression and hope.

The psalmist reflected these emotions, saying to himself, "My heart is breaking as I remember how it used to be: I walked among the crowds of worshipers, leading a great procession to the house of God, singing for joy and giving thanks amid the sound of a great celebration! Why am I discouraged? Why is my heart so sad? I will put my hope in God! I will praise him again—my Savior and my God! Now I am deeply discouraged, but I will remember you. . . . I will put my hope in God! I will praise him again—my Savior and my God!" (Psalm 42:4-6, 11).

Look how the psalmist improved his conscious contact with God. He talked to himself, commanding his emotions, "I will put my hope in God!" He repeated, "I will praise him again," even though he didn't feel that way right then. In the dark times he sang songs, thought about God's steadfast love, and prayed. We can do these things, too.

We will discover hope when we discard our inabilities for God's infinite ability.

Enjoying the "Calm"
Bible Reading: Matthew 16:24-26

> We sought through prayer and meditation to improve our
> conscious contact with God, praying only for knowledge of
> his will for us and the power to carry it out.

Some of us are addicted to chaos. We may be so used to crisis that we don't know how to enjoy the calm. Life in recovery may seem boring in comparison to our old ways. We may miss the excitement and danger. The rewards may seem too slow in coming.

The apostle Paul said, "So let's not get tired of doing what is good. At just the right time we will reap a harvest of blessing if we don't give up" (Galatians 6:9). Weeds spring up immediately. The good crops must be tended steadily even before we can see anything growing. It's only in time that we'll enjoy the fruit.

Jesus suggested that we expand our perspective even further, with a view toward eternity. "Jesus said to his disciples, 'If any of you wants to be my follower, you must turn from your selfish ways, take up your cross, and follow me. If you try to hang on to your life, you will lose it. But if you give up your life for my sake, you will save it. And what do you benefit if you gain the whole world but lose your own soul?'" (Matthew 16:24-26).

It is God's will for us to have a rewarding and fulfilled life. It may be easier to adjust to our new way of life if we remember that denying ourselves immediate pleasures will bring a harvest of rich rewards, in this life and the life to come.

❧

Immediate pleasures usually have razor blades planted in them.

Showing Love
Bible Reading: 1 Corinthians 13:1-7

> We sought through prayer and meditation to improve our
> conscious contact with God, praying only for knowledge of
> his will for us and the power to carry it out.

We may have given up on love. Perhaps we've waited for love to find us, only to be disappointed. Maybe our loved ones have hurt us so badly that we needed to numb ourselves from the pain. Our addictions helped to keep us numb. Now that we're in recovery we have to find a way to deal with the issue of love once again.

It's God's will that we love; without love nothing else matters (see 1 Corinthians 13:1-3). Love is more than a feeling. It's a choice of behavior that grows in our lives; it's a fruit of the Holy Spirit, produced in our lives as we yield to God. The Bible defines it this way: "Love is patient and kind. Love is not jealous or boastful or proud or rude. . . . Love never gives up, never loses faith, is always hopeful, and endures through every circumstance" (1 Corinthians 13:4-7).

No one loves perfectly, but we must not give up on loving. We can accept the responsibility to love others and stop playing the victim by waiting for them to love us. We can be patient with ourselves while love grows. When we choose to act lovingly, the emotions will follow. We'll also find that love comes back to us.

*The better we know God, the more we'll find
ourselves showing love.*

Love Is Waiting
Bible Reading: 1 John 4:7-10

> We sought through prayer and meditation to improve our
> conscious contact with God, praying only for knowledge of
> his will for us and the power to carry it out.

We may feel like love just doesn't seem to work for us. We may wonder if we're doing something wrong. Perhaps we have problems loving because we're disconnected from the source of true love.

The apostle John wrote, "Dear friends, let us continue to love one another, for love comes from God. . . . But anyone who does not love does not know God, for God is love" (1 John 4:7-8).

Jesus said, "I am giving you a new commandment: Love each other. Just as I have loved you, you should love each other" (John 13:34). Trying to love without first receiving God's love is like trying to water something with a hose that's disconnected from the faucet. When we receive God's unconditional love for us we can begin to love ourselves. We are then told to love others as we love ourselves and as Jesus has loved us. There is a boundless reservoir of love available to us; but without receiving the love of God in Christ we will run dry.

Jesus is waiting for us to open up and receive his love. He said, "Look! I stand at the door and knock. If you hear my voice and open the door, I will come in, and we will share a meal together as friends" (Revelation 3:20). Love is waiting. All we have to do is to open up to the love God offers us.

The more contact we have with God, the more
we're aware of his love for us.

Day 13

Loved by God
Bible Reading: Psalm 8:1-6

> We sought through prayer and meditation to improve our conscious contact with God, praying only for knowledge of his will for us and the power to carry it out.

We develop our self-perception by noticing how the important people in our lives see us. If we grew up in a dysfunctional family, their skewed view of us probably warped our ability to see ourselves as we truly are in God's eyes.

King David was amazed at the place God has made for us in his plan. He said, "What are mere mortals that you should think about them, human beings that you should care for them? Yet you made them only a little lower than God and crowned them with glory and honor. You gave them charge of everything you made, putting all things under their authority" (Psalm 8:4-6). "How precious are your thoughts about me, O God. They cannot be numbered! I can't even count them; they outnumber the grains of sand! And when I wake up, you are still with me!" (Psalm 139:17-18). The greatest demonstration of how precious we are in God's sight is that Jesus gave his life for us.

God wants us to realize how precious we are to him and to begin to see ourselves in the light of his love. Consider this: If we were worth God's giving up the most precious thing he had (his only Son), what does that say about our value?

❧

It is overwhelming when we begin to realize how much God really loves us.

A New Hiding Place

Bible Reading: 2 Samuel 22:1-33

> We sought through prayer and meditation to improve our
> conscious contact with God, praying only for knowledge of
> his will for us and the power to carry it out.

In the past we used our addictions as a hiding place when life became overwhelming. Now that we are in recovery, life can at times feel even more overwhelming. We'll need a new place of refuge to escape the storms and find protection.

King David experienced many battles. He said of God, "The LORD is my rock, my fortress, and my savior; my God is my rock, in whom I find protection. He is my shield, the power that saves me, and my place of safety. He is my refuge, my savior. . . . I called on the LORD, who is worthy of praise, and he saved me from my enemies. The waves of death overwhelmed me; floods of destruction swept over me. The grave wrapped its ropes around me; death laid a trap in my path. But in my distress I cried out to the LORD; yes, I cried to my God for help. He heard me from his sanctuary; my cry reached his ears. . . . He is a shield for all who look to him for protection. For who is God except the LORD? Who but our God is a solid rock? God is my strong fortress" (2 Samuel 22:2-7, 31-33).

There will always be times when we feel the need for a safe place to run and hide. God can be that hiding place. When we were in distress, and "death laid a trap" for us, we called to God and he brought us to where we are today. He's always there, ready to shield and protect us whenever we call on him.

When our lives are shaky, God is the only safe place for us to hide.

Day 15

A Time to Rest

Bible Reading: Exodus 20:8-11

> We sought through prayer and meditation to improve our conscious contact with God, praying only for knowledge of his will for us and the power to carry it out.

We need to have all our faculties about us as we seek to maintain our sobriety. If we allow ourselves to get overtired we'll be less able to cope with the demands of life and more susceptible to relapse.

Rest is essential to the maintenance of any kind of balanced life. Weekly rest was included as one of the Ten Commandments. God declared, "You have six days each week for your ordinary work, but the seventh day is a Sabbath day of rest dedicated to the LORD your God. On that day no one in your household may do any work. . . . For in six days the LORD made the heavens, the earth, the sea, and everything in them; but on the seventh day he rested. That is why the LORD blessed the Sabbath day and set it apart as holy" (Exodus 20:9-11). The Sabbath is described as "a permanent sign of my covenant with the people of Israel" (31:17).

God wants us to have rest and balance. A weekly "Sabbath" or intermission is a time to relax from our regular duties and allow our bodies to rest. It is also a time of spiritual refreshment, a time to reflect on God's promises. It is a day of renewing our contact with God and remembering that he sustains us in our sobriety.

We all need a day to draw close to God, his power, and his promises.

God Is for Me!

Bible Reading: Job 19:8-27

> We sought through prayer and meditation to improve our
> conscious contact with God, praying only for knowledge of
> his will for us and the power to carry it out.

When we experience pain and loss because of something that seems out of our control, we may feel like God is our enemy. We may never grasp why God allows such torment, but we can have faith that a time will come when we will understand his will for us.

Job felt this way, too. He said, "God has blocked my way so I cannot move. He has plunged my path into darkness. He has stripped me of my honor and removed the crown from my head. He has demolished me on every side, and I am finished. He has uprooted my hope like a fallen tree. His fury burns against me; he counts me as an enemy. His troops advance. They build up roads to attack me. They camp all around my tent. . . . My close friends detest me. Those I loved have turned against me. I have been reduced to skin and bones and have escaped death by the skin of my teeth. . . . Oh, that my words could be recorded. Oh, that they could be inscribed on a monument, carved with an iron chisel and filled with lead, engraved forever in the rock. But as for me, I know that my Redeemer lives, and he will stand upon the earth at last. And after my body has decayed, yet in my body I will see God! I will see him for myself. Yes, I will see him with my own eyes. I am overwhelmed at the thought!" (Job 19:8-27).

God is on our side, even if we can't see it now.

> We can be sure that God is on our side, even when
> life lets us down.

Day 17

Running to Win
Bible Reading: Hebrews 11:1–12:1

> We sought through prayer and meditation to improve our conscious contact with God, praying only for knowledge of his will for us and the power to carry it out.

Many of us feel like losers that have dropped out of the race of life. Faith in God can give us the motivation to run the race, with a real chance at life's rewards.

Chapter 11 of Hebrews has been called faith's "Hall of Fame." It refers to people whose lives were used by God because of their faith. The following chapter begins this way: "Since we are surrounded by such a huge crowd of witnesses to the life of faith, let us strip off every weight that slows us down, especially the sin that so easily trips us up. And let us run with endurance the race God has set before us" (12:1).

This illustration referred to the Olympic Games. In Bible times, men wore flowing robes. At the time of an event the athletes would strip off their robes and lay them aside to run without encumbrance. If someone tried to compete in his robes, he would get tangled up, losing both the race and the prize.

It is God's will for us to win the race of life. The robes of our recurrent sins need to be laid aside. There will be pain from the exertion, but we're told to pace ourselves and to bear it with patience. And remember, others who have run the same race and finished well are cheering us on!

The closer we come to God, the simpler our lives become.

Day 18

Rebuilding Our Faith
Bible Reading: Luke 22:31-34

> We sought through prayer and meditation to improve our
> conscious contact with God, praying only for knowledge of
> his will for us and the power to carry it out.

I t is easy to lose faith when we're troubled. As we're buffeted
about by life, we may feel like the faith we once had has slipped
away. We may begin to feel anger toward God.

Simon Peter had his ups and downs with God. On the night
Simon Peter would deny him, Jesus said to him, "Simon, Simon,
Satan has asked to sift each of you like wheat. But I have pleaded
in prayer for you, Simon, that your faith should not fail. So when
you have repented and turned to me again, strengthen your brothers" (Luke 22:31-32).

Jesus pointed out that Simon had an assailant in the spiritual realm. Jesus knew Peter would be attacked and "sifted," but
he also was confident that afterwards Peter would return to God.
Wheat is sifted by throwing it repeatedly into the air and catching
it. The kernels are separated from the chaff as the lighter chaff is
carried away by the wind. All that remain are the solid wheat kernels, which are good.

We should not be surprised that we face times when our
faith seems to disappear. We may feel like we are being ripped open
and our faith is being blown away. But we needn't worry. We'll find
the core of our faith again. And when we do, we'll be all the better
for it—and better able to encourage others, too.

With God's help, even our failures can be useful in our recovery.

329

A New Life

Bible Reading: 1 Chronicles 28:19-21

> We sought through prayer and meditation to improve our conscious contact with God, praying only for knowledge of his will for us and the power to carry it out.

Full recovery doesn't stop with repairing our brokenness. It includes building a new life that's free, full, and rich. It takes courage to let ourselves dream of the life we truly desire. What if we allow ourselves to hope only to be disappointed again? What if we start and fail, suffering public humiliation? These fears can paralyze us and keep us from life in all its fullness.

David dreamed of building a magnificent temple. In commissioning his son Solomon to do the work he said, "Every part of this plan . . . was given to me in writing from the hand of the LORD. . . . Be strong and courageous, and do the work. Don't be afraid or discouraged, for the LORD God, my God, is with you. He will not fail you or forsake you" (1 Chronicles 28:19-20). The apostle Paul said, "We [believers] are carefully joined together in him, becoming a holy temple for the Lord" (Ephesians 2:21).

Just as David dreamed of building a magnificent temple, we can dare to dream of building a magnificent new life. We need not be frightened by the size of the task, for "God, who began the good work within you, will continue his work until it is finally finished" (Philippians 1:6).

Our knowing God will provide the courage we need to build a new life.

Common Sense

Bible Reading: Proverbs 4:1-10

> We sought through prayer and meditation to improve our
> conscious contact with God, praying only for knowledge of
> his will for us and the power to carry it out.

We're learning to think in new ways. As we develop new thought processes we may lack confidence in our own wisdom and common sense. We may hesitate to carry out God's will if we are afraid of the criticism of the people around us.

Common sense could be defined as our ability to figure out in advance what the likely consequences of our choices and actions will be. We're told, "Getting wisdom is the wisest thing you can do! And whatever else you do, develop good judgment" (Proverbs 4:7). We can exercise our common sense by thinking about what we can do and then doing the things that we can.

A woman wanted to do something to display her love for Jesus. So she poured some expensive perfume on him. When she did this she was criticized by the disciples. Jesus came to her defense with these words: "Leave her alone. Why criticize her for doing such a good thing to me? . . . She has done what she could" (Mark 14:6-8). These are words we also can cling to.

God wants to renew our minds and help us develop wisdom and common sense. As we try to sort out our choices and develop common sense, people may criticize us. But we can trust that God will come to our defense as long as we do what we can.

❧

God will bring about our recovery as we seek
to do what we can.

Day 21

A Listening God
Bible Reading: Genesis 18:20-33

> We sought through prayer and meditation to improve our conscious contact with God, praying only for knowledge of his will for us and the power to carry it out.

Sometimes we become involved in extremely touchy situations. We may wonder if it's possible to change the circumstances while staying within God's will.

Here's what Abraham did in such a situation. "The LORD told Abraham, 'I have heard a great outcry from Sodom and Gomorrah, because their sin is so flagrant. I am going down to see if their actions are as wicked as I have heard.' . . . Abraham approached him and said, 'Will you sweep away both the righteous and the wicked? Suppose you find fifty righteous people living there in the city—will you still sweep it away and not spare it for their sakes? . . . Why, you would be treating the righteous and the wicked exactly the same! Surely you wouldn't do that! Should not the Judge of all the earth do what is right?' And the LORD replied, 'If I find fifty righteous people in Sodom, I will spare the entire city for their sake'" (Genesis 18:20-26). The bargaining went on: Suppose there are only forty-five . . . forty . . . thirty . . . twenty . . . ten? And God said, "Then I will not destroy it for the sake of the ten" (18:32).

Abraham wasn't sure what God's will was in this case; so he talked it over with him. When we don't know how much of a change we can—or even should—make, we can talk it over with God and then try to do as much as we feel confident doing.

✻

God is interested in us and will support our desires for change.

332

Selfishness

Bible Reading: Isaiah 14:12-15

We sought through prayer and meditation to improve our
conscious contact with God, praying only for knowledge of
his will for us and the power to carry it out.

When we were following after our addictions, we were pow-
erfully directed by our desires. We were driven. We didn't
think about the effect this had on others. Our selfishness
was in control and cut us off from life as it should have been.

Selfishness is at the heart of destructive behavior. The Bible
indicates that Satan was once a high-ranking angel in service of
the Lord. Isaiah gives us a glimpse of Satan's fall, writing, "How
you are fallen from heaven, O shining star, son of the morning!
You have been thrown down to the earth. . . . For you said to yourself, 'I will ascend to heaven and set my throne above God's stars.
. . . I will climb to the highest heavens and be like the Most High.'
Instead, you will be brought down to the place of the dead, down
to its lowest depths" (Isaiah 14:12-15).

The same kind of selfishness that brought Satan down
resides in the hearts of all people on earth. No one is exempt.
Addicts are no worse in nature than anyone else. It's just that the
ways we've chosen to meet our needs have led us to hit bottom
and go through our own personal hell. When we are free enough
to focus on God's will and his power to work in our lives, he will
show us a way to fulfill the needs we were trying to satisfy in vain.

❦

When our recovery becomes selfish, a relapse is just
around the corner.

The Highest Power
Bible Reading: John 14:6-10

> We sought through prayer and meditation to improve our conscious contact with God, praying only for knowledge of his will for us and the power to carry it out.

Christian people may have condemned us to the point that now we associate Jesus Christ with rejection and disapproval. These images may make us shy away from Jesus as a distinct representative of God. We may feel more comfortable with a nameless higher Power, whose nature is rather vague.

"Jesus shouted to the crowds, 'If you trust me, you are trusting not only me, but also God who sent me. For when you see me, you are seeing the one who sent me. I have come as a light to shine in this dark world, so that all who put their trust in me will no longer remain in the dark'" (John 12:44-46). Then he told his disciples, "I am the way, the truth, and the life. No one can come to the Father except through me. If you had really known me, you would know who my Father is. From now on, you do know him and have seen him! . . . The words I speak are not my own, but my Father who lives in me does his work through me" (14:6-7, 10).

Jesus said clearly, "This is the only work God wants from you: Believe in the one he has sent" (John 6:29). If we accept the Bible at all, we will see that the knowledge of God's will isn't vague and mysterious. It starts with believing in Jesus.

🌿

Following God's will starts by believing that Jesus is the highest power.

Friends of the Light

Bible Reading: John 3:18-21

We sought through prayer and meditation to improve our conscious contact with God, praying only for knowledge of his will for us and the power to carry it out.

Sometimes we don't want to know God's will because there are areas in our lives that we aren't ready to deal with yet. Recovery is a process for us. We may be ready to pray for God's will in some areas but feel uncomfortable with having God's light shine into the areas that are still hidden in shame.

When talking about those who refuse to trust him with their lives, Jesus said, "God's light came into the world, but people loved the darkness more than the light, for their actions were evil. All who do evil hate the light and refuse to go near it for fear their sins will be exposed" (John 3:19-20). "Jesus spoke to the people once more and said, 'I am the light of the world. If you follow me, you won't have to walk in darkness, because you will have the light that leads to life'" (8:12).

Darkness is great when we're trying to hide something; but light is needed when we're trying to walk without stumbling. When we were hiding the shameful issues of our lives and holding on to our addictions, the darkness seemed like our friend. Now that we're trying to walk in the steps of recovery, we need the light to keep us from stumbling. We don't have to be afraid of God's light anymore. He wants to safely guide us on the right path.

❧

The better we know God, the closer we will walk to the light of his will.

Day 25

Persistent Prayer
Bible Reading: Luke 11:5-10

> We sought through prayer and meditation to improve our
> conscious contact with God, praying only for knowledge of
> his will for us and the power to carry it out.

We may not pray because when we prayed in the past, it didn't seem to work. We may even have prayed for things that are promised in the Bible, but didn't get a response. This can be discouraging and make us want to give up on prayer.

While teaching about prayer, Jesus used this example: "Suppose you went to a friend's house at midnight, wanting to borrow three loaves of bread. . . . I tell you this—though he won't do it for friendship's sake, if you keep knocking long enough, he will get up and give you whatever you need because of your shameless persistence" (Luke 11:5-8).

In Old Testament times God had given promises to Israel regarding Jerusalem. Then he told them, "I have posted watchmen on your walls; they will pray day and night, continually. Take no rest, all you who pray to the LORD. Give the LORD no rest until he completes his work, until he makes Jerusalem the pride of the earth" (Isaiah 62:6-7).

Prayer takes persistence. It's not a magic button we push to make God move. We can be confident that if we persistently pray for the things that are God's will and don't rest from prayer until he fulfills his promises, we will see results.

※

When we ask persistently of a generous God, we will
receive a generous share.

God's Peace

Bible Reading: Philippians 4:4-7

> We sought through prayer and meditation to improve our conscious contact with God, praying only for knowledge of his will for us and the power to carry it out.

There are times when we're caught off guard by life. We are suddenly faced with problems that can wipe out our joy in an instant. Our hearts are disquieted and our minds begin to race. When we are grappling with unsettling problems that come our way and cause us to worry, it's time to run to God in prayer.

From his prison cell, Paul wrote this message: "Don't worry about anything; instead, pray about everything. Tell God what you need, and thank him for all he has done. Then you will experience God's peace, which exceeds anything we can understand" (Philippians 4:6-7).

The psalmist wrote, "Enter his gates with thanksgiving; go into his courts with praise. Give thanks to him and praise his name. For the LORD is good. His unfailing love continues forever, and his faithfulness continues to each generation" (Psalm 100:4-5).

God's gates are always open to us. He's waiting for us, whenever we're upset and in need of a friend. We'll still feel the painful emotions. We don't just hand them over to God and expect them to disappear. Prayer is a useful tool to help us work through our problems. He will give us his peace, reminding us that he's there with us. For this, we can be thankful.

A life bathed in prayer is the best antidote for worry.

Day 27

Knowing and Being Known
Bible Reading: Hosea 6:1-3

> We sought through prayer and meditation to improve our
> conscious contact with God, praying only for knowledge of
> his will for us and the power to carry it out.

Intimacy issues can be intimidating, especially for those of us who grew up in dysfunctional families. We may not feel safe to reveal our true selves to anyone. We may be afraid that if we were deeply intimate with others, if we let them into our hearts, they would reject us once they really knew us. We may find prayer intimidating for some of the same reasons.

Hosea once said, "Oh, that we might know the LORD! Let us press on to know him. He will respond to us as surely as the arrival of dawn or the coming of rains in early spring" (Hosea 6:3).

God wants us to know him; but he wants an intimate relationship with us, not just a surface one. The biblical word translated *know* is also used to describe sexual intimacy. It's the same word used in Genesis to describe the sexual intimacy between Adam and Eve (Genesis 4:1, NKJV). Coming to know God is an act of growing and deep intimacy. It is more than knowing him with our heads; it is a knowing that takes place in our hearts as well.

If we are afraid of knowing or being known deeply by God, we will want to avoid prayer. And yet it is those of us who are intimate with God who will have the strength to do great things. We are safe to reveal our true selves to God. As we dare to do so, he will surely respond.

❧

As our knowledge of God grows, so will our strength for recovery.

Day 28

Resting in God
Bible Reading: John 14:12-14

> We sought through prayer and meditation to improve our conscious contact with God, praying only for knowledge of his will for us and the power to carry it out.

We may have lived most of our lives trying to take care of our own needs. Our addictive behaviors may have been misplaced attempts to accomplish this very thing. Once we've given up our addictions, it's still hard to rely on others to do things for us, even when we don't have the power to handle them ourselves. This tendency to avoid reliance on others may come into play in our prayer lives, making it hard for us to depend on God.

Jesus told his disciples, "I tell you the truth, anyone who believes in me will do the same works I have done, and even greater works, because I am going to be with the Father. You can ask for anything in my name, and I will do it, so that the Son can bring glory to the Father. Yes, ask me for anything in my name, and I will do it!" (John 14:12-14).

Jesus has been given all authority in heaven and earth to do anything. He demonstrated this throughout his life by the mighty miracles he performed. We may feel that it would take a miracle to deal with some of our unresolved issues. But we may also be afraid of being disappointed if we rely on God to meet our needs. Jesus has given us an open door and strong assurances that there's no need too big or too small. We really can rely on him for anything!

When our requests are in line with God's will, he promises to answer.

A Trustworthy God
Bible Reading: Mark 11:22-24

We sought through prayer and meditation to improve our conscious contact with God, praying only for knowledge of his will for us and the power to carry it out.

We may have avoided prayer before we entered recovery and now find that we have questions about it. Maybe we find that our prayers go unanswered and wonder why. We may lack faith because we're not sure the things we're asking for are in God's will. Our faith may also be weak because of all the broken promises we've experienced with others. All of these things can discourage.

There are a few basic guidelines to follow when asking God for something in prayer. First, we need to ask: "You don't have what you want because you don't ask God for it" (James 4:2). Second, we need to ask in accordance with God's will: "Even when you ask, you don't get it because your motives are all wrong—you want only what will give you pleasure" (James 4:3). God won't give us the things that feed our lusts and addictions.

"Jesus said to the disciples, . . . 'You must really believe it will happen and have no doubt in your heart. I tell you, you can pray for anything, and if you believe that you've received it, it will be yours" (Mark 11:22-24). The way we develop a faith without doubt is to become sure about what is in God's will. This assurance comes from knowing what he has promised us in the Bible.

The better we know God, the more we will discover how trustworthy he is.

Thirst for God

Bible Reading: Psalm 27:1-6

> We sought through prayer and meditation to improve our
> conscious contact with God, praying only for knowledge of
> his will for us and the power to carry it out.

We may have started out going to God for the sake of
what he could do for us, namely, freeing us from the
power and effects of addiction. Now we may be surprised to find that we're going to God out of a desire to be near
someone who is wonderful, who loves us completely.

King David gave us a glimpse into his relationship with
God, saying, "The one thing I ask of the LORD—the thing I seek
most—is to live in the house of the LORD all the days of my life,
delighting in the LORD's perfections and meditating in his Temple.
For he will conceal me there when troubles come; he will hide
me in his sanctuary. He will place me out of reach on a high rock.
Then I will hold my head high above my enemies who surround
me. At his sanctuary I will offer sacrifices with shouts of joy, singing and praising the LORD with music" (Psalm 27:4-6).

David found great joy by improving his conscious contact
with God. God is always there, but we're not always aware of his
presence. When we began to go to God to get what we needed, we
grew more and more attracted to him. But when we begin to focus
on getting to know God as an end in itself, we will discover that he
will slowly and surely give us our hearts' desires. Then we will see
that he can be trusted with every area of our lives.

We should run to God every day—even on the best of days!

STEP TWELVE

Having had a spiritual awakening as the result of these steps,
we tried to carry this message to others and to practice
these principles in all our affairs.

*"The Spirit of the Sovereign LORD is upon me, for the LORD
has anointed me to bring good news to the poor. He has sent
me to comfort the brokenhearted and to proclaim that
captives will be released and prisoners will be freed"*
(Isaiah 61:1).

Our Stories
Bible Reading: Mark 16:14-18

> Having had a spiritual awakening as the result of these steps,
> we tried to carry this message to others and to practice
> these principles in all our affairs.

E ach one of us has a valuable story to tell. We may be shy and feel awkward about speaking. We may wonder if what we have to share is trivial. Is it actually going to help anyone else? We may struggle to get beyond the shame of our past. But our recovery story can help others who are trapped back where we were. Are we willing to allow God to use us to help free others?

Jesus left us with this vital task: "Go into all the world and preach the Good News [of salvation from the bondage and penalty of sin] to everyone" (Mark 16:15).

Paul traveled the world over telling everyone the story of his conversion. He ended up in chains, but his spirit was free. He presented his defense (and his own story of redemption) before kings. King Agrippa interrupted him to say, "'Do you think you can persuade me to become a Christian so quickly?' Paul replied, 'Whether quickly or not, I pray to God that both you and everyone here in this audience might become the same as I am, except for these chains'" (Acts 26:28-29).

Within each personal story of the journey from bondage to freedom is a microcosm of the gospel. When people hear our story, even if it seems trivial, we are offering them the chance to loosen their chains and begin a recovery story of their own.

All of our recovery stories are custom designed for
another person's encouragement.

Day 2

Never Forget
Bible Reading: Titus 3:1-5

Having had a spiritual awakening as the result of these steps,
we tried to carry this message to others and to practice
these principles in all our affairs.

A s we get further along in our recovery, the memory of how
bad it really was may begin to fade. Do we vividly remember what we once were? Can we recall the dark emotions
that filled our souls? Do we have true compassion and humble sym-
pathy for those to whom we try to carry the message?

When we take the message of recovery to others it is vital
that we never forget where we came from and how we got where
we are. Paul told Titus, "Once we, too, were foolish and disobedi-
ent. We were misled and became slaves to many lusts and pleasures.
. . . When God our Savior revealed his kindness and love, he saved
us, not because of the righteous things we had done, but because of
his mercy. He washed away our sins, giving us a new birth and new
life through the Holy Spirit" (Titus 3:3-5).

As we share our message, let us never forget the following
truths. We, too, were slaves just like they now are. Our hearts were
filled with the confusion and painful emotions that others still feel.
We were saved only because of the love and kindness of God, not
because we became good enough. We must also remember that
we are only able to stay free because God is with us, upholding us
every step of the way.

Sharing our recovery will remind us of how far we've
come and how much God loves us.

Sharing Together
Bible Reading: Galatians 6:1-3

> Having had a spiritual awakening as the result of these steps,
> we tried to carry this message to others and to practice
> these principles in all our affairs.

Since we have worked through the Twelve Steps, we are in a special position to carry the message to others. We can recognize the warning signs of addictive/compulsive tendencies in those around us, as well as in ourselves. When touching on such deep and sensitive issues it's important to speak in the language of love, not condemnation.

The Bible tells us that if someone "is overcome by some sin, you who are godly should gently and humbly help that person back onto the right path. And be careful not to fall into the same temptation yourself. Share each other's burdens, and in this way obey the law of Christ" (Galatians 6:1-2). The command was the one Jesus taught his disciples: "So now I am giving you a new commandment: Love each other. Just as I have loved you, you should love each other" (John 13:34). "This is my commandment: Love each other in the same way I have loved you. There is no greater love than to lay down one's life for one's friends" (15:12-13).

We are not the Savior, but we can love others as he has loved us. Love goes beyond mere words. Sometimes it is spoken in silence, when we don't condemn someone who's looking for help. Love doesn't just tell them what the problem is. It helps carry the weight of their burdens. We can be a part of a support network to help carry our friends until they are able to take steps toward recovery on their own initiative.

Sharing our own recovery will remind us of our need for others.

Day 4

Our Mission
Bible Reading: Isaiah 61:1-3

> Having had a spiritual awakening as the result of these steps,
> we tried to carry this message to others and to practice
> these principles in all our affairs.

A life that has been set free from addiction is a beautiful sight to behold. When we practice these principles, people will gain hope and see the glory of God in our lives. We know from experience the depths of suffering, affliction, and brokenness. We know the pain of being enslaved to our passions and blinded by our denial. We have endured our season of grieving. We can relate to those who struggle to be free. We also know that there is more to life than bondage. There is healing and freedom; there is clarity and mercy; there is beauty and joy; there is heaven as well as hell.

When Jesus came to earth he had a mission, which was expressed in these words, "The Spirit of the Sovereign LORD is upon me, for the LORD has anointed me to bring good news to the poor. He has sent me to comfort the brokenhearted and to proclaim that captives will be released and prisoners will be freed. He has sent me to tell those who mourn that the time of the LORD's favor has come. . . . To all who mourn . . . he will give a crown of beauty for ashes, a joyous blessing instead of mourning, festive praise instead of despair" (Isaiah 61:1-3).

This mission has been passed on to us. Some people talk about "preaching the gospel" but may alienate those who need the Good News the most. We're in a unique position to share our experience, strength, and hope in a way that broken people can receive it.

❦

Our mission is to share the "good news" of our recovery.

Celebrating Success
Bible Reading: Hebrews 10:25

> Having had a spiritual awakening as the result of these steps,
> we tried to carry this message to others and to practice
> these principles in all our affairs.

L ife flows in seasons. We all deal with life in terms of days and weeks, months and years. Special events, both personal and spiritual, are commemorated throughout the calendars of our lives. Birthdays, anniversaries, and holidays are woven into the fabric of our days to help keep us connected to God. They also remind us where we've come from and where we're headed.

The Bible is full of examples that show the importance of integrating the spiritual with the "practice of the principles" in our everyday lives. Daniel prayed three times a day, every day. The disciples of Jesus went to the Temple regularly for worship and prayer. Christians are told, "Let us not neglect our meeting together, as some people do, but encourage one another" (Hebrews 10:25). All faithful Jews were required to celebrate the sacred feasts three times each year.

God knows that we easily forget the deep truths of the spirit if we disconnect the spiritual from our daily lives. We need to take care to commemorate the victories we've had. We need to attend regular meetings, to encourage one another, to celebrate each year of our sobriety, to tell our story over and over again to our children and our children's children. That way, we will never forget and we will bring hope to others.

Celebrating our past victories can bring encouragement
to ourselves and others.

Day 6

The Narrow Road

Bible Reading: 1 Peter 4:1-4

Having had a spiritual awakening as the result of these steps,
we tried to carry this message to others and to practice
these principles in all our affairs.

We probably came into recovery because we'd had enough!
We'd had enough of the pain, the lies, and the destruction that addictive/compulsive behaviors bring with
them. One day at a time, we learned the principles on the road
to recovery. Now we're at a place we weren't sure we could ever
reach—Step Twelve. Now we're told to share the message with
others. We mustn't be discouraged when we find that not everyone
will welcome the message.

Peter pointed out, "You have had enough in the past of
the evil things that godless people enjoy—their immorality and
lust, their feasting and drunkenness and wild parties. . . . Your
former friends are surprised when you no longer plunge into the
flood of wild and destructive things they do. So they slander you"
(1 Peter 4:3-4).

Jesus said, "You can enter God's Kingdom only through the
narrow gate. The highway to hell is broad, and its gate is wide for
the many who choose that way. But the gateway to life is very narrow and the road is difficult, and only a few ever find it" (Matthew
7:13-14).

Our message won't be accepted by the masses. The people
on the "highway to hell" won't eagerly restrict themselves to the
clearly defined steps on the road to recovery.

❧

As we share our recovery with others, we bring new strength to
our own recovery journey.

Day 7

Talking the Walk
Bible Reading: 1 Timothy 4:14-16

Having had a spiritual awakening as the result of these steps,
we tried to carry this message to others and to practice
these principles in all our affairs.

When we wake up to realize everything we've gained by following the Twelve Steps, it will be natural to want to share this life-giving message with others. If we think back to the time before we entered recovery we'll probably recall that we didn't respond very well to "preaching." And yet, we also realize that there are people in our lives who our message could help. We are right in our estimation of how vital our message is to their lives. This is why we need to communicate in a way that they can receive.

The apostle Paul taught Timothy that to get the message across, we need to combine the practice of our beliefs with the telling of them. He said, "Throw yourself into your tasks so that everyone will see your progress. Keep a close watch on how you live and on your teaching. Stay true to what is right for . . . the salvation of those who hear you" (1 Timothy 4:15-16). When we practice the principles of the Twelve Steps, others will be watching and will notice the changes. This will open the door for us to be able to tell them our story as well.

We must never let ourselves forget that every addict is a precious lost soul whom God loves and wants to rescue. "If someone among you wanders away . . . , whoever brings the sinner back will save that person from death and bring about the forgiveness of many sins" (James 5:19-20).

Talking about our recovery helps us to keep ourselves on track.

Day 8

Ready to Help
Bible Reading: Romans 12:1-5

> Having had a spiritual awakening as the result of these steps,
> we tried to carry this message to others and to practice
> these principles in all our affairs.

We may feel like we're not good enough to be an example for others. We may realize that we need other people, but find it hard to believe that our story could help anyone else.

The apostle Paul said, "Just as our bodies have many parts and each part has a special function, so it is with Christ's body. We are many parts of one body, and we all belong to each other" (Romans 12:4-5).

To have a true view of where we fit in the scheme of things, we need to see that God has a purpose for our lives. God created each of us with abilities and talents. He likens us to a part of a body where every part is needed for the proper working of the whole. If you isolate any one part of a body and examine it, apart from its proper place among the other members, it may seem odd and useless. It is only when it is connected to the body and doing its appointed job that it realizes its usefulness. And so it is with us.

We need to find a place where our talents and abilities can be used to help others. Doing this will show that we have gained an honest understanding of whom God created us to be. He loves us and wants to help us realize our place in the body of Christ and our purpose in life.

❧

We're ready to help others when we've taken the
step they're about to take.

A Shield of Protection

Bible Reading: Ephesians 6:13-17

> Having had a spiritual awakening as the result of these steps,
> we tried to carry this message to others and to practice
> these principles in all our affairs.

R ecovery is not a battle anyone wins alone. We help each other to think and live in new ways. Alone we're vulnerable. Together we form a shield of protection for one another.

The apostle Paul wrote, "Hold up the shield of faith to stop the fiery arrows of the devil" (Ephesians 6:16). Faith here refers to trust in Christ for salvation. In general terms, it also means having constancy in our convictions. This can apply to our convictions about the Twelve Step principles. The shield of faith was likened to the shields carried by Roman soldiers, which were able to cover the entire body. To advance in battle, a group of soldiers would assemble together, making a wall of shields for protection as they moved.

Similarly, we are told to stick together, "not forsaking the assembling of ourselves together, as is the manner of some, but exhorting one another" (Hebrews 10:25, NKJV). We are to take our place in the unity that helps protect us and those with whom our lives are connected.

We need to assemble with others who share the common beliefs helpful in our recovery. Our encouragement of one another, our shared faith, and the principles of the Twelve Steps will be a form of protection as we continue to advance in recovery.

❧

By standing together, we form a shield against a
relapse and other dangers.

Listening First

Bible Reading: Acts 8:26-40

> Having had a spiritual awakening as the result of these steps,
> we tried to carry this message to others and to practice
> these principles in all our affairs.

We may be so excited about what God has done for us or so concerned for those in need of recovery that we want to rush right out and tell everyone our story. Or we may be very shy and hesitate to tell anyone, especially if we think they are better than us. We all have a valuable story to tell; we just need to learn how best to communicate it.

The apostle Philip was led to meet an influential traveler. "The eunuch had gone to Jerusalem to worship, and he was now returning. . . . he was reading aloud from the book of the prophet Isaiah. The Holy Spirit said to Philip, 'Go over and walk along beside the carriage.' Philip ran over and heard the man reading from the prophet Isaiah. Philip asked, 'Do you understand what you are reading?' The man replied, 'How can I, unless someone instructs me?' . . . So beginning with this same Scripture, Philip told him the Good News about Jesus" (Acts 8:27-31, 35).

The way Philip communicated can be a model for us. He was sensitive to allow God to lead him to someone who was ready. He wasn't so intimidated by the man's status that he hesitated in sharing his story. Philip began by listening carefully. He led the man's need and interests into the message he was prepared to share. Whether we are zealous or shy, following this model can help us communicate in a way that people can understand and receive.

We'll tell our own stories best, after we've listened first.

Raindrops of Truth

Bible Reading: Isaiah 55:10-11

> Having had a spiritual awakening as the result of these steps,
> we tried to carry this message to others and to practice
> these principles in all our affairs.

As we've practiced the principles of the Twelve Steps, we've seen growth in our lives. We have experienced a spiritual awakening, even if we weren't looking for one when we started. As the seasons passed, we worked at applying each step. We noticed that some of the hunger that used to drive us began to subside. We realized more of our human dignity.

God tells us that his Word in our lives has this kind of impact. He says, "The rain and snow come down from the heavens and stay on the ground to water the earth. They cause the grain to grow, producing seed for the farmer and bread for the hungry. It is the same with my word. I send it out, and it always produces fruit. It will accomplish all I want it to, and it will prosper everywhere I send it" (Isaiah 55:10-11).

The principles of the Twelve Steps are tremendously powerful to change lives. One reason is that they incorporate and apply many powerful truths from the Word of God. Sometimes they come to us in gentle showers or flurries. Sometimes the truth drenches us like a sudden downpour. The principles settle into our lives and seep down into our hearts. In time, they produce fruit in our lives that nourishes our souls. As we continue to soak in the godly principles found in the Twelve Steps we will prosper as God intended.

> Our recovery stories can soak into the lives of others,
> like rain into parched ground.

Fir Trees from Thorns

Bible Reading: Isaiah 55:12-13

> Having had a spiritual awakening as the result of these steps,
> we tried to carry this message to others and to practice
> these principles in all our affairs.

O nce we've been free from our addictions for a while we
start to feel great! So many people in our lives are relieved
of the pain and worry they used to suffer when we were in
bondage. The places in our lives that used to be wasted and over-
grown with thorns have been cleaned up. There's more joy and
peace in our lives.

A promise in the book of Isaiah can be applied to us. God
said, "You will live in joy and peace. The mountains and hills will
burst into song, and the trees of the field will clap their hands!
Where once there were thorns, cypress trees will grow. Where
nettles grew, myrtles will sprout up. These events will bring great
honor to the LORD's name; they will be an everlasting sign of his
power and love" (Isaiah 55:12-13).

As time passes and we continue to practice the principles
of the Twelve Steps, we will see good things developing in areas
of our lives that used to be thorny and wasted. The people around
us will happily get used to the new us, and there will be a lot more
joy in living. But we still need to look back and remember the
"thorns" of our addiction now and again. We need to be willing
to talk about our recovery at appropriate times. There are people
whose lives are still filled with "thorns," who need to hear our
story so they can receive the hope our recovery can offer.

🌿

> By remembering our thorny past, we will give hope
> to others of a glorious future.

Suffering That Heals
Bible Reading: Isaiah 53:1-12

> Having had a spiritual awakening as the result of these steps,
> we tried to carry this message to others and to practice
> these principles in all our affairs.

Those of us who have worked through the Twelve Steps will see life from a distinctive viewpoint. We'll see things differently from those who haven't acknowledged and dealt with their own pain. We've processed the depth of suffering that comes from growing up in this broken world. We're well acquainted with our own grief, and compassionate toward others who are hurting. The things we've suffered have helped us learn valuable lessons about life that can't be learned any other way. We have a message of hope for those still held prisoner by their addictions.

Even the Savior of the world learned from the things he'd suffered. Jesus spoke of himself by quoting Isaiah: "The Spirit of the Sovereign LORD is upon me, for the LORD has anointed me to bring good news to the poor. He has sent me to comfort the brokenhearted and to proclaim that captives will be released and prisoners will be freed. He has sent me to tell those who mourn that the time of the LORD's favor has come" (Isaiah 61:1-2). Isaiah told us that Christ would be, "a man of sorrows, acquainted with deepest grief" (53:3).

We're not the Savior of the world, but like him, we've learned through the things we've suffered. And we have good news for those who are brokenhearted and imprisoned.

> We have learned much through our painful steps toward recovery;
> we will learn even more as we share it with others.

God's Faithfulness

Bible Reading: Isaiah 38:1-20

> Having had a spiritual awakening as the result of these steps,
> we tried to carry this message to others and to practice
> these principles in all our affairs.

We may not have been on the verge of death, but something devastated our lives enough to lead us into recovery.

Once, King Hezekiah became deathly sick and was told to set his affairs in order because he was going to die. He broke down sobbing and prayed for God to heal him. God heard and spared his life. Here's part of a poem he wrote about his experience: "I waited patiently all night, but I was torn apart as though by lions. . . . Now I will walk humbly throughout my years because of this anguish I have felt. Lord, your discipline is good, for it leads to life and health. You restore my health and allow me to live! Yes, this anguish was good for me, for you have rescued me from death and forgiven all my sins. . . . Think of it—the LORD is ready to heal me! I will sing his praises with instruments every day of my life" (Isaiah 38:13, 15-17, 20).

We, too, can look back on the painful process of our recovery and say, "This anguish was good for me, for you have rescued me." We need to make God's faithfulness known to the next generation. We can do this by talking about our experiences and singing his praises every day we live.

> When our recovery is centered on God, his transforming power
> can turn our pain into gladness.

Known but Not Rejected

Bible Reading: John 4:28-42

> Having had a spiritual awakening as the result of these steps,
> we tried to carry this message to others and to practice
> these principles in all our affairs.

One thing we gain through recovery groups is the support of people who love and accept us, even though they know all about us. This kind of support is well worth telling others about.

Jesus met a Samaritan woman by a well in the middle of a hot day. She didn't have the best reputation. He knew she was thirsty for more than just water. She was thirsty for acceptance and love, something that Jesus gave her. After their talk, "the woman left her water jar beside the well and ran back to the village, telling everyone, 'Come and see a man who told me everything I ever did! Could he possibly be the Messiah?' So the people came streaming from the village to see him. . . . Many Samaritans from the village believed in Jesus because the woman had said, 'He told me everything I ever did!'" (John 4:28-30, 39).

This woman had gone through five broken marriages and was living with a man who wasn't her husband. She was despised in her community and rejected. When she met someone who knew all of this but accepted her anyway, she spread the news. We, too, can find God's love and acceptance in recovery groups and tell others about the support available. Then they can come and find recovery for themselves.

❧

> We will find new courage when we discover that we are
> known by God, but not rejected.

Day 16

Qualified to Encourage
Bible Reading: Luke 10:30-37

Having had a spiritual awakening as the result of these steps,
we tried to carry this message to others and to practice
these principles in all our affairs.

Maybe we've been treated like we're subhuman. Perhaps we've been despised and rejected because of the shameful effects of our addictions. We may feel like we aren't educated enough to help anyone recover. Don't they need a professional trained to deal with these issues? What do we have to offer that could really help?

The Samaritans of Jesus' day were a mixed race. They worshiped the Lord, but worshiped pagan gods as well (see 2 Kings 17:24-41). For these two reasons, they were hated and persecuted. Jesus tells a story about a Jew who was attacked and left bleeding on a roadside. "By chance a priest came along. But when he saw the man lying there, he crossed to the other side of the road and passed him by. A Temple assistant walked over and looked at him lying there, but he also passed by on the other side. Then a despised Samaritan came along, and when he saw the man, he felt compassion for him" (Luke 10:31-33). It was the Samaritan who helped the man recover.

The two spiritual professionals looked on the man's injuries but weren't moved to do anything. Perhaps they had never really suffered themselves! The despised Samaritan could feel deep pity because he knew what suffering and rejection were like. Who is better equipped to help a hurting person than someone who has been hurt himself and is able to display sincere compassion?

There is no one better qualified to help than someone
who's already been there.

Extending the Invitation
Bible Reading: Luke 14:16-24

> Having had a spiritual awakening as the result of these steps,
> we tried to carry this message to others and to practice
> these principles in all our affairs.

Some of us entered recovery or a relationship with God because someone encouraged us. Others of us had to find our own way because no one took an interest in us. Perhaps people thought we were too far gone to be worth their time; maybe they disqualified us for some other reason.

Jesus told this story about inviting people into the Kingdom of God. "A man prepared a great feast and sent out many invitations. When the banquet was ready, he sent his servant to tell the guests, 'Come, the banquet is ready.' But they all began making excuses. . . . The servant returned and told his master what they had said. His master was furious and said, 'Go quickly into the streets and alleys of the town and invite the poor, the crippled, the blind, and the lame.' After the servant had done this, he reported, 'There is still room for more.' So his master said, 'Go out into the country lanes and behind the hedges and urge anyone you find to come, so that the house will be full'" (Luke 14:16-18, 21-23).

Step Twelve says to "carry this message to others." "Go into all the world and preach the Good News to everyone" (Mark 16:15). In both regards, we should be careful not to prejudge and disqualify anyone from hearing the message. Our job is just to extend the invitation.

> Our part is to share our journey; God's part is
> to help others listen.

Day 18

Small Beginnings

Bible Reading: Matthew 13:31-32

> Having had a spiritual awakening as the result of these steps,
> we tried to carry this message to others and to practice
> these principles in all our affairs.

When we first decided to admit we were powerless and that our lives had become unmanageable, we took a tiny step. We probably had a hard time believing that we could go even one day without relapsing into our old ways. Now we're amazed to see how working the steps has caused a new life to grow and has positively impacted every area of our lives. We may shake our heads in wonder to realize how many days have passed (one day at a time) since we last fell.

Jesus gave this illustration: "The Kingdom of Heaven is like a mustard seed planted in a field. It is the smallest of all seeds, but it becomes the largest of garden plants; it grows into a tree, and birds come and make nests in its branches" (Matthew 13:31-32). The phrase "Kingdom of Heaven" refers to a realm or sphere in which, at any given time, God's rule is acknowledged.

When we turned our lives over to the care of God, we opened up our lives to becoming part of the sphere of God's rule. From such small beginnings we have seen a whole new life grow, and beyond our wildest expectations! The tiny seed of our being that was dwarfed by our addictions has now burst open with our spiritual awakening.

❧

When sharing, remember how God made great things
happen from small beginnings.

360

A Gradual Miracle

Bible Reading: Mark 8:22-26

Having had a spiritual awakening as the result of these steps,
we tried to carry this message to others and to practice
these principles in all our affairs.

Some of us have a spiritual awakening that's sudden. We're jolted to our senses—like being awakened by a splash of ice-cold water. For others of us the change is more gradual. We have a hard time shaking loose the darkness of our past. But whether we awoke in an instant or gradually, we have a valid message to take to others.

"Jesus took the blind man by the hand and led him out of the village. Then, spitting on the man's eyes, he laid his hands on him and asked, 'Can you see anything now?' The man looked around. 'Yes,' he said, 'I see people, but I can't see them very clearly. They look like trees walking around.' Then Jesus placed his hands on the man's eyes again, and his eyes were opened. His sight was completely restored, and he could see everything clearly. Jesus sent him away, saying, 'Don't go back into the village on your way home'" (Mark 8:23-26).

This miracle sounds like a messy process. It didn't all happen in an instant, but this doesn't make the story any less important. It's in the Bible right along with all the stories of instantaneous healing (see Matthew 9:27-31). If our awakening and recovery have taken a long and messy process, we still need to tell others. There are those who think there's something wrong with them because their recovery isn't a "sudden miracle." By hearing our stories of gradual recovery, they will be encouraged.

A gradual miracle is no less a miracle than an instant one.

Day 20

A Light of Hope

Bible Reading: 1 Thessalonians 5:5-8

Having had a spiritual awakening as the result of these steps,
we tried to carry this message to others and to practice
these principles in all our affairs.

N ow that we've had a spiritual awakening, we can see how
a daily practice of the principles in all our affairs is important. We can't just do things now and again, here and
there, and hope to stay alert.

Paul warned all believers to be alert and ready for the return
of Christ at any moment. "For you are all children of the light and
of the day; we don't belong to darkness and night. So be on your
guard, not asleep like the others. Stay alert and be clearheaded.
Night is the time when people sleep and drinkers get drunk. But
let us who live in the light be clearheaded, protected by the armor
of faith and love, and wearing as our helmet the confidence of our
salvation" (1 Thessalonians 5:5-8).

Just as we need sleep on a regular basis to keep us alert during the daytime, we need regular application of the Twelve Steps
to keep us sober. Jesus told his disciples, "You are the light of the
world—like a city on a hilltop that cannot be hidden. No one
lights a lamp and then puts it under a basket. Instead, a lamp is
placed on a stand, where it gives light to everyone in the house. In
the same way, let your good deeds shine out for all to see, so that
everyone will praise your heavenly Father" (Matthew 5:14-16).

Light makes itself evident by contrast. As we practice the
Twelve Steps in all of our affairs, we'll shine in a dark world. We
can be a light of hope for people still searching for answers. Let's
not hide our light, but let it shine!

❧

As our lives brighten through recovery, we can bring hope
to others by letting the light shine out.

A Solid Foundation
Bible Reading: Matthew 7:24-27

> Having had a spiritual awakening as the result of these steps,
> we tried to carry this message to others and to practice
> these principles in all our affairs.

A t this point in our recovery we've started to rebuild our lives. We came to realize that our past lives weren't able to hold up under the pressure of life's storms. Now we're trying to do things differently so we don't repeat past mistakes and see it all come crashing down again.

Jesus told a story that relates to this. "Anyone who listens to my teaching and follows it is wise, like a person who builds a house on solid rock. Though the rain comes in torrents and the floodwaters rise and the winds beat against that house, it won't collapse because it is built on bedrock. But anyone who hears my teaching and doesn't obey it is foolish, like a person who builds a house on sand. When the rains and floods come and the winds beat against that house, it will collapse with a mighty crash" (Matthew 7:24-27).

The instructions Jesus gave are integrated into the principles of the Twelve Steps. By practicing them we will be following Jesus' instructions. Life will always have storms and floods! We will face challenging problems and hurts in the future, as we have in the past. Practicing the principles of the Twelve Steps—honesty, humility, accountability, reliance upon God, self-evaluation, interdependence with others, openness to transformation, consideration, prayer, and diligence—will create a firm foundation for the new life we're working to build.

❧

> Our recovery takes time, but should reach and transform
> the very roots of our being.

Day 22

Transformation

Bible Reading: Romans 12:1-2

> Having had a spiritual awakening as the result of these steps, we tried to carry this message to others and to practice these principles in all our affairs.

Those of us who have sincerely practiced the Twelve Steps will begin to experience a transformation. The way we think and live will grow more and more in line with the satisfying life God intends for us. We're growing away from our old ways and experiencing more and more freedom.

Paul said, "Don't copy the behavior and customs of this world, but let God transform you into a new person by changing the way you think. Then you will learn to know God's will for you, which is good and pleasing and perfect" (Romans 12:2). He also said, "The Lord is the Spirit, and wherever the Spirit of the Lord is, there is freedom. . . . [We] reflect the glory of the Lord. And the Lord—who is the Spirit—makes us more and more like him as we are changed into his glorious image" (2 Corinthians 3:17-18).

By turning our lives over to the care of God, preparing for him to remove our defects of character, humbly asking him to remove our shortcomings, and seeking through prayer and meditation to improve our conscious contact with God, we have opened our lives up to the Holy Spirit. As he continues to work within us, and we continue to remain open to God, our transformation will continue. Our growing freedom is a reflection to others of the freedom they can have, too.

❧

Only a recovery that shares itself with others will be a transforming one.

Hanging On
Bible Reading: Genesis 32:24-31

Having had a spiritual awakening as the result of these steps,
we tried to carry this message to others and to practice
these principles in all our affairs.

For some of us our relationship with God has seemed like a
wrestling match at times. We almost see him as an opponent
who's fighting against us. And yet we don't dare let him go
because we know that without God's help we're lost.

Jacob had a strange experience. He was in camp alone "and
a man came and wrestled with him until the dawn began to break.
When the man saw that he would not win the match, he touched
Jacob's hip and wrenched it out of its socket. Then the man said,
'Let me go, for the dawn is breaking!' But Jacob said, 'I will not let
you go unless you bless me.' 'What is your name?' the man asked.
He replied, 'Jacob.' . . . 'From now on you will be called Israel,
because you have fought with God and with men and have won.'
'Please tell me your name,' Jacob said. 'Why do you want to know
my name?' the man replied. Then he blessed Jacob there. Jacob
named the place Peniel (which means 'face of God'), for he said,
'I have seen God face to face, yet my life has been spared.' The sun
was rising as Jacob left Peniel, and he was limping because of the
injury to his hip" (Genesis 32:24-31).

Jacob had a real wrestling match with God. He went away
with a new name and God's blessing, but he also was limping. We
may have to wrestle with God as he changes who we are. But if we
refuse to let go of God, he will bless us. Those of us who wrestle
with God may also come away with a "limp" to remind us of the
intensity of the struggle which led to our new identity.

Holding on to God is always rewarded by his blessing.

Day 24

Sharing Our Hope
Bible Reading: Acts 9:36-43

> Having had a spiritual awakening as the result of these steps,
> we tried to carry this message to others and to practice
> these principles in all our affairs.

Our spiritual awakening and recovery may seem to us like a resurrection from the dead. We have seen what the power of God can do. Now we're in a position to share that powerful message.

Jesus once referred to himself as "Petra," a massive rock. He renamed Simon "Petros," meaning a stone detached from the rock. Jesus was calling Simon a "chip off the old block"! One day Peter was brought in to see the body of a woman who had recently died. "The room was filled with widows who were weeping and showing him the coats and other clothes Dorcas [which in Aramaic is Tabitha] had made for them. But Peter asked them all to leave the room; then he knelt and prayed. Turning to the body he said, 'Get up, Tabitha.' And she opened her eyes!" (Acts 9:39-40).

We may wonder how Peter knew what to do in this situation. In Mark 5:22-43, we read about a time when Peter saw Jesus raise a girl from the dead in similar circumstances. Peter had been with Jesus when death was raised to new life. So later, Peter was able to take the power of God and the hope of renewed life to others.

We have seen how God can use the Twelve Steps to awaken us spiritually from lives that were killing us. We can recall what we saw God do for us. Then we can extend the life and the message of hope to others who are living lives that are killing them.

🌱

> We don't need eloquent words; we need only share
> what God has done in our lives.

Day 25

Freedom from Shame
Bible Reading: 2 Samuel 6:14-21

> Having had a spiritual awakening as the result of these steps,
> we tried to carry this message to others and to practice
> these principles in all our affairs.

When God does great things in our lives we may well be overjoyed. We may feel like dancing and singing! We might want to tell the whole world! But we may get some negative reactions.

David knew the feeling! "David danced before the LORD with all his might, wearing a priestly garment. So David and all the people of Israel brought up the Ark of the LORD with shouts of joy and the blowing of rams' horns. But as the Ark of the LORD entered the City of David, Michal, the daughter of Saul, looked down from her window. When she saw King David, . . . she was filled with contempt for him. . . . When David returned home to bless his own family, Michal, the daughter of Saul, came out to meet him. She said in disgust, 'How distinguished the king of Israel looked today, shamelessly exposing himself to the servant girls like any vulgar person might do!' David retorted to Michal, 'I was dancing before the LORD. . . . So I celebrate before the LORD. Yes, and I am willing to look even more foolish than this'" (2 Samuel 6:14-16, 20-22).

Michal wasn't a part of the celebration. She stayed back and fumed, rehearsing her criticisms, attempting to shame David. When we begin to express our joy over the great things God is doing for us, those who aren't in on the celebration will resent our display. They may try to shame us into being quiet. We don't have to be ashamed anymore! It's sad that they won't celebrate with us, but that's no reason for our party to stop.

God is able to remove our shame and replace it with joy.

367

Day 26

Something to Boast About

Bible Reading: Psalm 107:1-32

> Having had a spiritual awakening as the result of these steps,
> we tried to carry this message to others and to practice
> these principles in all our affairs.

Those of us who have worked through the Twelve Steps come from many different backgrounds. We could be categorized or labeled in many different ways. But we share a common past of imprisonment to the powerful effects of an addiction or compulsion. We can also share the common experience of having been rescued by God and set free from our peculiar prisons.

Psalm 107 is addressed to various groups of people who have been rescued by God. It says, "He satisfies the thirsty and fills the hungry with good things. . . . 'LORD, help!' they cried in their trouble, and he saved them from their distress. He led them from the darkness and deepest gloom; he snapped their chains. Let them praise the LORD for his great love and for the wonderful things he has done for them. For he broke down their prison gates of bronze; he cut apart their bars of iron. . . . Let them exalt him publicly before the congregation and before the leaders of the nation" (Psalm 107:9, 13-16, 32).

King David sang, "I will boast only in the LORD; let all who are helpless take heart. Come, let us tell of the LORD's greatness; let us exalt his name together" (Psalm 34:2-3).

Those of us who have been set free have something to boast about. We're called to praise God and to exalt him publicly.

❧

> Our natural response to recovery should be to
> shout our story from the rooftops!

Day 27

Never Too Late
Bible Reading: John 3:1-8

> Having had a spiritual awakening as the result of these steps,
> we tried to carry this message to others and to practice
> these principles in all our affairs.

Perhaps we thought we were too old and set in our ways to start all over again—but we found a new life anyway! In working the Twelve Steps we had a spiritual awakening. This may not be something we feel comfortable talking about openly, but we do want to carry the message to others.

"There was a man named Nicodemus. . . . After dark one evening, he came to speak with Jesus. 'Rabbi,' he said, 'we all know that God has sent you to teach us. Your miraculous signs are evidence that God is with you.' Jesus replied, 'I tell you the truth, unless you are born again, you cannot see the Kingdom of God.' 'What do you mean?' exclaimed Nicodemus. 'How can an old man go back into his mother's womb and be born again?' Jesus replied, '. . . Humans can reproduce only human life, but the Holy Spirit gives birth to spiritual life'" (John 3:1-6).

Nicodemus had spent many years working his way up in the religious and social hierarchy. He thought he was too old to change, but he experienced a spiritual awakening in his encounter with Jesus. There was at least one person with whom he shared his faith. After the crucifixion, he and another secret disciple, an influential Jew like himself, buried the body of Jesus. We may feel uncomfortable telling our story to the world, but there are other people like us who may be receptive, one on one.

※

God often works in the hearts of the people we
least expect him to.

Remembering the Lost
Bible Reading: Luke 15:1-7

> Having had a spiritual awakening as the result of these steps,
> we tried to carry this message to others and to practice
> these principles in all our affairs.

A s time goes by in our recovery we may find that some of our friends look down on us for attending meetings with "addicts and sinners." We may hear complaints about associating with this "kind of people." Or we may find that we forget about those who are still lost in the wilderness of addiction.

"Tax collectors and other notorious sinners often came to listen to Jesus teach. This made the Pharisees and teachers of religious law complain that he was associating with such sinful people—even eating with them! So Jesus told them this story: 'If a man has a hundred sheep and one of them gets lost, what will he do? Won't he leave the ninety-nine others in the wilderness and go to search for the one that is lost until he finds it? And when he has found it, he will joyfully carry it home on his shoulders. When he arrives, he will call together his friends and neighbors, saying, "Rejoice with me because I have found my lost sheep." In the same way, there is more joy in heaven over one lost sinner who repents and returns to God than over ninety-nine others who are righteous and haven't strayed away!'" (Luke 15:1-7).

God doesn't see people as either despicable or good. He sees them all as precious, whether they are lost or found. Now that we have been found, we must not forget those who are still lost.

> God loves us so much that he seeks each one of us out
> and rejoices when we are found.

A Spiritual Recovery
Bible Reading: Luke 12:16-21

> Having had a spiritual awakening as the result of these steps,
> we tried to carry this message to others and to practice
> these principles in all our affairs.

Being free from our addictions and compulsions is wonderful! We have the chance to build a life that's rich in every way. We may know people who have used the Twelve Steps to find freedom from their addictions, but who have never accepted Jesus Christ as the Savior of their souls. Perhaps, we are in this situation. We've found a better life, but our eternal life is still in jeopardy.

Jesus gave this illustration: "A rich man had a fertile farm that produced fine crops. He said to himself, 'What should I do? I don't have room for all my crops.' Then he said, 'I know! I'll tear down my barns and build bigger ones. Then I'll have room enough to store all my wheat and other goods. And I'll sit back and say to myself, "My friend, you have enough stored away for years to come. Now take it easy!"'. . . But God said to him, 'You fool! You will die this very night. Then who will get everything you worked for?' Yes, a person is a fool to store up earthly wealth but not have a rich relationship with God" (Luke 12:16-21). Another time Jesus said, "What do you benefit if you gain the whole world but lose your own soul? Is anything worth more than your soul?" (Matthew 16:26).

Our earthly life may be wonderful now that our addictions are under control. But, God's "kindness is intended to turn you from your sin" (Romans 2:4). In the final evaluation, recovery is wasted if we lose our eternal souls. We need to keep this in mind for ourselves and those with whom we share our message.

❧

> What is the use of recovery in this life if we are still
> eternally lost?

371

Day 30

We Will Make It!
Bible Reading: Philippians 1:3-11

> Having had a spiritual awakening as the result of these steps, we tried to carry this message to others and to practice these principles in all our affairs.

We may have gotten through the Twelve Steps (for the first time or for the tenth time), but we are all still in process. God began a work within us which is continuing each day we live. His grace is at work within us, as we practice the principles we've learned, and as we carry the message of recovery to others.

The apostle Paul wrote a message for the Philippians which applies to us in many ways. He wrote, "I am certain that God, who began the good work within you, will continue his work until it is finally finished on the day when Christ Jesus returns. . . . I pray that your love will overflow more and more, and that you will keep on growing in knowledge and understanding. For I want you to understand what really matters, so that you may live pure and blameless lives until the day of Christ's return" (Philippians 1:6, 9-10).

Grace is the gift of God's unearned favor. God favored us when we were still held in bondage by our addictions. He took us in his arms when no one else would touch us. He bought us when no one else was sure we were worth much. He is the author and finisher of our faith. We can be sure we will make it, because he has lavished his grace on us and committed himself to our recovery.

When God starts a project, he finishes it!

STARTING OVER

"And I am convinced that nothing can ever separate us from God's love. Neither death nor life, neither angels nor demons, neither our fears for today nor our worries about tomorrow—not even the powers of hell can separate us from God's love. No power in the sky above or in the earth below— indeed, nothing in all creation will ever be able to separate us from the love of God that is revealed in Christ Jesus our Lord" (Romans 8:38-39).

Day 1

The Morning After
Bible Reading: Matthew 26:33-35, 74-75

Yesterday we may have sworn there was no way we were going to fall again. Things were going well. But what happened? Now we're sitting here, aching inside, and cursing ourselves. Maybe we allowed ourselves to be lured into a risky situation. We convinced ourselves there was good reason—that it would be all right. Maybe we just felt like we could handle it—but we couldn't—or at least we didn't. And now we're miserable!

Peter had his own "morning after" experience. He had sworn to Jesus, "'Even if everyone else deserts you, I will never desert you.' Jesus replied, 'I tell you the truth, Peter—this very night, before the rooster crows, you will deny three times that you even know me.' 'No!' Peter insisted. 'Even if I have to die with you, I will never deny you!'" (Matthew 26:33-35). Jesus had been right, as always! Jesus was betrayed, arrested, tried, and beaten. It was more than Peter could bear; but he couldn't walk away. So he followed. He was suspected of being a collaborator. Each time he lied to protect himself. The third time, "Peter swore, 'A curse on me if I'm lying—I don't know the man!' And immediately the rooster crowed. Suddenly, Jesus' words flashed through Peter's mind: 'Before the rooster crows, you will deny three times that you even know me.' And he went away, weeping bitterly" (Matthew 26:74-75).

Jesus knew Peter was going to fall in advance; and his love didn't skip a beat! God doesn't hate us on the morning after. He loves us every bit as much today as he did before we fell.

❧

God's love for us never changes, even when we've failed.

Not Disqualified
Bible Reading: Matthew 4:18-20

We may accept God's forgiveness, but feel that our fall has disqualified us from serving God or aspiring to great things. We may conclude that we're only fit for the kind of position in life we had before we began to hope and work for something better.

The apostle Peter started out as a fisherman named Simon. That was all he was qualified for, at least before Jesus came along. "One day as Jesus was walking along the shore of the Sea of Galilee, he saw two brothers—Simon, also called Peter, and Andrew—throwing a net into the water, for they fished for a living. Jesus called out to them, 'Come, follow me, and I will show you how to fish for people!' And they left their nets at once and followed him" (Matthew 4:18-20). For the next three years Jesus trained him to "fish for souls," and during that time Peter witnessed many miracles. But then he blew it! In the end he denied Jesus. He went through three days of utter hell, and then the greatest miracle of all happened. Jesus was alive again! But Peter still thought of himself as disqualified. He started up his fishing business again. That's where Jesus found him, back in his old life. It was on that same shore that Jesus reaffirmed his call. Again he said to Peter, "Follow me" (John 21:19).

We may consider ourselves disqualified after a fall, but God doesn't. The apostle Paul said, "For God's gifts and his call can never be withdrawn" (Romans 11:29). Just because we've blown it doesn't mean that we should give up and go back to our old lives. God still has a wonderful future for us.

We only really fail when we refuse to get up and start again.

God Still Loves Us

Bible Reading: Romans 8:38-39

We may feel like God hates us. We may hate ourselves right now. We wonder how God's love can continue when we've disappointed him so. It's a wonder that God doesn't just throw us away! It's a wonder that he keeps us at all!

This may be how we feel, but it isn't true! The apostle Paul once wrote, "And I am convinced that nothing can ever separate us from God's love. Neither death nor life, neither angels nor demons, neither our fears for today nor our worries about tomorrow—not even the powers of hell can separate us from God's love. No power in the sky above or in the earth below—indeed, nothing in all creation will ever be able to separate us from the love of God that is revealed in Christ Jesus our Lord" (Romans 8:38-39). King David prayed, "O LORD, you have examined my heart and know everything about me. . . . You know what I am going to say even before I say it, LORD. You go before me and follow me. You place your hand of blessing on my head. Such knowledge is too wonderful for me, too great for me to understand! I can never escape from your Spirit! I can never get away from your presence!" (Psalm 139:1, 4-7).

Once we've accepted Christ's death as payment for our sins, there's absolutely nothing we can do to escape the love of God! God knows everything we've done—every thought, word, and deed. In fact, he knew things would happen as they did before they ever happened. He is determined to bless us, to love us, and to keep us. He'll never throw us away!

❦

There is absolutely nothing we can do to make God love us any less.

Wanting to Die

Bible Reading: 1 Kings 19:3-7

When we fall, we may wish we could just die. We may feel like the struggle is just too much for us. We've tried but failed again; now we're exhausted! When we feel this way we may withdraw from those who could help us. Our shame over the failure makes us want to hide. We feel like the journey is over. The last thing we want to do is start back on the steps of recovery.

Elijah, the great prophet, had similar feelings. Almost immediately after winning one of his greatest victories for God, he became overwhelmed by a threat from wicked Queen Jezebel. "Elijah . . . fled for his life. . . . He went on alone into the wilderness . . . and prayed that he might die. 'I have had enough, LORD,' he said. 'Take my life, for I am no better than my ancestors who have already died.' Then he lay down and slept under the broom tree. But as he was sleeping, an angel touched him and told him, 'Get up and eat!' He looked around and there beside his head was some bread baked on hot stones and a jar of water! So he ate and drank and lay down again. Then the angel of the LORD came again and touched him and said, 'Get up and eat some more, or the journey ahead will be too much for you'" (1 Kings 19:3-7).

After this dark moment, Elijah lived to experience many more great victories. We will too! We probably are exhausted. Right now we need to give ourselves some rest and nourishment. We need someone by our side who will encourage us to get up and get going again. There's still a long journey ahead of us.

❦

When we want to quit we need to look for loving people
who will encourage and nourish us.

Day 5

No Condemnation
Bible Reading: Romans 7:15–8:1

We may be punishing ourselves. We certainly feel like we deserve it! We don't just feel guilty; we feel like this last fall proves that we're rotten to the core. Our feelings of self-condemnation may go beyond guilt for the wrong behavior, convincing us of our worthlessness. It seems futile to keep trying.

The apostle Paul talked about how frustrating it can be to fall back into the very things we hate (see Romans 7). But then he concludes, "So now there is no condemnation for those who belong to Christ Jesus. And because you belong to him, the power of the life-giving Spirit has freed you from the power of sin that leads to death" (Romans 8:1-2).

Our feelings of condemnation come from ourselves and Satan, not from God. The Bible calls Satan "the accuser." Looking to a future day, it says, "It has come at last—salvation and power and the Kingdom of our God, and the authority of his Christ. For the accuser of our brothers and sisters has been thrown down to earth—the one who accuses them before our God day and night" (Revelation 12:10).

God will convict us of the wrong of our behavior, so we can confess it and receive cleansing forgiveness. Remember, "If we confess our sins to him, he is faithful and just to forgive us our sins and to cleanse us from all wickedness" (1 John 1:9). Let's not give in to the condemnation. We're not hopeless and worthless! We just fell. God wants to dust us off and set us back on the path to a better life.

❦

God never condemns those who look to him for forgiveness, even after the greatest of failures.

Check out these great resources to help you on your path to recovery:

The Life Recovery Journal has been carefully created to guide you through the recovery process. The questions and quotes will help you to write honest reflections, reinforce what you're learning, and give insight into your recovery as a whole person.

The Life Recovery Workbook is about transformation: from death to life, from addiction to recovery. As you work through each of the Twelve Steps, the challenging spiritual lessons will strengthen you to live free from addiction.

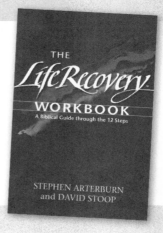

The easy-to-read, down-to-earth meditations in *The Life Recovery Devotional* are designed to help you find the recovery, rest, and peace that Jesus promises. They will help you understand the struggles we all face— in recovery, in overcoming temptation, and in getting back on track after a relapse.

CP0324